dBASE 5
FOR WINDOWS
PROGRAMMING
FOR
DUMMIES

dBASE 5 FOR WINDOWS PROGRAMMING FOR DUMMIES

Ted Coombs

and

Jason Coombs

**IDG
BOOKS**

IDG Books Worldwide, Inc.
An International Data Group Company

Foster City, CA • Chicago, IL • Indianapolis, IN • Braintree, MA • Dallas, TX

dBASE 5 for Windows Programming For Dummies

Published by
IDG Books Worldwide, Inc.
An International Data Group Company
155 Bovet Road, Suite 310
San Mateo, CA 94402

ISBN: 1-56884-215-5

Library of Congress Catalog Card No.: 94-072738

Printed in the United States of America

First Printing, October, 1994

10 9 8 7 6 5 4 3 2 1

Distributed in the United States by IDG Books Worldwide, Inc.

About IDG Books Worldwide

Welcome to the world of IDG Books Worldwide.

IDG Books Worldwide, Inc., is a subsidiary of International Data Group, the world's largest publisher of business- and computer-related information and the leading global provider of information services on information technology. IDG was founded over 25 years ago and now employs more than 5700 people worldwide. IDG publishes over 195 publications in 62 countries. Forty million people read one or more IDG publications each month.

Launched in 1990, IDG Books is today the fastest growing publisher of computer and business books in the United States. We are proud to have received three awards from the Computer Press Association in recognition of editorial excellence, and our best-selling ...For Dummies series has over ten million copies in print with translations in more than twenty languages. IDG Books, through a recent joint venture with IDG's Hi-Tech Beijing, became the first U.S. publisher to publish a computer book in the People's Republic of China. In record time, IDG Books has become the first choice for millions of readers around the world who want to learn how to better manage their businesses.

Our mission is simple: Every IDG book is designed to bring extra value and skill-building instruction to the reader. Our books are written by experts who understand and care about our readers. The knowledge base of our editorial staff comes from years of experience in publishing, education, and journalism—experience which we use to produce books for the 90s. In short, we care about books, so we attract the best people. We devote special attention to details such as audience, interior design, and illustrations. And because we write, edit, and produce our books electronically, we can spend more time ensuring superior content and spend less time on the technicalities of making books.

You can count on our commitment to deliver high-quality books at competitive prices on topics you want to read about. At IDG, we value quality, and we have been delivering quality for over 25 years. You'll find no better book than an IDG book.

John Kilcullen
President and CEO
IDG Books Worldwide, Inc.

For More Information

For general information on IDG Books in the U.S., including information on discounts and premiums, contact IDG Books at 800-434-3422 or 415-312-0650.

For information on where to purchase IDG's books outside the U.S., contact Christina Turner at 415-312-0633.

For information on translations, contact Marc Jeffrey Mikulich, Foreign Rights Manager, at IDG Books Worldwide; fax number: 415-358-1260.

For sales inquires and special prices for bulk quantities, contact Tony Real at 415-312-0644 or 800-434-3422.

For information on using IDG Books in the classroom and ordering examination copies, contact Jim Kelley at 800-434-2086.

The ...*For Dummies* book series is distributed in the United States by IDG Books Worldwide, Inc. It is distributed in Canada by Macmillan of Canada, a Division of Canada Publishing Corporation; in South America and the Caribbean by Computer and Technical Books of Miami, Florida; in Singapore, Malaysia, Thailand, and Korea by Longman Singapore; in Japan by Toppan Co. Ltd.; in Hong Kong by Asia Computerworld; in Australia and New Zealand by Woodslane Pty. Ltd.; and in the U.K. and Europe by Transworld Publishers Ltd.

IDG Books Worldwide, Inc. is a subsidiary of International Data Group. The officers are Patrick J. McGovern, Founder and Board Chairman, and Walter Boyd, President.

International Data Group's Publications

ARGENTINA'S Computerworld Argentina, Infoworld Argentina; AUSTRALIA'S Computerworld Australia, Australian PC World, Australian Macworld, Network World, Mobile Business Australia, Reseller, IDG Sources; AUSTRIA'S Computerwelt Oesterreich, PC Test; BRAZIL'S Computerworld, Gamepro, Game Power, Mundo IBM, Mundo Unix, PC World, Super Game; BELGIUM'S Data News (CW); BULGARIA'S Computerworld Bulgaria, Ediworld, PC & Mac World Bulgaria, Network World Bulgaria; CANADA'S CIO Canada, Computerworld Canada, Graduate Computerworld, InfoCanada, Network World Canada; CHILE'S Computerworld Chile, Informatica; COLOMBIA'S Computerworld Colombia, PC World; CZECH REPUBLIC'S Computerworld, Elektronika, PC World; DENMARK'S Communications World, Computerworld Danmark, Macintosh Produktkatalog, Macworld Danmark, PC World Danmark, PC World Produktguide, Tech World, Windows World; ECUADOR'S PC World Ecuador; EGYPT'S Computerworld (CW) Middle East, PC World Middle East; FINLAND'S MikroPC, Tietoviikko, Tietoverkko; FRANCE'S Distributique, GOLDEN MAC, InfoPC, Languages & Systems, Le Guide du Monde Informatique, Le Monde Informatique, Telecoms & Reseaux; GERMANY'S Computerwoche, Computerwoche Focus, Computerwoche Extra, Computerwoche Karriere, Information Management, Macwelt, Netzwelt, PC Welt, PC Woche, Publish, Unit; GREECE'S Infoworld, PC Games; HUNGARY'S Computerworld SZT, PC World; HONG KONG'S Computerworld Hong Kong, PC World Hong Kong; INDIA'S Computers & Communications; IRELAND'S ComputerScope; ISRAEL'S Computerworld Israel, PC World Israel; ITALY'S Computerworld Italia, Lotus Magazine, Macworld Italia, Networking Italia, PC Shopping, PC World Italia; JAPAN'S Computerworld Today, Information Systems World, Macworld Japan, Nikkei Personal Computing, SunWorld Japan, Windows World; KENYA'S East African Computer News; KOREA'S Computerworld Korea, Macworld Korea, PC World Korea; MEXICO'S Compu Edicion, Compu Manufactura, Computacion/Punto de Venta, Computerworld Mexico, MacWorld, Mundo Unix, PC World, Windows; THE NETHERLANDS' Computer! Totaal, Computable (CW), LAN Magazine, MacWorld, Totaal "Windows"; NEW ZEALAND'S Computer Listings, Computerworld New Zealand, New Zealand PC World, Network World; NIGERIA'S PC World Africa; NORWAY'S Computerworld Norge, C/World, Lotusworld Norge, Macworld Norge, Networld, PC World Ekspress, PC World Norge, PC World's Produktguide, Publish& Multimedia World, Student Data, Unix World, Windowsworld; IDG Direct Response; PAKISTAN'S PC World Pakistan; PANAMA'S PC World Panama; PERU'S Computerworld Peru, PC World; PEOPLE'S REPUBLIC OF CHINA'S China Computerworld, China Infoworld, Electronics Today/Multimedia World, Electronics International, Electronic Product World, China Network World, PC and Communications Magazine, PC World China, Software World Magazine, Telecom Product World; IDG HIGH TECH BEIJING'S New Product World; IDG SHENZHEN'S Computer News Digest; PHILIPPINES' Computerworld Philippines, PC Digest (PCW); POLAND'S Computerworld Poland, PC World/Komputer; PORTUGAL'S Cerebro/PC World, Correio Informatico/Computerworld, Informatica & Comunicacoes Catalogo, MacIn, Nacional de Produtos; ROMANIA'S Computerworld, PC World; RUSSIA'S Computerworld-Moscow, Mir - PC, Sety; SINGAPORE'S Computerworld Southeast Asia, PC World Singapore; SLOVENIA'S Monitor Magazine; SOUTH AFRICA'S Computer Mail (CIO),Computing S.A.,Network World S.A., Software World; SPAIN'S Advanced Systems, Amiga World, Computerworld Espana, Communicaciones World, Macworld Espana, NeXTWORLD, Super Juegos Magazine (GamePro), PC World Espana, Publish; SWEDEN'S Attack, ComputerSweden, Corporate Computing, Natverk & Kommunikation, Macworld, Mikrodatorn, PC World, Publishing & Design (CAP), Datalngenjoren, Maxi Data,Windows World; SWITZERLAND'S Computerworld Schweiz, Macworld Schweiz, PC Tip; TAIWAN'S Computerworld Taiwan, PC World Taiwan; THAILAND'S Thai Computerworld; TURKEY'S Computerworld Monitor, Macworld Turkiye, PC World Turkiye; UKRAINE'S Computerworld; UNITED KINGDOM'S Computing /Computerworld, Connexion/Network World, Lotus Magazine, Macworld, Open Computing/Sunworld; UNITED STATES' Advanced Systems, AmigaWorld, Cable in the Classroom, CD Review, CIO, Computerworld, Digital Video, DOS Resource Guide, Electronic Entertainment Magazine, Federal Computer Week, Federal Integrator, GamePro, IDG Books, Infoworld, Infoworld Direct, Laser Event, Macworld, Multimedia World, Network World, PC Letter, PC World, PlayRight, Power PC World, Publish, SWATPro, Video Event; VENEZUELA'S Computerworld Venezuela, PC World; VIETNAM'S PC World Vietnam.

About the Authors

Ted Coombs began using dBASE in 1982. He has written hundreds of dBASE programs for hospitals, retail point-of-sale, engineering firms, non-profit organizations, bowling alleys, and private investigators. Most recently, he was a consultant on the dBASE 5 for Windows development team.

Jason Coombs manages to keep himself planted firmly in the way of oncoming knowledge and experience. Somehow, he survives each collision with his sense of humor and passion for learning intact. In addition to working with a wide array of software development tools on several hardware platforms, he has helped develop several commercial dBASE applications.

Credits

Vice President and Publisher
Christopher J. Williams

Editorial Director
Trudy Neuhaus

Brand Manager
Amorette Pedersen

Project Editor
Susan Pink

Manuscript Editor
John Pont

Technical Reviewer
Carl Jackson

Editorial Assistant
Berta G. Hyken

Production Manager
Beth A. Roberts

Proofreader
Vicki L. Hochstedler

Indexer
Seth A. Maislin

Composition and Layout
Publishers' Design & Production Services

Book Design
University Graphics

Cover Design
Kavish + Kavish

Dedication

To our family.

Acknowledgments

This book has been a monumental effort on the part of many people. Special thanks to our dear friend, Nan Borreson, who made this book possible in so many ways. She not only arranged everything to get this project underway, she also kept us inspired by taking us on long walks and feeding us.

To Trudy Neuhaus, the woman with nerves of steel, thank you for being so supportive. Susan Pink laughed at all our jokes, and most importantly, cared about us and this book. And a big thank you to John Pont for guiding us through the development of the manuscript.

We'd like to thank Carl Jackson for his insightful technical review. When Carl writes a book, buy it, because it's sure to be excellent. To the entire dBASE for Windows team, a.k.a Big Bladerunners, thanks for the support you gave us in getting this book finished.

Ted Coombs would also like to acknowledge some special people in his life who helped make this book possible. To Dr. John Blank of Cleveland State University for first sitting me down in front of a PC with a copy of dBASE. To the late Jim Mersefelder for giving me my first job programming in dBASE. To Jafar Abbas for teaching me systems analysis. To Mike Gardner for letting me work on the dBASE for Windows Development team — it was a dream come true. Last but not least, to Richard Mainz of the Toner Corporation, technical recruiter extrodinaire. What a guy. Thank you all very much.

There is a special tribute to the late NASCAR driver Davey Allison in Help | About. Press Alt-28 to see it. Thanks to Kevin Brown for sharing this with all of us.

The publisher would like to give special thanks to Patrick J. McGovern, without whom this book would not have been possible.

Contents at a Glance

Cartoons at a Glance

by Rich Tennant

page 291

page 1

page 1

page 39

page 1

page 107

page 333

page 191

page 355

page 5

page 237

Table of Contents

Introduction

● ●

*W*elcome home! This is the book about dBASE 5 for Windows that treats
you like a member of the family. First, it cares about helping you
understand. If you don't grasp something the first time, this book will be
patient and explain it again. Second, it really believes in you. Third, it'll stick
by you through good times and bad.

What more could you ask for? No, that's out of the question. If you don't do
the dishes, who will?

The 5th Wave
By Rich Tennant

"I STARTED DESIGNING DATABASE SOFTWARE SYSTEMS AFTER SEEING HOW EASY IT
WAS TO DESIGN OFFICE FURNITURE."

About This Book

The power of dBASE has been combined with the simplicity of Windows in Borland International's new product, dBASE 5 for Windows.

Since the 1980s, dBASE has been the database of choice for millions of users. Large businesses, small community groups, students, educators, and individuals all over the world use dBASE to simplify the management of their information.

Millions of computer users rely also on Windows to provide a simple, user-friendly computing environment. With dBASE simplifying the challenge of managing information, and Windows easing the struggle of using a computer, dBASE 5 for Windows promises to be an enjoyable, productive database tool.

In writing this book, we've asked ourselves a few basic questions:

- ✔ What are you most interested in doing with dBASE for Windows?
- ✔ What have we learned that you've just got to know?
- ✔ What's funny about dBASE for Windows?

We hope you enjoy the answers we've found. We've tried to explain them in an entertaining, readable format.

Who This Book Is For

This book is for anyone who wants to learn about dBASE 5 for Windows programming. If you're new to dBASE for Windows, this book will have you writing programs in no time. If you're an experienced dBASE for DOS programmer, this book can help ease your transition to dBASE for Windows.

And, if other computer books bore you or leave you confused, this book will delight you with clarity and humor.

How This Book Is Organized

This book is packed with information, so you may want to sit in a comfortable chair and get something cool to drink. But don't go too far from your computer, because you'll want to follow along by experimenting with the sample programs.

This book has eight parts:

- ✔ Part I shows you how to use dBASE for Windows building blocks to create a Windows-style user interface for your programs.
- ✔ Part II teaches you how to build database tables as well as how to use them with your Windows-style user interface.
- ✔ Part III introduces some more programming concepts and shows you how to apply them in your programs.
- ✔ Part IV helps you build programs that can generate attractive, informative reports.
- ✔ Part V shows you how to get more out of dBASE for Windows by using objects.
- ✔ Part VI provides several ways to work with data in your applications.
- ✔ Part VII shows you how to use OLE and DDE to talk to other Windows applications.
- ✔ Part VIII is the Part of Tens, where you'll find tips on upgrading from dBASE III Plus and dBASE IV, plus our favorite dBASE for Windows functions.

Icons Used in This Book

Several icons are sprinkled throughout this book. These icons highlight important or useful tidbits of knowledge. Here's what they look like and why they're used:

Points out one of two things. It may alert you to important things that you should try to remember. Or, it may remind you about something you've already learned. ∎

Identifies technical discussions that aren't essential to the material being covered. You can skip these if you'd like. ▪

Psst! Here's a suggestion that you might find useful. ▪

Watch out! This icon points out potential disasters, and tells you how to avoid them. ▪

And a little gray square, like the one at the end of this sentence, is used to indicate the end of the iconed text. ▪

Part I

Building a User Interface

"THE LCD DISPLAY WAS GOOD, PLASMA DISPLAYS WERE A LITTLE BETTER, BUT WE THINK THE LIQUID LAVA DISPLAY THAT JERRY'S DEVELOPED IS GONNA ROCK THE WEST COAST."

In This Part...

You've made it! The book is open, you've conquered the table of contents, and the passion and excitement are beginning to build. There's that certain feeling in the air, a slight hint of blooming flowers as the possibilities of creation present themselves. You just know this is going to be fun.

Your adventure begins with an introduction to objects, the building blocks for programming in dBASE for Windows. You learn how to customize these building blocks and use them to build Windows applications. By the end of Part I, you'll be able to create impressive programs in a short amount of time, and you'll have a strong foundation for handling more advanced programming topics.

Chapter 1

Creating a Window
Isn't a Pane

● ●

In This Chapter
▶ Using objects as building blocks
▶ Creating a form
▶ Adding some window dressing

● ●

*R*emember how creative you were as a toddler, surrounded by colored building blocks? Your imagination knew no boundaries. You could build anything and bring it to life, from small wilderness cottages to vast factories. With the building blocks of dBASE for Windows and some of that overactive imagination, you can write programs to automate the information management for those cottages and industrial complexes! In the graphical world of dBASE for Windows, imagination counts.

The building blocks for writing programs are referred to as *objects*. Like the building blocks from your childhood, objects come in many shapes, sizes, colors, and political orientations. However, objects are more sophisticated than typical building blocks.

Building Blocks

When you started the dBASE for Windows program, you probably noticed all the things you can click with the mouse. Each of those things is an object. An object has a size, a shape, maybe even a picture, and it does something when you click on it. The size, shape, color, and other qualities of an object are known as its *attributes*. The things an object can do are referred to as its *capabilities*. Attributes and capabilities are known collectively as *properties*.

Each object in dBASE for Windows has properties that you can customize to give the object just the right personality and appearance. For example, an object such as a PushButton can be as large or as small as you'd like. It can even display a picture, and do anything you want when it is clicked.

The personality and appearance of an object are defined by the following characteristics:

- *Properties*. Each object has properties that describe its appearance and determine how it behaves. For example, most objects in dBASE for Windows have a property that describes their foreground and background colors.

- *Events*. Like the ringing of Dr. Pavlov's bell, events are stimuli, or signals that an object responds to. (Pavlov would ring a bell whenever he gave his dog a piece of meat. As a result, Pavlov's bell became a signal to his dog, and the poor mutt would drool whenever it heard the bell.) When an object "hears" an event signal, it reacts in the way your program tells it to.

- *Methods*. These properties define special capabilities of an object. For example, a window is an object that can be opened, closed, or resized, to name just a few of its capabilities. All dBASE for Windows objects have methods. You can use these methods to control the actions of objects. You can also write custom methods that give your objects additional capabilities.

Looking under the hood

When buying a car, some people like to look closely at the engine. Others make sure the heater and radio work, and hope that just hearing the engine after they turn the key means everything's okay. As a programmer, it's your job to look under the hood and get your hands dirty. Here's how you look under the hood of an object in dBASE for Windows:

1. While you are working in the Form Designer, use the right mouse button to click an object that you'd like to know more about. dBASE for Windows displays a pop-up menu that allows you to change the Form Designer properties; cut, copy, and paste objects; and select the Controls window, the Object Properties window, or the Procedures window.

2. Check Object Properties on the pop-up menu. (If there's already a check mark to the left of Object Properties, you can skip this step.)

3. Click the title bar of the Object Properties window to bring it to the top.

4. Dive in! Inspect the object until you run out of air, then surface by clicking again on the object you are inspecting or on another object. Watch out for sharks!

If your mouse has only one button, now would be a good time to buy a new one (a mouse, that is, not a button). When you program visually in dBASE for Windows, you'll want at least two buttons on your mouse. ▨

You've just looked at one of your most important visual programming tools. You use the Object Properties window, which is also known as the Object Inspector, to view or modify an object's properties and events.

In Figure 1-1, the Object Properties window is being used to inspect a fictitious object resembling a culinary treat. The three tabs at the bottom of the window are used to switch between viewing the properties, events, and methods of an object. To switch views, you simply click on the appropriate tab.

Figure 1-1:
The Object
Properties
window lets
you view
details
about an
object's
properties,
events, and
methods.

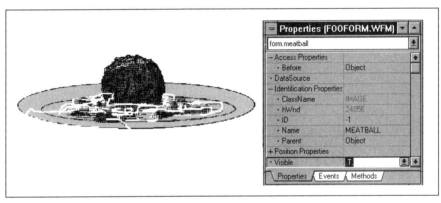

The Object Properties window can display properties either by type or alphabetically. To change the display, select Desktop from the Properties menu. This displays the Desktop Properties window, which is shown in Figure 1-2. Select the Application tab and check the Object Properties Outline option to display object properties by type, or uncheck it for an alphabetical listing.

When the Object Properties are listed in outline form, you'll notice that a plus sign (+) is displayed to the left of some property names. This indicates that multiple properties of this type are available; they just aren't being displayed at the moment. To see the individual properties in the type, double click the row containing the plus sign. The plus sign changes to a minus sign (–), which indicates that the property type is being viewed in detail, and each property appears on a row by itself below the type name. To hide the detail, double click the row containing the minus sign.

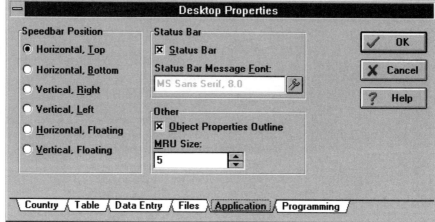

Figure 1-2:
The Desktop
Properties
window
allows you
to modify
the way you
work with
dBASE for
Windows.

Changing object properties

To change a property or an event, find the one you want to change in the Object Properties window and click it. For some properties and events, a special tool icon is displayed to help you make changes. If no tool icon appears, you can make changes by typing over the current value and pressing Enter.

Table 1-1 shows the tool icons you may encounter and how they are used.

Table 1-1: Tool icons found in the Object Properties window

Icon	Description
![wrench icon]	Displays yet another window that lets you access special editing options. The window that is displayed depends on the property or event you're editing. It can be anything from a color palette to a text editor. This icon looks a little like a venus flytrap, but we think it's supposed to be a wrench.
![down arrow icon]	Allows you to choose from a list of available settings.
![up/down arrow icon]	Scrolls through a range of possible values. Clicking the up-arrow icon scrolls up through the range, clicking the down-arrow icon scrolls down.

Not all properties can be changed using the Object Properties window. Some properties appear grayed out, or disabled, which means they contain a fixed value that must stay the same. All properties that appear in the Object Properties window are used by the object, whether you can change them or not. Some properties are used only when your program is running. For example, the following objects have properties that keep track of values:

- ✔ EntryFields
- ✔ ListBoxes and ComboBoxes
- ✔ SpinBoxes
- ✔ CheckBoxes and RadioButtons

In some cases, you may want an object to have a specific value when the program starts. You may set these initial values and then allow users to change them while the program is running.

Creating the Sandbox of All Objects, the Form

User interfaces in dBASE for Windows are built on objects called *forms*. Like a child's sandbox, a form is a place where you can use your building blocks to create incredible worlds. Forms are sometimes referred to as windows. However, to follow the convention used in the dBASE for Windows on-line help system and the dBASE for Windows manuals, we will refer to them in this book as forms. This will also help differentiate between the form you are building and the multi-scadzillion other windows and dialog boxes used by dBASE for Windows.

To create a blank form, enter the following command in the Command window:

```
CREATE FORM
```

The Command window has the title Command. If it isn't displayed on your screen, you can bring it up by clicking on the magic lamp icon in the tool bar. You know, "Your wish is my command!" Let's hope you get more than three wishes. ■

Watching what happens when you give the CREATE FORM command is as much fun as adding water to a magic crystal set. Windows start popping up everywhere. Your screen ends up looking something like Figure 1-3. The blank window with the rather informative title of Form Designer (Untitled), usually found in the upper-left part of the screen, is the new form.

The Object Properties window and the Controls window should appear on the screen next to the blank form. If they don't, click on the form with the

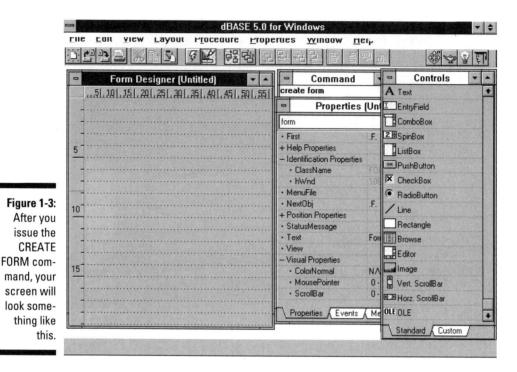

Figure 1-3:
After you
issue the
CREATE
FORM com-
mand, your
screen will
look some-
thing like
this.

right mouse button. This displays a pop-up menu that lists the available windows. If Object Properties and Controls have check marks, those windows are open somewhere on the screen, and you just have to hunt for them. If those windows aren't open, click their names in the pop-up menu.

One of the more challenging characteristics of dBASE for Windows is the shooting-gallery-like window interface. You're never really sure whether dBASE for Windows will display the windows you want, and if so, where. Sometimes, the window you want is completely hidden. At other times, it is only partially visible beneath another window. To make a partially hidden window pop to the top, click its title bar. It's like hitting the little ducks in the carnival shooting gallery. If you lose a window because it's totally hidden, select it from the Window menu, which lists the currently open windows. ■

Let's Play

Hurray! You've created your first form, and there were no casualties! Now you can poke around, contort, and otherwise annoy your form, all in the name of learning. Go ahead, it won't bite.

For now, the form is like a car without a steering wheel, gas pedal, brake pedal, or speedometer. You can start it, but you can't really go anywhere with it yet. If someone gave you a car like that, the first thing you would want to do is put some controls in it, such as a steering wheel. Your form doesn't need a steering wheel, but you do need to add controls if you want the form to be useful.

Controls on a form are objects that let users of your program select, enter, browse, change, and delete information. These controls are the building blocks of your application. dBASE for Windows provides a window full of controls. This Controls window is also called the Controls Palette, because you can paint the form with controls.

You're probably itching to play with the Controls window by now, so let's jump ahead for a moment and do just that. Conventional wisdom says to look before you leap. Sometimes we like to pretend we're conventional. So you know what we're getting you into, Figure 1-4 shows the Controls window.

To select a control type to place on the form, click one of the items in the Controls window. Now click on the form in the area you'd like the control to appear. If your computer likes you, a control appears on the form. If a control doesn't appear on the form, maybe you should spend more time with your computer, or call it during the day to let it know you care.

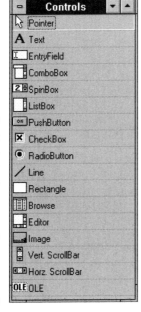

Figure 1-4:
The Controls window acts as your control palette, displaying the types of controls you can paint on a form.

Keep adding controls to your form until you get bored, the ball on your mouse reaches 50,000 miles, or you create perfection. You can move a control by using the left mouse button to click and drag the control to a new position on the form. You can also change the size and shape of a control by clicking and dragging the little rectangles that appear on the control when you select it.

Two Lovely Acres in Tarzana

Fortunately, you don't need a real estate agent to explore the properties of a form. You won't find any No Trespassing signs, and if you're lucky, the guard dogs may leave you alone. Bring a large steak just in case.

Getting to the properties

To open the Properties window for the form, click on the form using your right mouse button, and select Object Properties from the pop-up menu that's displayed. Then, click on the Properties tab at the bottom of the Properties window. The window should look like Figure 1-5.

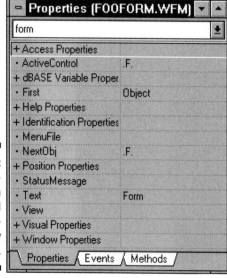

Figure 1-5: Object properties can be listed alphabetically or by type.

There are two ways to view an object's properties in the Properties window, alphabetically or by type. This example uses the Object Properties Outline method to display by property type. To change a property, use the tool icon that appears when you select the property, or type over the existing value and press Enter. ■

Positioning the form on your screen

The property type called Position Properties contains properties related to the position of the form on the screen. The form's Position Properties are

- ✔ *Height.* The height of the form.
- ✔ *Left.* The distance from the left side of the screen to the left side of the form.
- ✔ *Top.* The distance from the top of the screen to the top of the form.
- ✔ *Width.* The width of the form.

You can click and drag the border of the form to increase or decrease the form's size. To change the Left and Top positions, click the title bar and drag the form to a new location.

Changing the way a form looks

Each form has a title bar that can contain informative text. The Text property allows you to change the text that's displayed in a form's title bar.

Some forms are really obnoxious; they like to tell you what to do as soon as possible. You use the StatusMessage property to enter a message that will be displayed at the bottom of the screen when the form is used. Try not to be rude.

To change the form's color, modify the ColorNormal property in the Visual Properties type. This property allows you to change the foreground and background colors of the form.

The N/W means in the ColorNormal property is a holdover from earlier versions of dBASE. In those versions, foreground and background colors were represented by a letter. The letter N happens to represent black. N means None, you see. The W stands for white, but it means gray (don't ask why). In the old style of colors, you could make a color brighter by adding a plus sign. If you wanted white, you would enter W+. The first letter is the foreground color and the second is the background. Therefore, N/W gets you black letters on a gray background. ▪

Helping the form be on its best behavior

Many programs allow the user to close windows by pressing the Esc key. To tell your form to close when the user presses Esc, you need to set the EscExit property, which is found in the Window Properties type. By setting this property to .T. (True), you specify that the form should close when the user presses the Esc key. If you don't want the user to close the form by pressing Esc, set this property to .F. (False).

Several Window Properties have true or false values that determine which window features are available when the form is used. These properties include:

✔ *Maximize*. This property determines whether an up-arrow icon is included in the right corner of the form to let the user expand the form to full-screen size.

✔ *Minimize*. This property determines whether a down-arrow icon is included in the right corner of the form to let the user shrink the form to an icon.

✔ *Moveable*. This property determines whether the user can move the form around the screen.

✔ *Sizeable*. This property determines whether the user can change the size of the form by dragging its corners and sides.

✔ *SysMenu*. This property determines whether the System menu appears in the upper-left corner of the form.

The size of objects on a form is calculated according to a consistent scale. This scale is set by choosing a font in the following Window Properties:

✔ *ScaleFontName*. This property identifies the font that's used when calculating the dimensions of an object on the form.

✔ *ScaleFontSize*. This property identifies the size of the font that's used when calculating the dimensions of an object on the form.

One unit of size equals one character in the font you've selected. You don't usually need to change the ScaleFont properties of a form. ▪

Save Your Form, We Like You Just the Way You Are

There are several ways to save your form:

- ✔ Press Ctrl-W to save the form and exit the Form Designer.

- ✔ Press Ctrl-F4 to close the form. dBASE for Windows will tell you if changes have been made and ask whether you'd like to save them.

- ✔ Choose <u>S</u>ave from the <u>F</u>ile menu to save the form and continue in the Form Designer.

The key combination Ctrl-W can be used to save almost anything in dBASE for Windows. This saves whatever you're working on and closes the editor you're using. ■

Hang out your shingle, you're a Windows programmer. You already know a lot about putting windows on the screen. You can place them where you want; change their size, shape, and color; and even change the way they behave. You even know how to put controls on the form. The next chapter takes you deeper into controls. You learn how they are used and why you would want them on your form.

Chapter 2

Making Your Form Perform

In This Chapter

▶ Placing controls on the form

▶ Convincing controls to do something useful

▶ Designing and using menus, so you won't go hungry

▶ Open the window; it's warm in here

A blank form isn't that exciting. You want a form with personality, skill, daring, a sense of humor, and the ability to listen. Wait, those are things you look for in a partner! Well then, as long as you're forming an intimate relationship with your form, it might as well be interesting and attractive, not to mention useful. This chapter shows you how to give your form all these qualities by adding controls and a menu.

Control Yourself

Controls are the most important objects in a program's user interface. Controls allow users to interact with the form, giving them something to click on, type in, or select from. Adding controls to your form makes it useful.

When you're familiar with the different control types and what they're used for, you may have trouble holding back the flood of creativity that suddenly overcomes you. For now, go slow and try not to giggle too hard when you find out how easy this is. With practice, you can learn to add controls to a form without bursting into uncontrollable laughter.

To place controls on a form, you edit the form using the Form Designer. To modify an existing form called MyForm, you would click in the Command window, which is usually located in the upper-right corner of your screen, and type the following command:

```
MODIFY FORM MyForm
```

The Form Designer appears on your screen and displays your form.

Of course, this assumes that you already have a form and now you want to modify it. (Which should be the case, unless you skipped Chapter 1.) Don't worry though, creating a new form with the Form Designer is easy. All you do is type CREATE FORM in the Command window. ■

Once you're using the Form Designer, follow these steps to add a new control to the form:

1. Open the Controls window (if it's not already open) by clicking on the form with the right mouse button and then checking the Controls option on the pop-up menu that's displayed. The Controls window is shown in Figure 2-1.

2. Select the control type to place on the form from the Controls window.

3. Click on the form in the location you'd like a new control to appear.

4. Call your mother and tell her what you did.

Table 2-1 describes the control types that you'll find in the Controls window.

Figure 2-1:
The Controls window helps you add controls to a form.

Table 2-1: Control types in the Controls window

Control type	Description
Pointer	The Pointer isn't a control; it's the tool you use to manipulate controls that are already on the form. Confused yet?
A Text	Displays text on a form that the user can't edit.
EntryField	Displays text that the user can edit, or allows the user to type a single line of text in the control.
ComboBox	Gives the user a choice of selecting an option from a drop-down list or typing in a value. If necessary, you can also force the user to choose from the list.
SpinBox	Lets the user scroll through a range of valid entries for the control.
ListBox	Displays a list that the user can scroll through and select from. A ListBox control can respond immediately when the user clicks on the list or it can simply highlight the option.
PushButton	Gives users a button they can click that causes something to happen.
CheckBox	Displays a box that can be either checked or empty, giving a choice between two possibilities.
RadioButton	Displays a group of choices and allows only one to be selected.
Line	Draws lines on the form.
Rectangle	Draws rectangles on the form.
Browse	Displays or allows editing of information from the database.
Editor	Displays or allows editing of a text file or memo field.
Image	Displays an image from a file, resource, or binary database field.
Vert. ScrollBar	Displays a vertical scroll bar that is not connected to any other control.
Horz. ScrollBar	Displays a horizontal scroll bar that is not connected to any other control.
OLE	Displays an OLE object from an OLE database field.

You can continue selecting and placing controls until your computer runs out of memory. To see how much memory you have left, select Help | About ... from the dBASE for Windows menu.

To remove a control from the form, you should:

1. Click on the object to select it.
2. Press the Del key.
3. Marvel as the control vanishes.

Text with static cling

Have you ever gone to work with cotton socks stuck to your back? If so, they probably stuck there without moving. They certainly didn't serve any purpose. The word *static* means unmoving and unchanging. The second object listed in Table 2-1 is a Text control, which is a static object. Almost every form you create will use Text controls. These controls are called static for two reasons:

- ✔ They stick to a form and just sit there like bumps on a log.
- ✔ Users can't change them.

However, static doesn't mean cast in stone. You can make the following types of changes to a Text control:

- ✔ You can change the text by using the Text property in the Properties window.
- ✔ You can change the Font properties using the Properties window.
- ✔ You can resize a Text control either by entering new values in the Height and Width properties, or by clicking and dragging the handles that surround the control when you select it in the Form Designer.

Even though a Text control is static, you can do many useful things with it. Figures 2-2 through 2-4 give you some creative examples.

Figure 2-2:
Static text
controls can
display sim-
ple
thoughts.

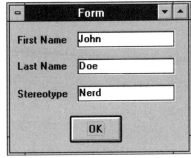

Figure 2-3:
Static text
controls
can label
other
controls.

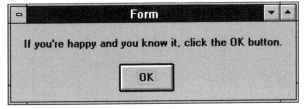

Figure 2-4:
Static text
controls
can give
instructions
to the user.

Push me!

PushButtons play an important role in the government of your forms. They present a clear and simple course of action with slogans such as OK, CANCEL, SAVE, or TAX-AND-SPEND. Armed with little more than these catchy slogans, PushButtons convince the user that clicking them is a good idea. Some users even click a PushButton more than once, though their reasons aren't always clear.

Although PushButtons may appear to be extremely powerful, most PushButtons get work done only when they are clicked. A PushButton's purpose is usually limited, and it doesn't change. When you want the user to do something simple and repetitive, a PushButton is an excellent choice.

Figure 2-5 shows a PushButton in the Form Designer, with its properties displayed in the Properties window.

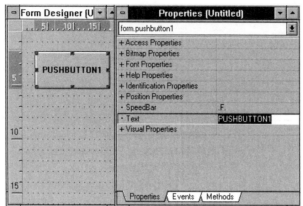

Figure 2-5:
This
PushButton
has a really
weak
slogan.

You use the PushButton's Text property to define the text that appears on the button. To change the text that appears on a PushButton, select the Text property in the Properties window and type over the existing value. You can change the font by changing the PushButton's Font Properties.

You've got the look

You can spice up a PushButton's appearance by adding bitmap graphics to the button. To do this, edit the button's Bitmap Properties, and choose the bitmaps you want for any or all of the four button states:

- *Disabled.* The button can't be used at this time. In other words, nothing happens if the user clicks it.

- *Down.* The button is depressed (poor thing). In other words, it is being clicked.

- *Focus.* The button has input focus. *Focus* means the control has the full attention of dBASE for Windows. When you click on a control, you "focus" the attention of the program on that control.

- *Up.* The button is in its normal state, that is, the state it returns to after being depressed.

Figure 2-6 shows a button with a bitmap in the Up state.

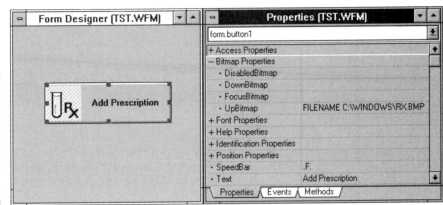

Figure 2-6:
You can use
bitmaps to
enhance
the appear-
ance of
buttons.

Defining hot keys

A hot key allows the user to select a button using a key combination rather than the mouse. For example, you could define Alt-S as the hot key for a PushButton labeled SAVE. Then, the user could choose the PushButton with the mouse or by pressing Alt-S.

To define a hot key for a PushButton, include an ampersand (&) in the Text property of the button. As shown in Figure 2-7, the letter, number, or symbol

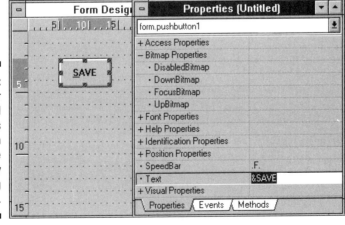

Figure 2-7:
A user
could
choose this
PushButton
with the
mouse or by
pressing
Alt-S.

following the & is underlined on the PushButton. When a hot key is defined, the user can select the PushButton by pressing Alt together with the underlined letter, number, or symbol.

Hmm, I'd like one of those, and one of those, and...

When you were a child, or acting like a child, most of the things that involved picking were bad—picking a fight, picking at your food, picking the wrong friends. However, picking in dBASE for Windows is a good thing. Three types of controls let users pick things from lists:

- ComboBoxes
- SpinBoxes
- ListBoxes

Oh no, now you have to pick which control to use!

ComboBoxes

There are three styles of ComboBoxes. To change the style of a ComboBox control, set the Style property, which is found in the Visual Properties, to one of the following:

- Simple
- DropDown
- DropDownList

Art as a function of society

You aren't a programmer. You're an information artist. The controls and colors you use—how your form looks and "feels"—should reflect life around you. Artists are an important part of society because they help us see and think in new ways. Powerful artwork can have a significant impact on people's attitudes and change their expectations of life. As an information artist, you can give people new understanding of and appreciation for the information in their lives. Now, don't come crying to us if you cut off your ear.

The simple ComboBox has two parts, an EntryField and a ListBox. You can fill in the EntryField by typing text or by selecting an entry from the ListBox. Figure 2-8 shows a simple ComboBox.

In the DropDown style, the ComboBox starts working its magic. It looks like an EntryField with a small arrow icon on the right. When the user clicks the arrow icon, the ComboBox displays a selection list that the user can choose from. After the user selects from the list, the selection appears in the EntryField, and the list disappears. Figure 2-9 shows a DropDown ComboBox.

Now for the super-slick ComboBox, the DropDownList. Like the DropDown style, this ComboBox style displays an EntryField with a small arrow icon on the right, which the user can click to select from a list. However, the user can also enter text in the EntryField. Figure 2-10 shows a DropDownList ComboBox.

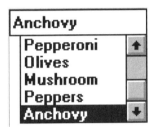

Figure 2-8: A simple ComboBox shows its list all the time.

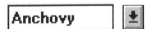

Figure 2-9: A DropDown ComboBox shows its list only when the user wants to see it.

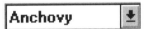

Figure 2-10: A DropDownList ComboBox is both an EntryField and a DropDown ComboBox.

SpinBoxes

As shown in Figure 2-11, SpinBoxes allow the user to scroll through a range of numeric values. You might use a SpinBox control to scroll through amounts in a quantity field or dates in an invoice date field. Sometimes it's easier to scroll through numbers or dates rather than retype them.

Figure 2-11: Use a SpinBox control to spin through numbers and dates.

You can define a range of values for the SpinBox by setting the Rangemax and Rangemin properties in the Edit Properties type. Set the SpinOnly property to .T. (true) if you don't want to allow the user to type in the SpinBox.

As you'll find out in Chapter 8, many of the operators you use in dBASE for Windows are enclosed by periods. These are known as *dot-delimited operators*. For now, you need to remember only that .T. means true and .F. means false. ■

ListBoxes

A ListBox control allows users to choose from a list. Unlike a ComboBox control, a ListBox doesn't display the user's choice. As you can see in Figure 2-12, a ListBox doesn't offer an EntryField.

Figure 2-12: Use a ListBox control to select choices from a list.

ListBoxes have two important properties:

> ✔ *DataSource*. This property identifies where a ListBox control gets the choices it displays. When a DataSource is specified, the ListBox fills in its choices. As you'll see in Chapter 4, a ListBox can have a number of possible DataSources.

> ✔ *DataLink*. This property identifies which field in a table is updated when a user chooses an item from the ListBox. (You'll learn more about tables and fields in Chapter 3.)

You might use a ListBox to allow a user to select from a list of customers.

You would use the DataSource property to supply the ListBox with the source of its list of customers. By entering the DataLink property, you allow the control to accept the user's selection.

On the other hand, you might want a ListBox that displays a list but doesn't allow the user to select anything. For example, the ListBox might list the last ten items purchased by a customer. It's pretty easy to create a ListBox like this because a ListBox is display-only until you establish a DataLink.

Teaching Your Objects to Do Tricks

Did you ever have a guinea pig as a pet? If so, have you ever wondered why? They really don't do much. They won't come if you call them, brush against your leg, catch mice, amaze your friends, or lick your face when you're sad.

Objects are better (though not cuter) than guinea pigs, because you can teach objects to do tricks. Pets do tricks in response to vocal commands or hand signals. Objects receive event notices, and respond by executing event procedures.

Event programming

Windows keeps track of things like when you click your mouse and what you click on. Each time an event such as a mouse click occurs, Windows sends a signal to the affected object. Writing Windows programs consists of issuing commands that are to be executed when one of these events takes place. This is known as *event programming*.

Each object can respond to events. Here are some typical events that objects in dBASE for Windows will respond to:

- ✔ OnClick. This event takes place when the user clicks an object with the left mouse button.

- ✔ OnLeftDblClick. This event occurs when the user double clicks an object with the left mouse button.

- ✔ OnLeftMouseDown. This event occurs when the user presses the left mouse button.

- ✔ OnLeftMouseUp. This event is triggered as soon as the user releases the left mouse button.

This is only a sampling of the types of events that dBASE for Windows responds to. The programs you write that tell dBASE for Windows how to respond to these events are known as *event handlers*.

When we say that you can teach your objects to do tricks, we are actually referring to writing event handlers to respond to different events.

Event notices are delivered to an object when something occurs that the object needs to know about. For example, when the user clicks a PushButton, an OnClick event notice is sent to the PushButton. dBASE for Windows has events for anything that can happen to an object, and you can write event procedures for each of them.

To see which events an object responds to, select the Events tab in the Properties window. Figure 2-13 shows a PushButton's events displayed in the Properties window.

Clicking the tool icon to the right of an event's name opens the Procedure Editor, which is shown in Figure 2-14. The Procedure Editor allows you to enter instructions that tell an object what it should do when events occur. There are many events in Windows, and most applications need only a few of them to function exactly as you'd like.

OK, so what's a procedure?

Procedures are sets of instructions that tell the computer what you want it to do. They are written in the dBASE for Windows Command Language.

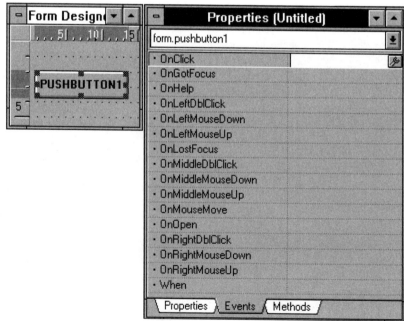

Figure 2-13:
A Push-
Button will
respond to
various
events.

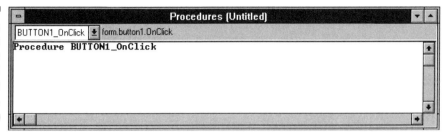

Figure 2-14:
You use the
Procedure
Editor to tell
objects
what to do.

The simplest procedures tell dBASE for Windows what actions to take by giving instructions in two ways:

✔ *Commands*. These are simple directives such as CLOSE FORM or QUIT.

✔ *Functions*. These are more versatile instructions, such as DATE( ) or TIME( ), which may return a value.

The dBASE for Windows Command Language consists of hundreds of commands and functions. Several pounds of them can be found in the dBASE for Windows manuals. Chapter 8 covers more complex procedures that can make decisions, loop, and store information in variables.

All procedures, simple and complex, begin with the word Procedure, followed by a name. This is how dBASE for Windows recognizes a procedure. Procedure names can be as long as needed.

dBASE for Windows assigns default names to the procedures that you write. You can change the names if you wish. Figure 2-15 shows a simple event

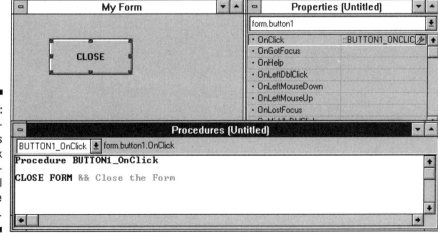

Figure 2-15:
This Push-
Button's
OnClick
event pro-
cedure will
close the
form.

procedure for a PushButton. When a user clicks the PushButton, this event procedure tells dBASE for Windows to close the form.

Windows make good parents

Before we go any further, you need to know how to talk to objects. When you want to talk to someone, it usually helps to know their name. The same is true with objects.

In dBASE for Windows, a form is considered a *parent object*, and the objects you place on the form are considered its *children*. An object's name has two parts. The first part is sort of like the family name. The second part is the object's unique name.

When you refer to a child object, you must use its full name. As children of the form, controls carry the family name. The name of a child object is preceded by the name of its parent, separated by a dot (period). For example, if your form includes a PushButton named DESIRE, you would refer to the Push-Button as:

```
FORM.DESIRE
```

To refer to a property of an object, add the property's name to the object's name, separated by a period. For example, you would refer to the Text attribute of a PushButton named DESIRE as:

```
FORM.DESIRE.Text
```

To change a property of an object within a procedure:

1. Begin a new line in the procedure.
2. Type the full name of the object, followed by the property name (*parent.object.property*).
3. Type an equal sign (=).
4. Type the new value for the property after the equal sign. Be sure to enclose text in quotation marks.

Figure 2-16 shows how you would change the Text property of a Text control from a PushButton's OnClick event procedure.

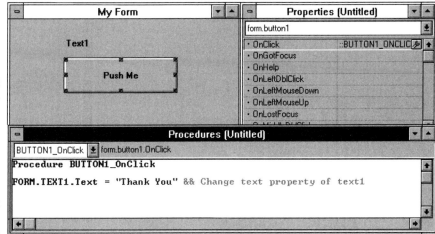

Figure 2-16:
When the
button is
clicked, this
procedure
changes the
text in a
Text
control.

There's a method to the madness

The preceding sections show how you can give objects capabilities by writing procedures that are triggered when an event occurs. You can also give an object capabilities that are not attached to events. These procedures, which are triggered by requests from the user or other objects, are called *methods*.

Some methods are already built in. For example, each form has an Open method. If another object calls this method, the form opens. In dBASE for Windows, you can create new capabilities for your form by adding methods to it.

As detailed in the preceding section, you need to get the name right when you call an object's methods. For example, the PushButton control has a Move( ) method. This built-in method can resize and reposition the PushButton. The following example shows how you call this method:

```
Form.PushButton1.Move(2,2,10,5)
```

The name of the parent—in this case the form—comes first, followed by the name of the object, and then the method. The names are separated by dots.

To create a new method, select Procedures | New Method from the menu at the top of the Form Designer screen. (The Procedures menu selection is available only while you are running the Form Designer.) This brings up the Procedure Editor. The default name for methods is PROCEDURE Method.

For fun, you can give your form the ability to blush. When the following method is called, the form turns bright red:

```
PROCEDURE Blush
FORM.ColorNormal = "N/R*"
```

You can now call the Blush method as you would any of the built-in methods such as FORM.Open( ), or you can link methods to events.

What's on the Menu?

Menus, menus, everywhere, and not a thing to eat.

Anyone who uses Windows software has grown accustomed to choosing from menus. Menus provide users with a simple, structured method for navigating through a program. A well-designed menu makes your application easier to use.

When designing menus for your programs, consistency with other Windows programs is an important consideration. Most menus in Windows follow a common style. Because most applications work with files in some way, the menus in Windows applications begin with a File option. Most applications also provide on-line help to the user, so most menus end with a Help option. You'll notice that this is true of dBASE for Windows as well. For more ideas about menu style, look through the dBASE for Windows menu and the menus of other Windows programs.

Building a menu

Menus provide fast, direct access to the different parts of your program. Boy, that sounds like an ad for pizza delivery. Although menus are not required in dBASE for Windows programs, they do make your programs more user-friendly.

A menu has two parts:

- The menu bar. This is the top bar that has selections such as File and Help.
- The pull-down menu. This is the menu that appears when you select an item from the menu bar.

The Menu Designer helps you build a menu quickly. To access the Menu Designer, type the following command in the Command window:

```
CREATE MENU
```

The Menu Designer is shown in Figure 2-17.

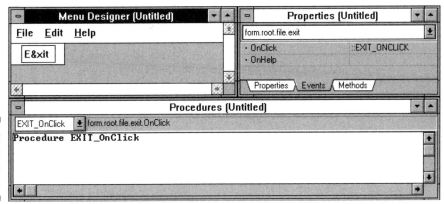

Figure 2-17:
The Menu
Designer in
action.

After opening the Menu Designer, you begin creating your menu by entering the first menu bar item, which is usually File. To do this, you simply type File at the current cursor position.

In the dBASE for Windows menu bar, you have probably noticed that the letter *F* in the word File is underlined. This means it is a *hot key*. Hot keys allow users to access menu choices by holding down the Alt key and typing the underlined letter. To access the File pull-down menu, you press Alt-F.

To create hot keys for your menus, type an ampersand (&) before the appropriate letter in the menu item that you are creating. The ampersand isn't displayed in the menu. Instead, the letter following the ampersand is underlined, which means it is a hot key.

Once you have entered your first menu bar selection, press Enter. This lets you enter the first choice on the File drop-down menu (assuming that File is the first choice in your menu bar). The File drop-down menu usually includes such choices as New, Open, and Exit. Continue adding drop-down menu choices until you have completed the choices under the first menu bar selection.

Exit is usually the last choice in the File drop-down menu. The hot key is usually the letter *x*. Once again, you should pay close attention to menu designs in other programs. You want to give your programs a professional look and feel.

You can also create a sub-menu for any drop-down menu choice. To add a sub-menu, press the right-arrow key on your keyboard. A sub-menu will appear next to your menu selection.

When you are ready to begin your next menu bar selection, press the up-arrow key until the cursor moves up to the menu bar, then press Tab. The cursor moves to the right, and you can begin entering a new menu bar item and its drop-down menu choices.

To exit the Menu Designer and save your menu, press Ctrl-W. When prompted, enter a name for your menu file. Once your menu structure is complete, you will want to create the procedures that allow your menu to actually do something. The next section shows you how to add procedures to each menu choice.

Drop down! Pop up! Fight! Fight! Fight!

Now that you are an expert menu builder and know how to write procedures, it's time to put the two together. You use the Properties window to add a procedure to a menu selection. To modify the meny you just created, enter the MODIFY MENU command followed by the name of your menu file. Your new menu should be on the screen. To open the Properties window, click on the menu selection with your right mouse button, and select Object Properties from the pop-up menu that is displayed.

As you can see in the Properties window shown back in Figure 2-17, each menu choice has two events:

- ✔ The OnClick event, which is triggered by a mouse click on the menu choice.
- ✔ The OnHelp event, which is triggered when the user highlights the menu choice and presses F1.

You can write procedures or link methods to these menu choice events. A common menu choice is Exit. With this menu choice, you probably want to close the form. To add this capability to your menu do the following:

1. Click the Exit menu item in the Menu Designer.
2. Find the Properties window and click the Events tab to display the events for the Exit menu item.
3. Click the OnClick row to display the tool icon for the OnClick event.
4. Click the tool icon to access the Procedure Editor.
5. Enter the OnClick event procedure for the Exit menu item. When you're finished, the Procedure Editor will contain the following code:

```
PROCEDURE Exit_OnClick
FORM.Close()
```

As you become more proficient at writing programs in dBASE for Windows, your menu items can become more complex.

Saving your menu

When you have defined all your menu items and written your procedures, you should save the menu. To save the menu, press Ctrl-W. If it is brand new, you will be prompted for a filename. All of your menus are saved with a file-name and the extension .MNU. You need to remember the menu filename to attach it to a form. A menu cannot be run without a form.

Attaching the menu to your form

Imagine that you're walking down the street one sunny day. It would be a per-fect day if you weren't so hungry. Then, you hear something crunch under your foot. Looking down, you see a paper with the words "à la carte" staring back at you. You lean over and start reading. (You don't pick it up, because picking up things off the street is another bad picking thing.) Pretty soon you can smell and almost taste the delicious food described on the menu. This is because you are bent over and all the blood is rushing to your noggin. You stagger a bit when you stand up too quickly. You look around and there are no restaurants to be found, not even a fast-food joint. A menu without a restaurant, what a cruel thing.

The moral of this story is that a menu by itself is worthless. The wonderful menu you have so artfully created needs to be attached to a form. In the Properties window for the form, you will find a property called MenuFile. If you click on the tool icon for this property, you are prompted to select the menu file you have created. This bonds the menu to the form, avoiding sad stories like the one you just read.

If you have multiple forms in your application, you can associate a different menu with each form. As the user moves from form to form, the menu at the top of the screen changes.

The Big Event! Running the Form

Building forms is like putting a kite together. It isn't much fun if you can't play with it. Along the top of the screen, dBASE for Windows provides a toolbar containing a number of icons. Some icons in dBASE for Windows have light-ning bolts. The lightning bolt signifies doing something. The icon in Figure 2-18 is a lightning bolt all by itself. Clicking on this icon runs your form.

When you select this Run icon, dBASE for Windows checks your program for errors. How could there be errors? Well, we don't want to shatter your

Figure 2-18: The lightning bolt icon lets you run your form.

dreamy image of computers, but they make mistakes too. If an error window appears on your screen, select Cancel and see the dBASE for Windows on-line help. Error messages are listed alphabetically and numerically.

To stop running your form and re-enter the playworld of design mode, click on the icon shown in Figure 2-19.

Figure 2-19: The Design Mode icon stops running your form and returns you to the Form Designer.

In this chapter, you have explored some of the most important elements in developing a dBASE for Windows application. Controls are the building blocks that make your forms useful. Adding procedures and methods to your controls gives them real capabilities. Menus are objects that allow you to run procedures and access parts of your program by calling them with event procedures. We cover a lot more programming in this book, and this chapter should give you a solid foundation. You may want to review this chapter as you become more proficient with the dBASE for Windows language. Part II covers creating database tables and using them with your forms and controls.

Part II

Creating Data Tables and Making Them Useful

The 5th Wave — By Rich Tennant

"YO-I THINK WE'VE GOT A NEW KIND OF VIRUS HERE!"

In This Part...

Managing information is the heart of dBASE for Windows. (Other vital organs include the lungs, brain, and kidneys, but that's not important right now.) Effective information management begins with creating and perfecting a table—the storage container for your data. Then, you need to organize your data in useful ways, and develop the forms and controls that make it easy to access the data. When you've finished this part of the book, you'll know what it feels like to get what you ask for every time. You're about to learn how to put dBASE for Windows to work managing your data.

Chapter 3

Evolving Your Database

● ●

In This Chapter

▶ Getting ready to store information

▶ Storing your data so that it doesn't clutter up the office

▶ Making sense of data by sorting it

▶ Browsing the shelves

▶ Getting data out once it's in there

▶ Modifying information when you've found it

● ●

A table is a place for storing information. In written tables (such as the ones you find in books), information is listed in columns and rows. In the world of databases, information is stored in fields and records. Like a column, a *field* is a place to store individual pieces of information. One field (or column) might contain names, another might contain addresses. A *record* (or a row in a written table) contains a group of related fields. For example, a record might consist of a name field and an address field. When building a database table, you want to create a structure that makes it easy and efficient to store and find the information you need. This chapter shows you how to construct a table using the dBASE for Windows Table Designer.

Creating Tables the Easy Way

In most kitchens, there's a drawer containing knives, forks, and spoons, all neatly laid out in a plastic organizer. The organizer has molded indentations that vaguely resemble the utensils that are stored in them. There are places for big spoons and little spoons, long spaces for the knives, and shorter ones for the forks.

Data tables are a lot like your kitchen organizer; they must be molded to hold the information you want to store in them. dBASE for Windows has a very useful tool for doing just that. It's called the Table Designer.

However, we shouldn't get ahead of ourselves. You need to do a few things before you use the Table Designer:

1. Figure out which information you want to collect.

2. Arrange the information into logical groups.

3. Order a pizza.

4. Type CREATE in the Command window.

Getting the best table

Designing the table structure is the key to creating a successful application. A poor table design makes it extremely difficult to develop the rest of the program, and this difficulty only increases as you try to accomplish more sophisticated tasks with the information in your table.

Knowing what you want from your table will help you determine what you need to put into it. In other words, you need to anticipate how the information in your table will be used. Imagine the output you'd like, and think about what you'll have to do to get it. This will help you organize information in your tables.

Working things out on paper is one of the most effective planning tools you can use. Your design plan should explain the flow of information by answering such questions as:

✔ Where does the information come from?

✔ How is the information processed?

✔ How is the information used?

✔ How is the information stored?

✔ What happens when you have too much information?

✔ How is the information backed up?

Review the plan in detail with the people who will use your program. Risk boring them with too much information. Many users try to distance themselves from the details, believing that it is your job to work magic, read minds, and know their job better than they do. In many cases, you will have to do all of that and more.

When you create that ideal design, you should treat yourself to a nice dinner. As a successful table designer, you can expect to be seated at the very best table in any good restaurant. Here are some tips for getting just the right table:

✔ Call ahead for reservations.

✔ Ask if the restaurant accepts Platinum cards.

✔ Ask if they would be embarrassed by a 25% gratuity.

✔ Inquire if they stock Dom Perignon.

✔ Intimate that you might be a food editor.

✔ Buy the restaurant.

Deciding what to plant in your fields

When designing data tables, it's usually a good idea to create a list of the information you want to collect. Match this list against any reports you need. This will help you identify calculations you might need, fields you hadn't thought of, and maybe a table of summary information.

Your table will probably include different types of data, including text, numbers, dates, and logical information. Once you have a definitive list of the information you want to collect, you can design the places where you will put the information—that is, the fields that will make up your table.

In dBASE for Windows, you can store the following types of information:

✔ Character data, such as names, addresses, or other text data.

✔ Numeric data, such as amounts, ages, and other numbers you may want to use in mathematical operations.

✔ Dates, such as birthdays.

✔ Logical data, which is yes and no, or true and false data. For example, you might want to store data about whether or not customers like your product.

✔ Memo fields, which are used for storing large amounts of text data. You can use memo fields to write accounts of conversations with people, or biographies, or short novels.

✔ Binary data, such as sounds or graphics. For example, you can store employees' pictures in binary fields.

✔ OLE fields, which can contain documents or links to documents from other applications. You might use an OLE field to store an Excel spreadsheet or a Word document.

As suggested by this list, a database doesn't have to be a boring collection of text and numbers. A picture is worth a thousand words, and the binary field type lets you put pictures in your table. If you're hot on multimedia, you can create another binary field to store some sounds. In fact, you can store many types of binary information in this field type. For example, you can store the mechanical drawings you created in your favorite CAD package.

Binary fields store non-text information in binary format—that is, ones and zeros that only a computer could love, or even understand. This is a common format for storing complex information such as graphics or sounds. To look at the pictures or hear the sounds, you must use the tools supplied with dBASE for Windows. You can store other binary files here, but dBASE for Windows doesn't give you any tools to access them.

In some cases, you might decide that it's best to store certain information in another application that you can link to your dBASE for Windows table using object linking and embedding (OLE). Perhaps you have a considerable amount of numeric information that must be recalculated whenever any of the values change. It might be easier to create this type of procedure in a spreadsheet program and then store the entire spreadsheet in an OLE field.

Although the variety of possible field types might seem a bit daunting at first, you'll find that it's usually very straightforward deciding which field type to use for a particular piece of data.

Building a table with no legs

When creating a table, you use the Table Designer to define the table structure. As shown in Figure 3-1, this definition includes such information as the name, type, and width of each field.

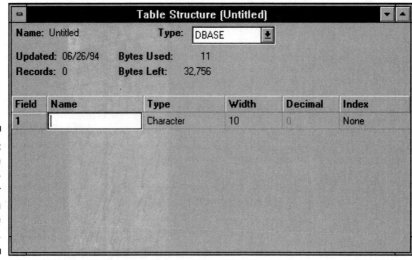

Figure 3-1:
You create the structure of your data table in the Table Designer.

You may feel a little important when you issue the CREATE command in the Command window, optionally followed by the name you would like to give your new table:

```
CREATE Universe
```

This command opens the Table Designer and creates a new table named Universe.

Designing a table is a little like creating a questionnaire. Your questionnaire would have blank spaces for entering information. For example, you might have spaces for a name, telephone number, and today's date. You can think of each space as a field. The word that identifies what to put in a specific field, such as Name or Date, is the *field name*. Figure 3-1 shows the Table Designer prompting for a field name.

There are a few important rules for creating field names:

- ✔ They can be up to 10 characters long.
- ✔ They must start with a letter.
- ✔ They can't contain spaces.
- ✔ You can separate words by using underscores instead of spaces.

Although field names in tables are capitalized, dBASE for Windows is not sensitive about case. You can use all capital letters or mix upper- and lower-case letters. However, when you write programs and procedures, it's helpful to develop a style and stick with it. This will make your programs easier to read. ■

Tables typically have meaningful field names, such as LASTNAME, FIRST-NAME, ADDRESS, CITY, STATE, and ZIPCODE. It's a good idea to break proper names into first and last names. This makes retrieving information by name much easier.

Try to come up with descriptive field names. Imagine trying to fill out a form with blanks labeled Info, Data, Stuff, or worse yet, SBJK12_1. You may not be the only person to use the table, so it's important to choose field names that another user will understand. ■

Next, you must decide on the field type. The default type is character. If you click on the word Character, the Table Designer displays a ListBox arrow. You can drop down a list of field types by clicking this arrow. Table 3-1 provides some simple guidelines for choosing the right field type.

Table 3-1: Which field type should you use?

Field type	Description
Character	Text information, including numbers and letters
Numeric	Numbers that you plan to use in math operations
Memo	Lots of text
Logical	Yes or no, true or false
Date	A valid day of the year, not your friend
Float	Floating-point numbers, not fishing
OLE	Documents and links to other applications
Binary	Binary data such as pictures or sounds

When you get really slick at building tables, you'll want some shortcuts. You can automatically fill in the field type by typing the first letter of the type instead of dropping down the list. For example, you can type N for numeric, or D for date. ■

You must specify a width for some of the field types; others have default widths. The width of a character field is simply the number of characters you want the user to be able to enter in that field. For numeric and floating-point fields, you can enter both the field width and the number of decimal places.

When calculating the width for numeric and floating-point fields, you must count the decimal point as part of the width. For example, 99999.99 requires a width of 8 and a decimal width of 2. ■

Memo, binary, and OLE fields have a default width of 10. dBASE for Windows uses those 10 characters as a link to the external file that contains the data for the memo, binary, or OLE field.

The last column in the Table Designer is labeled Index. In a nutshell, you can arrange the information in the table in ascending or descending order based on a particular field. The default value for this column is None. Indexes are explained in considerable detail later in this chapter, so stay tuned.

When you are finished creating your table structure, you can save the new structure by pressing Ctrl-W or by selecting Close from the System menu in the upper-left corner of the Table Designer.

Tips for some common fields

It's usually a good idea to create separate fields for first names, last names, and sometimes middle names. This makes it easier to index or sort the information. A good width for first name fields is 15, and 18 works well for last name fields.

Address, city, state, and zip code fields are all character information. A zip code doesn't need to be a numeric field because you don't need to use a zip code in mathematical operations. For example, you wouldn't calculate the average zip code in a particular county, or the standard deviation of zip codes in a three state area. The same is true for telephone numbers and social security numbers.

Ages are usually stored as numeric fields, or they can be calculated from a birthdate that is stored as a date field. You might want to be able to calculate the average age.

Sorting your data with simple indexes

As you saw in Figure 3-1, the last column in the Table Designer is called Index. If you click in this column, the Table Designer displays a ListBox arrow.

You create a simple index by clicking the List Box arrow and choosing either Ascending or Descending from the drop-down list. It's known as a simple index because the computer finds it simple to put your data in order. The simple index orders your data based on a single field.

Only certain field types can be indexed. However, you may create as many simple indexes as you have fields that can be indexed. For example, if you have a table structure with NAME, ADDRESS, and ZIPCODE fields, you might create indexes on both the NAME field and the ZIPCODE field. Of course, you could also create an index on the ADDRESS field.

The following field types can be indexed:

- ✔ Character
- ✔ Numeric
- ✔ Date
- ✔ Float

More Address Book than You'll Ever Need

The first application many people create is an address book. This always makes us smile because addresses are usually the one thing that people have organized in their lives. What else in your life is always alphabetized either in a book or in a card file? Not only that, how many addresses can one person have anyway? Maybe 100? If you have an extensive business card collection from the past 30 years, maybe you have 300. So, why would you need a computer program that can handle thousands (or even millions) of names and addresses?

Like any table you create, your address book is actually limited by the size of your hard disk. Let's say the address and other information for each person takes about 200 bytes, and your hard drive holds about 200 million bytes. After using roughly 50 million bytes for Windows, dBASE for Windows, and other important software programs, you still have room for 750,000 names and addresses. Personally, we wouldn't want to have that many friends and acquaintances. ■

If you still want to create an address book application, it's perfectly okay with us. However, a program to predict global weather patterns might be a loftier goal. The bottom line here is that you can enter a lot of information.

Using Your Table

Before you can add information to a table, you must open the table. In dBASE terminology, you need to USE a particular table. In the Command window, enter the USE command and the name of the table you want to open:

```
USE MyTable
```

The only way to know whether you have successfully opened the table is by looking at the status bar at the bottom of the screen. The status bar helps you keep track of what's going on in dBASE for Windows. Figure 3-2 shows the status bar shedding some light on things.

The status bar shows you:

- The name of your open table
- Whether you have exclusive use or are sharing the table with others on the network

Figure 3-2:
The status
bar keeps
you
informed.

✔ The current record number

✔ The total number of records in the table

When dBASE for Windows opens a table, it always points to the top or first record. If an index is active, the top of the file may not be record number one.

Adding Information to Your Table

Once a table is open, you can start adding records. To add new records to the table, type the following command in the Command window:

```
APPEND
```

As shown in Figure 3-3, the Append command opens the Table Records window, which allows you to enter values for each field in the table. You can move forward or backward through the records you add by pressing PgUp or PgDn respectively.

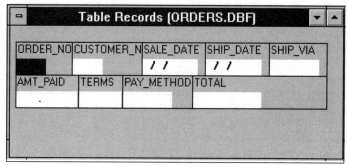

Figure 3-3:
You use the
Table
Records
window to
add, modify,
or view
records.

When adding records, you should remember two important points:

✔ When you finish adding information, don't press the Esc key. If you do, you will lose the information in the record you are working on. Instead use Ctrl-W to save your information.

✔ If you're in a blank record when you finish adding records, move back one record before saving; otherwise dBASE for Windows will save the blank record. ▪

I browse

The Browse window is the most versatile way to view and change information in a table. The Browse window presents your data in a columnar format similar to a spreadsheet. For you couch potatoes, it also looks like the prime-time-at-a-glance listings in your weekly TV directory.

To start browsing, you must:

✔ Be sitting at your computer

✔ Be using your table

✔ Have at least one record in the table

You open a Browse window by typing BROWSE in the Command window.

In the Browse window, you can scroll through the records using the vertical scroll bar or the up-arrow and down-arrow keys. If all the data columns don't fit across the Browse window, you can scroll to the right by pressing Tab or by using the horizontal scroll bar. Figure 3-4 shows the Browse window displaying records from the Orders table.

		Table Records [ORDERS.DBF]						
Rec	ORDER_NO	CUSTOMER_N	SALE_DATE	SHIP_DATE	SHIP_VIA	AMT_PAID	TERMS	PAY_METHOD
74	1730	5515	05/12/97	05/20/97	FedEx	0.00	Net 30	MC
75	1741	6215	06/01/97	06/02/97	UPS	179.00	FOB	MC
76	1750	6312	06/01/97	06/05/97	FedEx	500.00	FOB	Check
77	1751	6312	06/02/97	06/10/97	UPS	20.00	Net 30	Check
78	1760	6516	06/02/97	06/03/97	UPS	525.00	Net 30	MC
79	1775	6582	06/02/97	06/10/97	UPS	100.00	FOB	MC
80	1781	6812	06/02/97	06/11/97	FedEx	300.00	Net 30	MC
81	1785	6812	06/03/97	06/06/97	UPS	0.00	FOB	Visa
82	1789	6812	06/03/97	06/11/97	FedEx	0.00	Net 30	Visa

Figure 3-4:
You can use
the Browse
window to
view, edit,
delete,
and add
records.

Here's how to add data when you're in the Browse window. From the last record in the table, press the down-arrow key and dBASE for Windows will ask whether you'd like to add more records. If you answer yes, you can add records by filling in each field and pressing Enter. When you fill all the fields for one record, dBASE for Windows automatically adds a new record for you to fill in. You can continue adding records until you either exit Browse or press the up-arrow key. ▪

Filling your table with junk food

An empty table is like an empty wallet. It looks good, it smells good, it opens and closes, but you can't pull anything out of it. An empty wallet is a very sad thing indeed. An empty database table is even sadder. A wallet might be empty because you just bought a hot tub. Even though your wallet is empty, you can still enjoy your new hot tub. However, you can't have much fun with an empty table. You can't browse it, edit it, or list its contents. All you can do is open it, close it, and append records to it. But then it won't be empty anymore.

If you want to avoid having an empty table, you can generate records. Nuclear reactors generate, the Hoover Dam generates. Now, you can generate too.

The Generate feature allows you to fill up your table with gibberish. This might come in handy if you're a student and your homework is late. You can use this feature and then tell the teacher you must have a printer problem because your history assignment looked fine on the screen.

Why would you want to do something as silly as filling a table with nonsense? I'm glad you asked. When you are building applications, you need to have something in the table so you can browse, edit, or test controls on a form. You can use Generate to create that test data. Simply specify how many records you want, send in a box top or proof-of-purchase seal, and Generate will gladly comply. To generate 13 records, type the following command:

```
GENERATE 13
```

Here are some other things you can do with generated records:

- ✔ Look for cryptic anagrams.
- ✔ Tell your spouse that it's an encrypted file of old lovers.
- ✔ Try to recreate Shakespeare by generating enough records.
- ✔ On April Fools day, tell your boss the computer has a virus.

Moving through the Records

There are many ways to get around in a table full of data, though some are more efficient than others. You usually move through the records because you are looking for specific information. Browsing is cool, especially if you are being paid by the hour. But be sure your glasses are handy and a pot of coffee is brewing. You'll need them. Another equally inefficient method of looking for data is using the EDIT command. With EDIT, you use the Table Records window to view records one at a time.

When you move through the records, you also move an imaginary pointer called the record pointer. No matter how you arrive at a record, the record pointer doggedly follows you there, pointing like an Irish Setter.

Skipping through your records

In some cases, you might not be interested in what's stored in a record. You just want to move past it. The SKIP command lets you move through records without looking at them. In other words, SKIP moves the record pointer through the records. You can see the record number change in the status bar when you type SKIP in the Command window.

You can use the SKIP command over and over again. You also can skip several records at once. To do this, simply specify the number of records you want skipped at the end of the command. For example, this command skips 50 records at a time:

```
SKIP 50
```

You can also SKIP backward. You do this by following the SKIP command with a negative number. The following command moves you back one record:

```
SKIP -1
```

Getting there directly with GOTO

The GOTO command is useful for moving through the records. It is like the automated phone answering systems that tell you, "If you know the extension of the party you are trying to reach, please enter it now." If you know the record number you are trying to reach, please enter it after the GOTO command in the Command window:

```
GOTO 6
```

This command moves you to record number 6. If the table is in index order, you still move to record number 6, regardless of the record's position in the index.

You can also shorten this command to GO *RecordNumber*:

```
GO 6
```

The most common uses of the GO command are GO TOP and GO BOTTOM. The GO TOP command lets you move to the first record. With an index, GO TOP moves the record pointer to the first record in the index. In other words, GO TOP might take you to some record other than record 1. The GO BOTTOM command moves the record pointer to the last record in the table. ■

Looking for Mr. Goodbar

Rather than using the commands we've discussed so far, you might want to give your eyes a break and let dBASE for Windows do all the searching for you. (This is a much better way to look for information if you are paid on commission instead of by the hour.) When you need to find something, LOCATE and SEEK are very useful commands.

The LOCATE command starts at the beginning of the table and faithfully looks through the records one-by-one, like a persistent hound, a trained ferret, or a very hungry bear that's convinced you have food in your backpack. The LOCATE command tries to match the information you have given it with similar information in a table.

You type the LOCATE command in the Command window, followed by the information you are looking for. For example, the following command tells dBASE for Windows to find the first record in which the LASTNAME field contains the text "Jones":

```
LOCATE FOR LASTNAME = "Jones"
```

To use the LOCATE command, you must know the field name that has the information you are looking for. If you're like us, you forget field names two seconds after you create them. Type the following command:

```
DISPLAY STRUCTURE
```

to display the field names from your table in the Results window. ■

The LOCATE command moves through the table and looks for a match. LOCATE stops as soon as it finds a match. No fanfare, beeps, bells, or parades; it just stops. To determine whether the search was successful, you need to check the status bar at the bottom of the screen. If the record pointer isn't at the end of the file, a match was found.

LOCATE is okay if you don't have to look through too many records. However, if your table has a lot of records, you could find yourself staring at your fingernails and humming the song you heard on the way to work. In such cases, the SEEK command is much faster:

```
SEEK "Jones"
```

To find data with the SEEK command, your table must be indexed. Regardless of the size of your indexed table, the SEEK operation is almost instantaneous because SEEK uses the index file as a high-speed lookup.

Just as you did with the LOCATE command, you have to check the status bar to find out whether dBASE for Windows finds a last name of Jones. It's too modest to tell you the search was successful.

Changing What's Already in There

Seek and you shall find. Use and the file shall be opened. Enter data and you shall err. But don't worry, that's why you have the EDIT command.

Before you can edit the contents of a record, you need to move the record pointer to that record using one of the methods described in the previous sections. When the record pointer is on the correct record, you can use the EDIT command or the BROWSE command to display the record for editing.

If you're changing only one record, the EDIT command is probably simpler than the Browse window, because you can see all the information at once. With the Browse window, you will probably have to scroll to the right to see the entire record. If browsing is easier for you, you can use the Browse window to find the record you want, and then switch to the EDIT view of your data by pressing F2. Pressing F2 again takes you to another type of Edit view. Pressing F2 yet again takes you back to Browse. ■

After making all the necessary changes, you can save those changes by pressing Ctrl-W, or by selecting <u>C</u>lose from the Browse window System menu.

If you haven't moved from the record you are editing, you can abandon your changes by pressing Esc.

In general, you shouldn't finish your editing by pressing the Esc key. If you press the Esc key before leaving the record you have edited, all of your changes will be lost. You can press the Esc key without losing your edits *only* if you have moved to another record. However, it's safest to simply avoid using the Esc key. Ctrl-W is a much safer way to stop editing and ensure that your changes are saved. ■

Getting Rid of Records

Remember the big pink eraser you had in grade school? Or maybe you preferred the two-tone eraser that could handle both ink and lead. Either way, erasers were an important part of your life. Of course, you never made mistakes—it was just fun to erase stuff. Well, get ready to have some more fun, because dBASE for Windows makes it easy to get rid of stuff. And you won't have those little chunks of pink rubber all over your desk like you did when you erased something in school.

Most applications allow you to delete records. In dBASE for Windows, you can delete one or many records at the same time. In fact, if you're just tired of the whole mess, you can use the ZAP command, which permanently removes all records from the table in one fell swoop. So don't use ZAP out of anger or frustration, because not even your mother can find those records again. They're history.

Some commands that affect the table, such as ZAP, must have exclusive use of the table. If your computer is connected to a network, *exclusive use* means the table isn't shared with the other computers on the network. If you aren't connected to a network, you should set up dBASE for Windows to use the tables exclusively at all times. For more information on configuring dBASE for Windows for network or single-user operation, please refer to your user manual.

You indicate that you want exclusive use of a table by entering the keyword EXCLUSIVE at the end of the USE command:

```
USE MyTable EXCLUSIVE
```

The SET EXCLUSIVE command allows you to temporarily open any file for your exclusive use. This command affects any other tables opened from this point, until you exit dBASE for Windows or SET EXCLUSIVE OFF again. If you want all of your tables opened exclusively throughout your program, you can set this value in the beginning of your program. You may want to put this:

```
SET EXCLUSIVE ON
USE MyTable
```

in the OnOpen event of your form. ▪

Make it go away, Mommy

Getting rid of records is a two-step process. First, you need to mark the records you want to delete. Then, you tell dBASE for Windows to get rid of them. This section tells you all about marking records for deletion. The next section tells you how to finish them off.

dBASE for Windows gives you several ways to mark records for deletion. If you're in Browse, Edit, or Append mode, you can move to the record you want to delete and press Ctrl-U.

A dBASE for Windows environment variable called DELETED lets you ignore records that are marked for deletion:

```
SET DELETED ON
```

When this variable is set to ON, records that are marked for deletion aren't visible and are ignored by most commands. With DELETED set to ON, deleted records will not appear in the Browse window. Therefore, deleting records in Browse mode causes them to disappear. If DELETED is set to OFF, records that are marked for deletion are not ignored. Because these records show up in the Browse window, an extra column appears next to the record number to show which records are marked for deletion. ▪

You can also delete records by entering the DELETE command in the Command window. If you're on the record you want to delete, simply type DELETE and press Enter.

You can also enter a command such as DELETE 12, where 12 is the record number of the record you want to delete. Don't worry, this command isn't like SKIP. You won't delete 12 records.

The following command searches the entire table and deletes any records where the last-name field contains Jones:

```
DELETE FOR LASTNAME = "Jones"
```

The DELETE command doesn't use the index. It automatically starts at the top of the table, searches the entire table, and marks all the appropriate records for deletion.

 When records are marked for deletion, they still exist. When you issue the command SET DELETED ON in the Command window, dBASE for Windows ignores the records that are marked for deletion. It sort of shuns them. Enter the following command:

```
SET DELETED OFF
```

if you need to view all records, including those marked for deletion. ▪

A call from the governor is necessary to bring back records that you have marked for deletion. The RECALL command lets you rescue these records from oblivion. You use this command exactly like the DELETE command. The only difference is that the RECALL command unmarks records.

The Packers are my team

The command to remove records that you've marked for deletion is PACK. It doesn't get much simpler than this. There's nothing to type before the command or after it, just type PACK. If your computer is on a network, you need to remember that PACK is one of those commands that requires you to have exclusive use of your table.

 PACK permanently removes all records that you have marked for deletion. You won't find any commands, clever DOS files, or nifty utilities that will bring these records back. They're gone. ▪

The PACK command makes a new copy of your table, minus the deleted records. You have permanently deleted records, so don't expect the remaining records to have the same record numbers. The records have been copied to an entirely new table, so records have filled in where the deleted records were removed.

Managing information in tables is challenging—and rewarding if you do it well. You have learned to construct tables, enter information into them, and delete information from them. The next chapter shows you how to manage table information with a form.

Chapter 4

Managing Your Data with a Form

*W*ell-designed tools are physically beautiful, structurally sound, and above all, functional. You already know how to make the form physically beautiful and structurally sound. You also understand the heart of data management, the table. Now you're ready to make your information management tool functional by linking the form and its controls to the table.

Houston, We Have Established a Link

In most dBASE for Windows applications, a form lets the user work with information that's been stored in database tables. You provide access to the information in a table by linking controls on a form to fields in a table. By using the following properties to define these links, you can let users view and edit the table's contents:

▶ *DataLink*. This property establishes a link between a control and a field in a table. By establishing such a link, the DataLink property allows direct editing of information that's stored in a table.

▶ *DataSource*. This property specifies where ComboBoxes and ListBoxes get the information that makes up their lists.

When you view a control's properties, you might see a DataLinkage property type. For example, ComboBoxes and Browse controls have DataLinkage properties. For these controls, DataLink and DataSource aren't the only properties that affect table access; other properties are listed under the DataLinkage property type.

In such cases, the DataLinkage property type contains all of the properties that determine the control's access to information in tables. For example, the Browse control has two properties under the DataLinkage type: Alias and Fields. These properties determine which table the Browse control is attached to and which fields it will display. The DataLinkage property type is described in more detail a bit later in this chapter.

Linking controls to fields

By defining the DataLink property for a control, you allow users to view and edit information stored in a table. Here are the steps for creating this link between a control and a field in a table:

1. In the Form Designer, use the right mouse button to click on the control that is to be linked to a field, and select Object Properties from the pop-up menu that's displayed.

2. In the Properties window, select the DataLink property and click the tool icon for this property. As shown in Figure 4-1, dBASE for Windows displays the Choose Field dialog box.

3. Choose a table from the list of open tables on the left side of the Choose Field dialog box. If the table you want to link with is not open, you can click the View button to open a table or a .QBE file.

4. To the right of the list of tables is a field list for the currently selected table. After selecting a table, choose the field that is to be linked with your control.

5. After selecting a field, click the OK button.

After you link your control using the DataLink property, the selected table name and field name appear in the Properties window to the right of the word DataLink. If the selected field contains data, the data is displayed in the control on the form, even while the form is still in design mode. When you run your form, the data will automatically appear in the control.

By linking controls to fields, you are giving users of your program direct access to your table. In other words, they are free to modify the information stored in the table. If correct data entry is an important part of your application, you should use the Valid property to give error-checking capabilities. ■

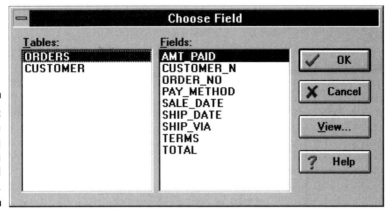

Figure 4-1:
The Choose
Field dialog
box lets you
link a field
to a control.

The psychology of linked controls

Each type of control behaves differently when it has access to information through the DataLink property:

- ✔ EntryFields allow the user to change the field data by typing over it.

- ✔ ComboBoxes might allow the user to type over the data in an EntryField, select data from a ListBox, or do a little of both. It all depends on the style of ComboBox you choose for your form.

- ✔ SpinBoxes allow the user to increase or decrease numeric values or dates by clicking on up-arrow and down-arrow icons.

- ✔ CheckBoxes change logical fields to either true of false, depending on whether these controls are checked or not.

- ✔ RadioButtons enter the data you've stored in their text properties into the field, when they're selected by the user.

- ✔ Editor controls let the user enter and edit formatted information that is stored in memo fields and text files.

- ✔ Vertical and horizontal scroll bars don't accept keyboard input . Instead, they allow the user to change numeric field values by sliding the position box in the scroll bar up and down or back and forth with the mouse.

- ✔ OLE controls are linked to OLE fields, allowing the user to edit documents that were created with other applications. With an OLE control, any changes the user makes to a document are processed by the application that created the document.

Filling ListBoxes from Your Tables

When building an application, you often want to create a list of choices for the user. For example, an order entry system might include a ListBox that allows users to choose from a list of product names. There are a few ways to get these choices into a ListBox. One way is to specify the choices permanently in the program. Experienced programmers call this *hard-coding* the choices. You only want to hard-code choices if they will absolutely, never, ever change. This is a rare occurrence, and it's usually a better idea to store the choices for your lists in tables.

There are several good reasons for storing ListBox information in a table rather than making it a permanent part of the application:

- *Greater flexibility.* If information is stored in a table, users can easily change it, delete it, or add to it.

- *Smaller programs.* Storing data in your programs makes the programs large and unwieldy. It's much easier to update the information used in your list if you store it in a table.

- *Happier users.* Users want to feel like they have control over the program. Giving them power makes them happy.

You can specify the source of the choices that are displayed in a ListBox by setting the DataSource property for the ListBox. To set the DataSource property, do the following.

1. In the Form Designer, use your right mouse button to click on the ListBox, and select Object Properties from the pop-up menu that is displayed.

2. In the Properties window, select the DataSource property and click the tool icon for this property. As shown in Figure 4-2, dBASE for Windows displays the Choose Data Source dialog box.

3. Select a DataSource and click OK. Table 4-1 lists the types of Data-Sources you can use for a ListBox or ComboBox.

Figure 4-2:
The Choose Data Source dialog box lets you set a control's DataSource property.

Table 4-1: DataSources for ListBoxes and ComboBoxes

DataSource	Description
Array	The choices listed in the control are the elements of an array, which is a group of memory variables. Using an array as a DataSource is a way of hard-coding your choices. (Arrays are described in detail later in this book.)
Field	The choices listed in the control are taken from a field in a dBASE for Windows table.
File	The choices listed in the control are the names of files from the current DOS directory.
Structure	The choices listed in the control are field names from a specific table.
Tables	The choices listed in the control are table names from the current DOS directory.

For example, let's assume that you want to create a ListBox, and its DataSource will be a field called PRODUCTS, which is part of an existing table named BUSINESS. Here are the basic steps for creating this ListBox and defining its DataSource:

1. Indicate that you want to use the BUSINESS table by entering the following command in the Command window:

   ```
   USE BUSINESS
   ```

2. Create a form by issuing the CREATE FORM command in the Command window.

3. If the Controls window isn't already open, open it by clicking on the form with the right mouse button and then checking the Controls option on the pop-up menu that's displayed.

4. Place a ListBox on the form by selecting it from the Controls window and clicking on the form.

5. In the Form Designer, click the ListBox using the right mouse button, and select Object Properties from the pop-up menu. dBASE for Windows displays the Properties window.

6. Select the DataSource property and click its tool icon to access the Choose DataSource dialog box.

7. Select Field as the DataSource Type, and click the tool icon.

8. Select BUSINESS as the table and PRODUCTS as the field.

9. Click OK, and your ListBox is ready to run. Whenever the form is run, the ListBox will fill its choices with product names from your BUSINESS table.

Your Very Own Browse Object

The Browse control is one of the most versatile tools for accessing information in a table. Whether you need to change information, delete it, or simply view it, the Browse control has numerous properties that allow you to create powerful data access forms using only this type of control. For example, as shown in Figure 4-3, you could use Browse controls to view several tables at the same time.

The process of creating a Browse control involves the following steps:

1. Placing a Browse control on your form.

2. Resizing the Browse control by using the mouse to drag its sides or corners.

3. Using the DataLinkage properties to tie the control to a table.

4. Customizing the visual and editing properties of the control.

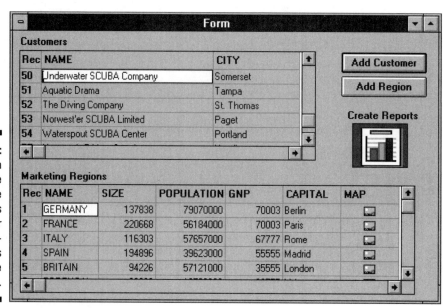

Figure 4-3: A form with multiple Browse controls lets the user view several tables at the same time.

You already know how to add controls to your form. In the following sections, you learn how to set the essential properties of a powerful Browse control.

Before you can link your Browse control to a table, you must USE a table. If you haven't already opened a table, you can click in the Command window while you are defining a form and USE the table that the Browse control will be linked to. Then you can continue in design mode by clicking on the form again. ■

Setting the DataLinkage properties

If one or more tables are open while you are creating your form, the Browse control tries to attach itself to one of the tables and it begins displaying table information, even though you are still in design mode. Don't worry if the information is from the wrong table; this is easily corrected. You need to link the Browse control to the correct table, even if the control is already displaying information from the correct table. Even when the Browse control displays information in design mode, it isn't necessarily linked to a table.

When linking a Browse control to a table, you need to set two DataLinkage properties:

- *Alias*. This property identifies the table to which you are linking.
- *Field*. The Field property lets you choose which fields you want to display in the Browse control.

To set the Alias property:

1. Click the tool icon next to the Alias property.

2. Select a table from the list that's displayed, or choose View to scroll through the directories and find the desired table. Choosing View also sets the View property on the form.

3. After selecting a table, click the OK button to return to the Properties window.

Now you need to choose the fields that you want to display in your Browse control. When you click the tool icon next to the Field property, dBASE for Windows displays the Browse Fields Picker, which is shown in Figure 4-4.

Use the Browse Fields Picker to move fields between the Available Fields box and the Selected Fields box, until all of the fields you want displayed are in the Selected Fields box. The arrow buttons between the Available Fields and Selected Fields boxes let you move fields from one box to the other. The single arrow (>) moves one field at a time. The double arrows (>>) move all the fields.

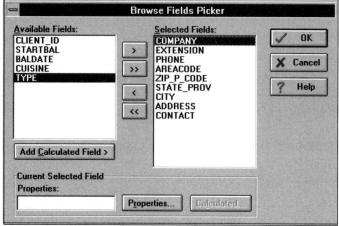

Figure 4-4:
The Browse
Fields
Picker lets
you select
the fields
that you
want to dis-
play in your
Browse
control.

Customizing the Browse control

Setting the DataLinkage properties is only part of the fun. You also have complete control over the appearance and behavior of the Browse control, all the
way down to the field level. It's almost like being able to send signals to the
quarterback from your seat on the 50-yard line.

For added thrills with the Browse Fields Picker, highlight a field and click the
Properties... button. As shown in Figure 4-5, dBASE for Windows displays the
Field Properties dialog box.

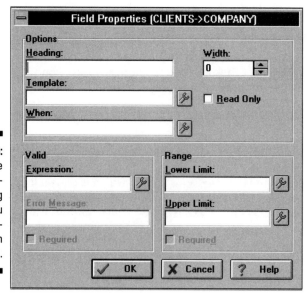

Figure 4-5:
With the
Field Prop-
erties dialog
box, you
can cus-
tomize each
field.

As detailed in Table 4-2, the Field Properties dialog box gives you control over the display and editing of the fields that appear in your Browse control.

Table 4-2: Customizing field display and editing

Field Property	Description
Heading	Changes the column heading to something other than the field name, which is the default setting.
Template	Uses special characters to define a format for displaying or editing the field.
When	Allows editing of the field only when a specified expression is true.
Width	Sets the width of the data entry field. Many controls allow users to enter information wider than the field in the table.
Read Only	Displays the field without letting the user change it.
Valid	Creates a validity check for the information entered by a user.
Range	Restricts data entry to a range of values. Restricts numbers and dates to a range.

In addition to the field-level customization that you've just seen in the Field Properties dialog box, various properties apply to the entire Browse control. Let's go back to the Properties window and continue customizing your Browse control. For example, you might want to set the following basic properties:

- *Enabled.* Set this property to .T. if you want to activate the scroll bars and editing capabilities.

- *Tabstop.* Set this property to .F. if you want to prevent users from moving to the Browse control by pressing the Tab key.

- *Visible.* Set this property to .T. if you want to see the Browse control, or set it to .F. to make the control disappear.

You can modify your Browse control in so many ways that it quickly loses any resemblance to the control you originally placed on your form. Another group of properties that helps with this amazing transformation are the Edit property types:

- *Append.* If you set this property to .T., the user is allowed to add new records to the table. By setting this property to .F., you prevent users from adding records to the table.

Creating templates

A template allows you to specify how information is entered or displayed in your control. When you click the tool icon next to the Template option in the Field Properties dialog box, dBASE for Windows displays a dialog box that helps you create the template. You create a template by using special characters to define a format for displaying or editing the field. Each of these characters is explained in the Template dialog box.

The template characters that are preceded by the @ sign are called functions. However, you shouldn't confuse them with the regular dBASE for Windows Command Language functions. These template functions have a global effect over the entire field. For example, @! causes all letters to be entered as uppercase.

You can also combine template functions. For example, @!A means allow only alpha characters, no numbers, and make them all uppercase.

In addition to the template functions, you can select other characters to create a data entry pattern. The most common example is the telephone number template:

    @R (999) 999-9999

The @R function in this template tells dBASE for Windows to store only the numbers and to ignore such characters as the parentheses and the dash. As shown in the following example, this function is also used in the template for social security numbers:

    @R 999-99-9999

When saving this information in a table, dBASE for Windows ignores the dashes, spaces, and parentheses. The template is used when you view or change the information. For example, a telephone number would be saved as 4155551212 and displayed as (415) 555-1212.

✔ *Modify*. Setting this property to .T. allows users to change the information that is displayed in the Browse control. If you set this property to .F., the information is displayed in read-only format.

✔ *Delete*. If you set this property to .T., the user is allowed to delete records by pressing Ctrl-U. When this property is set to .F., the user cannot delete records in the Browse control.

The Follow property changes how the Browse control behaves when a new record is added. If the new record affects the index key and the Follow property is set to .T., Browse follows the information to its new logical place in the table. With Follow set to .F., the new record moves to its correct position in the table, but Browse stays where it is.

Toggle is a very cool property. You'll like it. You can have three different views of your data. If the Toggle property is set to .T., the user can switch between these three views by pressing F2:

More fun with Browse controls

We are spending quite a bit of time on Browse because it is the most powerful of all the controls. You can build entire applications around this one control.

You can use Browse controls to create different ways of looking at the information stored in your tables. Here are a few possibilities:

✔ Several Browse controls can be open at the same time, looking at either the same table or different tables. For example you might create an order entry form in which one Browse control displays the order information while another Browse control shows the details of each item in the order.

✔ A Browse control can be small enough to display only one record at a time. You could use this format for the first Browse control in the order entry example.

✔ A Browse control can be used for editing a single record while another displays all of the records in the table. You can specify which format Browse uses to display your information. You can also let the user switch between Browse and the other two Edit display formats by pressing the F2 key.

✔ A Browse control can create a calculated field. This field appears to be part of the table but is actually created on the fly. For example, your Browse control might have a commission field that is calculated from a percentage and the value in a total sales field. Although the commission appears as though it is stored in the table, it is actually calculated using values from two other fields.

✔ Browse Layout lets you see several records at a time in a column-and-row format (see Figure 4-6).

✔ Form Layout displays a single record with the fields arranged horizontally. If there are too many fields, they wrap to the next line (see Figure 4-7).

✔ Columnar Layout displays a single record with the fields arranged in one vertical column (see Figure 4-8).

Finally, the following properties let you add a little more polish to your Browse control:

✔ *Text.* This property lets you enter a title for your Browse control.

✔ *ShowRecNo.* You can turn off the record numbers by setting this property to .F.

✔ *ShowDeleted.* If you set this property to .F., the control displays only undeleted records. In other words, the control doesn't display records that you have marked for deletion.

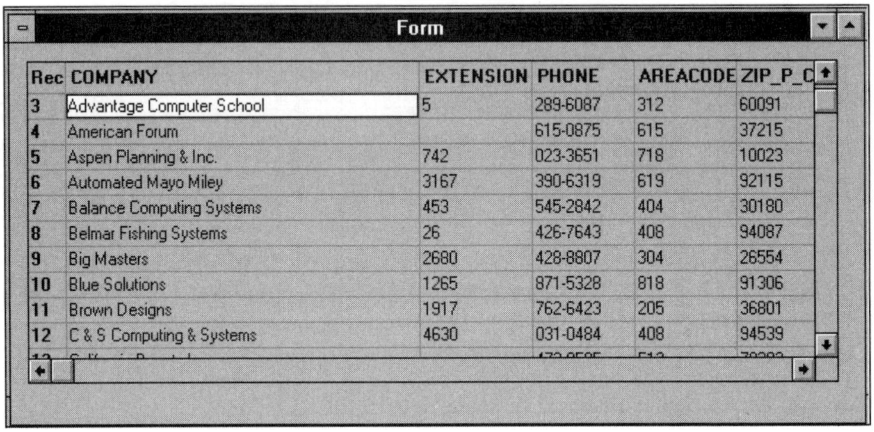

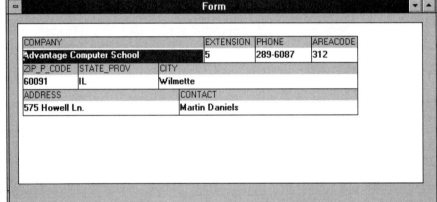

Figure 4-6:
Browse
Layout is
the default
view for a
Browse
control.

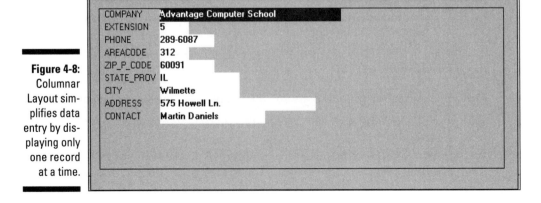

Figure 4-7:
With the
Form Lay-
out, the dis-
play is
limited to
one record
at a time.

Figure 4-8:
Columnar
Layout sim-
plifies data
entry by dis-
playing only
one record
at a time.

Taking a Novel Approach with the Editor

If you tend to be a bit verbose, the Editor is the control for you. This object is a full-blown text editor. By linking this control to memo fields, text files, or long character fields, you can provide word processing-like editing features in your application.

Table 4-3 describes the properties you can use to customize an Editor control.

Table 4-3: Customizing an Editor control

Property	Description
LineNo	Moves you to a specified line number.
Wrap	Turns word wrap on and off.
Scrollbar	Turns the scroll bars on and off.
Modify	Controls whether text is displayed in read-only mode.
Value	Inserts default text.

The Properties window lets you specify the DataLink for an Editor control. If the Editor control is accessing memo fields, the information stored in each record is automatically displayed with all formatting intact.

This chapter has covered linking controls on a form to the information in your tables. You will find that linking all of your controls to fields in a table makes managing data very simple and straightforward. The next chapter helps you organize the information stored in your tables.

Chapter 5

Adding More Indexes

● ●

In This Chapter

▶ Managing indexes with the Index Designer

▶ Designing simple and complex indexes

▶ Using dBASE III and dBASE IV indexes

● ●

*A*n index makes it easier for your program to find information in a table. Without an index, a program has to search the records in your table one by one until it finds the requested information. That's like trying to find someone at Dodger Stadium by starting at seat A-1 and looking in each seat until you find the person.

An index is a file that dBASE for Windows uses to give you high-speed look-up access to a table. You can't directly edit an index. You design an index and then let dBASE for Windows manage the information in the index.

Effective indexes are often the difference between an efficient program and an unusable one. Users won't care about a snazzy user interface if they have to stare at it for hours while they wait for the data they requested. If your application keeps them waiting, they'll go back to using their 3-by-5 cards in no time. By indexing on the right information, you can create more efficient applications and avoid a lot of aggravation for the users.

We Have Plans for You

Creating indexes that really work for you isn't hard, it just takes a little planning. Here are a few ideas to you help plan your indexes:

> ✔ Make a list of all the fields you want to search on. For example, in an application that keeps track of employee data, you might want to search on the fields that contain employee ID numbers, employee names, and zip codes.

✔ List all the key fields in relationships. Applications often use more than one table, and these tables are tied together by certain fields that are common to the tables. For example, the tables used by our employee application might be linked by a field called EMPLOYEEID. Each table in the application would include this key field. (Chapter 6 provides a detailed discussion of relationships.)

✔ Determine whether any reports require sorted output. In our example, it will be easier to create reports if the data for paid time off is arranged in EMPLOYEEID order.

✔ Think about the order in which information should be presented to the user. Again, in our example, the information will probably be presented in report form by employee name or employee ID number.

Creating a Simple Index

Most of the indexes you create are simple indexes. These indexes are based on the values in a single field. This type of index is most easily created using the Table Designer.

To create a simple index using the Table Designer:

1. Open the Table Designer by entering the MODIFY STRUCTURE command in the Command window. If no table is in use, the Open Table dialog box will prompt you for the name of the table you want to modify.

2. Find the field you want to index on, and choose either Ascend or Descend in the column labeled Index.

3. Save the table structure and exit the Table Designer by pressing Ctrl-W.

When you save the table, this index, or tag, is added to a file called the production index. Simple indexes have filenames with the extension .MDX.

Complex indexes are built from multiple fields, expressions, and the values that are returned by functions. You use the Index Designer to add these indexes to the index file. The Index Designer helps you select the fields, create the expressions, and enter the functions that will order your data.

You should remember a few important points when you are working with indexes:

✔ Tags are the names of the indexes in an index file.

✔ The production index file has the same name as the table, but the extension for its filename is .MDX.

✔ The production index file opens automatically when you open the table.

✔ No tags are active when the production index is opened. The SET ORDER command lets you choose a specific tag to activate an index.

As you change information in the data table, all of the index tags are updated. The more tags you have, the more time it takes for dBASE for Windows to update all of them. If you create too many indexes, it may take too long to add or edit information. ■

What If the Phone Book Was Random?

If you're one in a million, there are nine of you in Los Angeles. The importance of ordered information becomes evident when you try to do something as simple as finding a name in the phone book. If the phone book was in random order, you might consider writing a letter instead of calling.

In some cases, you might want your information ordered by more than one field. For example, the phone book is indexed on both last names and first names. This makes it easy to find the phone number you're looking for, even if the person has a very common last name. Indexes that are based on more than one field are known as complex indexes.

The Index Designer Is Your Friend

You can manage your indexes in a production index by using the Index Designer. You open the Index Designer by selecting Table | Table Utilities | Manage Indexes from the dBASE for Windows menu. As shown in Figure 5-1, dBASE for Windows displays the Manage Indexes window.

Figure 5-1:
The Manage Indexes window lets you create, modify, or delete indexes.

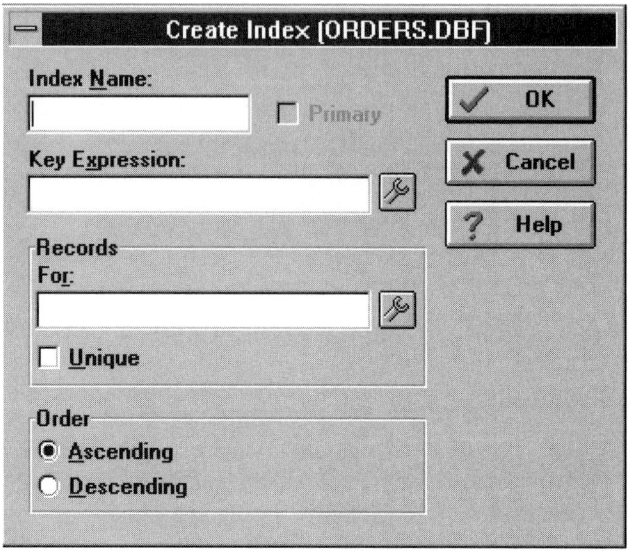

Create Index [ORDERS.DBF]

Index **N**ame:

☐ Primary

✓ OK

Key E**x**pression:

✗ Cancel

? Help

Records
Fo**r**:

☐ **U**nique

Order
● **A**scending
○ **D**escending

Figure 5-2:
The Create
Index win-
dow allows
you to
create new
indexes for
a table.

When you click the **C**reate button, dBASE for Windows displays the Create
Index window, which is shown in Figure 5-2.

The Create Index window lets you define the following information about the
new index:

✔ The name of the index.

✔ An expression to index on.

✔ Which records you want to index.

✔ Whether the index is unique.

✔ Whether the index is a Primary index. This CheckBox is usually inactive
   because it applies only to Paradox tables.

✔ The index order, which is either ascending or descending.

Don't use the TRIM( ) function in indexes. This function confuses an index
very badly. You won't be able to find your data using SEEK, your data tables
won't relate, and the moon and stars will come crashing down on your computer. In other words, don't use TRIM( ). ■

The Create Index window lets you define a scope, or range of records that
you want to index. You can index all the records in the table, or you can

choose to index a subset of your table. If necessary, you can click a tool icon for help in choosing the records you want indexed.

The CheckBox labeled Unique is pretty important. A unique index is one in which only the first occurrence of any duplicate record is included in the index. This type of index is useful for creating ListBoxes. You usually want a ListBox to display each choice only once. It would be pretty boring to have a ListBox filled with the same choice over and over again.

On top of everything else, dBASE for Windows wants to know if your index should be in ascending or descending order. For example, you might want your data arranged to display the most recent records first, or the oldest age, or the highest score, and so on. The search features work the same no matter which index order you use.

The index order depends on the type of data:

- *Character.* Ascending orders letters from A to Z. Descending is from Z to A.

- *Numeric or Float.* Ascending is from the smallest number to the largest. Descending is from the largest to the smallest.

- *Date.* Ascending orders dates from past toward the future. Descending is from future to past. ■

Tag, you're it

Your production .MDX index file can contain as many index files as you need. However, you can only see your records in one index order at a time (unless you're raising tropical toads and you just licked your fingers). In other words, only one tag can order your records at a time. This tag is called the controlling or active index. The following command lets you specify which tag is ordering your data:

```
SET ORDER TO MyTagName
```

When data is changed, all of the index tags are updated, regardless of the order of your tags or which one is the active index. ■

Creating complex indexes

Don't let the word complex scare you. A complex index simply means that the index is built on more than one field. It can also mean that the index is built using the results of a function, instead of fields.

To index a table on both last and first names, you simply add the fields together and give the new index a tag name:

```
INDEX ON LASTNAME + FIRSTNAME TagName
```

In an index, uppercase letters come before lowercase letters. As a result, the UPPER() function is particularly useful when you are indexing on character fields. This function returns the contents of the field as all uppercase letters. The information stored in the table remains unchanged.

For example, assume that information in your table is stored in upper- and lowercase letters, such as the name "Smith." In this case, a search for "Smith" will find the record, but searching for "SMITH" or "smith" will not find the record.

Indexing on UPPER(LASTNAME) converts all the last names to uppercase letters in the index only. You can then search on "SMITH" and find it. This makes a program a little more forgiving for the user. You can either use a template that forces the user to enter all uppercase letters, or you can use the UPPER() function to convert whatever they enter to uppercase letters.

The following command finds the record if the table is indexed using the UPPER() function:

```
SEEK UPPER("smith")
```

The following command also finds the record if the table is indexed using the UPPER() function:

```
SEEK "SMITH" ▪
```

You can also create index files that are not production indexes. These index files do not open automatically when the table is opened. Non-production indexes are useful if you have seldom-used indexes, or indexes for tables that never change.

Non-production indexes must be opened using the SET INDEX command, or they won't be updated when information changes in your table. ▪

You may need to create indexes from within a procedure. If so, you won't be able to use the very cool Index Designer. In such cases, you're stuck with using the INDEX command, which has the following general form:

```
INDEX ON Expression TAG Tag Name OF MDX Filename FOR Condition
             DESCENDING UNIQUE
```

You can supply the following information in the INDEX command:

✔ *Expression* is the field or expression by which you want the table indexed.

✔ *Tag Name* is a unique name you give the index.

✔ *MDX Filename* is the name of the index file that contains one or more indexes (tags). If you don't specify a filename, the index file is given the same name as the table.

✔ *Condition* can be used to limit which records are indexed. This is an optional parameter.

✔ DESCENDING lets you specify descending order instead of ascending, which is the default order.

✔ UNIQUE allows you to create a unique index in which duplicate records are ignored. This keyword is optional.

Using Chronologically-Challenged dBASE Indexes

For those of you who are upgrading from dBASE III Plus or dBASE IV, it's possible that your dBASE files already have indexes that you are compelled to use. Or, perhaps you believe that tradition is important, even in programming. It's easy to identify these old dBASE indexes because their filenames have the extension .NDX.

Although dBASE for Windows can maintain the older style index files, using these files is a less efficient way to maintain indexes because:

✔ .NDX files don't open automatically. If tables are updated while the index is closed, the index will no longer match the table. The index must be opened to be updated.

✔ Opening more files takes additional time and wastes limited DOS file handles.

✔ The additional files will make your application harder to maintain.

The syntax of the INDEX command is a little different for .NDX indexes:

```
INDEX ON Expression TO NDX FileName UNIQUE
```

Unlike production indexes, you can have only one index in each .NDX index file. To access more than one index, you must open each of the .NDX index files. To open more than one index file, separate their names with commas:

```
SET INDEX TO MyNDX1,MyNDX2,MyNDX3
```

To change the active index, enter the SET ORDER command with the number of the index that you want to make active. In the preceding example, MyNDX1 is opened first, so it is considered index number 1. The following command sets the order to the second index opened:

```
SET ORDER TO 2
```

The following command does the same thing:

```
SET ORDER TO MyNDX2
```

Both of these commands make MyNDX2 the active index.

As you've seen in this chapter, indexes order the information in your table, provide high-speed lookups, and enable you to create relationships between tables. Two types of indexes are available in dBASE for Windows: production (recommended) and the older style .NDX file, which was added for compatibility with earlier versions of dBASE.

Creating indexes takes a little planning. Barring unforeseen circumstances, the beauty of indexes is that once they're created you almost never have to mess with them. dBASE for Windows takes care of opening, updating, and closing your indexes. All you need to do is specify which tag within the index file should be the active index.

The next chapter shows you how to open several tables at the same time. Indexing plays a big part in creating relationships between these tables.

Chapter 6

Juggle Your Files, Not Your Books

* *

In This Chapter

▶ Opening more than one table at a time

▶ Selecting multiple work areas

▶ Linking tables together

▶ Viewing many tables as one table

* *

*T*hese are the days of multitasking. You can be driving the car, talking on the phone, listening to the radio, scolding the kids, and gulping down a cup of coffee, all at the same time. In keeping with these exciting times, dBASE for Windows allows you to open several tables at the same time. Not only can you open them, you can tie them together as though they were one large table.

You will want to have more than one table open for the same reason that you might want two or more file folders open on your desk. For example, you might need to compare information in a sales file with information in an expense file and the listings in a salary file. This is most easily accomplished by opening all three files, or tables, at the same time. When you open several tables at the same time, each table is opened in a special area called a *work area* or *select area*.

New Work Areas, Opening Soon

If you were starting a business, you would want an office that was just right for your business, and you wouldn't want to put more than one business in that office. If you wanted to start a second business, you might lease another office in the same building. Each open table in dBASE for Windows is like a business; it needs its own place to work.

Instead of an office, each open table has a *work area*. Only one table and its indexes can be open in a work area. If you want to open another table while leaving the first table open for business, you need another work area.

Selecting a work area

Being a perfect world, dBASE for Windows has an unlimited number of work areas, and they're all free. To access another work area, you simply select it with the SELECT command. For example, the following command selects work area number two:

```
SELECT 2
```

After entering this command, you can open a table and its indexes in this work area. The following example selects a third work area and opens a table:

```
SELECT 3
USE MyTable
```

When you select a work area, you are "in" that work area. When you issue commands that operate on a table, such as LIST or DISPLAY, dBASE for Windows assumes that you mean the table in the currently selected work area.

The FILES= statement in your CONFIG.SYS file controls the number of files that can be open at one time. To increase the number of files you can open at one time:

1. Save your tables and exit dBASE for Windows.

2. Open CONFIG.SYS with your text editor and change the FILES= statement to FILES=100. If CONFIG.SYS doesn't include this statement, add it now.

3. Save your changes to CONFIG.SYS and exit your text editor.

4. Exit Windows and reboot your computer. This step is necessary because changes to CONFIG.SYS don't take affect until you reboot. ■

It is possible to open tables in other work areas without changing the currently selected work area. Let's assume that you have already selected work area 1. The following example opens 3 tables and leaves work area 1 as the currently selected work area:

```
USE Table1 IN 1
USE Table2 IN 2
USE Table3 IN 3
```

The IN keyword identifies the work area in which each table is opened.

Once tables are open in different work areas, you can use the SELECT command to change which work area is currently selected. The following example selects work area 3 as the currently selected work area:

```
SELECT 3
```

As shown in the following example, you can also change the currently selected work area by selecting the table that is open in the desired work area:

```
SELECT Table3
```

You can also select work areas by using the SELECT( ) function instead of the SELECT command. If you enter the SELECT( ) function with no parameters, it returns the number of the next available work area.

It's a good idea to include comments that describe what's happening in the different parts of your program. A comment is simply explanatory text that you insert in a program. dBASE for Windows ignores these comments when it is executing the commands that make up your program.

Two special symbols allow you to put comments in your programs. If you precede text with either a double ampersand (&&) or an asterisk (*), the text that follows is a comment. The difference between the two symbols is simple. You can use an asterisk only when a comment is on a line that contains no program code. If you try to use an asterisk on a line that contains code, it will be mistaken for a multiplication sign. You can use the double ampersand on any line, as long as the comment is the last thing on the line. In other words, you can't embed comments within a line of program code. ▪

The following examples show how you can use the SELECT( ) function:

```
SELECT("Table1") && This selects work area 1, and returns a 1
SELECT(1)   && This also selects work area 1, and returns a 1
```

The following example uses the SELECT( ) function to open a table in a new work area:

```
USE Table4 in SELECT()
```

In the preceding example, the SELECT( ) function opens Table4 in the next available work area, and the function returns the number of that new work area.

Choosing an alias

Once a table is open in a work area, you can refer to that work area by either its number or the table's name or *alias*. When a table is in use, you refer to it by its name without the .DBF extension. Because this isn't the complete DOS filename, it is considered the table's alias. You can use that name, or you may temporarily give the table another alias:

```
SELECT 1
USE MyTable ALIAS GoodStuf
```

This example doesn't change the name of the table. However, while it remains open, you must refer to the table as GoodStuf. You would select the table in the preceding example like this:

```
SELECT GoodStuf
```

Tables with aliases are like actors in a play. When they're in their parts, they may not respond to their own names. Just don't call your tables Roxanne or Cyrano.

Just as actors sometimes use stage names, you might want to use an alias to better identify a table. If your tables have names like emp1, emp2, and emp3, you may want to give them aliases that better identify their contents. For example, you might use PersInfo as an alias for emp1.

Finding the right table

By using a table's name, you can refer to a table that isn't in the currently selected work area. For example, if three tables are open and each table contains a field named LASTNAME, you need to make sure you are referring to the right table. You do this by preceding the field name with the name of the table. The table name and field name are separated with a hyphen-greater-than sign (–>).

The following example uses the ? command to ask for a last name from each table without selecting different work areas:

```
? Table1->LASTNAME
? Table2->LASTNAME
? Table3->LASTNAME
```

Assuming that the information in the three tables is different, the result of this example would be three different last names.

Although it isn't required, it's a good idea to precede the name of your field with the table name or alias, as in the preceding example. Do not include the .DBF extension. This helps to avoid confusion for you (and dBASE for Windows), because conflicts can arise when more than one table uses the same field name. ■

As mentioned, each work area is numbered. You may choose to open your table in any numbered work area. Once a table is open in a work area, you can refer to a field in that table in two ways:

- ✔ The Alias of the table—for example, MyTable–>LASTNAME.
- ✔ The letter of the alphabet that corresponds to the work area's number—for example, A–>LASTNAME. In this method, A is 1, B is 2, C is 3, and so on.

Closing tables

Now you know how to open several tables, select them, and call them by other names. What about closing them? You can close them all with one sweep of the keyboard by issuing the following command:

```
CLOSE ALL
```

This command closes the tables and their indexes in all of the work areas.

You can close a table by issuing the USE command with no table name:

```
USE
```

This is one of the oddities of early dBASE versions that has followed the program through the years. If you tell the program to open something, but you don't tell it what to open, it closes whatever is in the active work area. The same logic is applied to many of the SET commands.

The USE command provides a handy method for closing tables in other work areas. For example, the following command closes the table in work area 3 without making work area 3 the active work area:

```
USE IN 3
```

This is like having a remote control that lets you turn off the lights in every room of the house without leaving your favorite chair.

Better Relations without Dr. Ruth

You may be wondering why opening several tables at the same time is such a big deal. After all, the command USE MyTable is shorter than SELECT MyTable. Well, hold on to your hats. This is the exciting part. You can tie them together as though they are one big table.

Remember grandmother's house on Thanksgiving? You pushed all the tables together, and then you threw a tablecloth over them. With the tablecloth across all the tables, it looked like you were all seated at one big table. Now you can do the same thing with data tables—that is, you can put them together like one big table.

Let's use the example of collecting employee information. You could easily put the employees' names, addresses, ID numbers, and so on in a single table. However, if you tried to put their payroll information in the same table, you would have a problem. If the employees are paid weekly, you would need at least 52 fields just to collect the check numbers for a year.

Rather than create a huge table, you can put the payroll information in a table of its own. To identify which records in the payroll table belong to each employee, you need a unique identifier, such as the employee ID number. This identifier lets you link related information in the different tables.

Names aren't very effective as unique identifiers because you would need at least two fields to identify each employee: first name and last name. In addition, two employees might have the same name. Finally, long or complex identifiers such as proper names are more susceptible to typing errors during data entry. If your company doesn't use employee numbers, you can create your own employee ID numbers.

They'll relate if they have something in common

Most of the people at grandmother's house on Thanksgiving are related; just one big happy family. Figuring out the relations is always fun. "Let's see, you're my great aunt's second cousin on my mother's side. I guess that makes you Uncle Bob."

You might have heard someone refer to dBASE for Windows as a relational database. Tables that share information about a particular subject are said to be related. The capability to link related tables is what makes a database relational.

As shown in Figure 6-1, related tables are linked together by a *key field*. This is the unique identifier we mentioned earlier. Each of the related tables contains this key field. The key field must be identical in all of the related tables. In other words, the key field must have the same type and width in each table you are going to relate. Like a jigsaw puzzle, the pieces must match.

Like the relationships in your family, tables have parent-child relationships. The table that best identifies the subject, such as the Employee table in our example, is usually the parent, or master table.

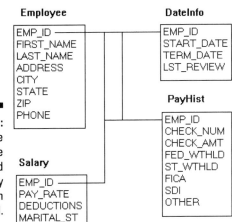

Employee Information Tables

You can have one parent table and several child, or slave, tables. In a child table, the records that match the key field are forced to match the key field in the parent table. In other words, when the parent table is referring to employee ID number 78654, the records in the child table are also referring to employee ID number 78654. As the record pointer moves in the parent table, the record pointer in the child table moves to find a match to the key field in the parent table.

The key field in the child table must be indexed. When you move the record pointer in the parent table, the record pointer in the child table uses the index to perform a high-speed search and find a match. ▪

Now that you know you can tie tables together, you may be asking yourself why you would ever want to do such a thing. Maybe having fun isn't a good enough reason. There are several reasons why you might want to relate several tables:

- ✔ You'll always have enough places to store repeating information, such as the weekly payroll information in our example. The child table can have as many payroll records as you need for each employee.

- ✔ You can hold down the size of your parent table by distributing the information throughout several smaller child tables.

- ✔ You can save space in the parent table by creating a separate child table for information that is not commonly entered. This table helps to minimize the number of empty fields in the parent table. For example, your employee information system might include biographical data only for the senior officers of the company. Because this information relates to only a few people, it goes in a separate table.

✔ By linking all the related information that's stored in separate tables, you can create one virtual table. You have seen how easy it is to get information out of a table using controls. If all the information in each of the tables rushes to match the parent table, you can use the controls on your form to view and edit information in all the tables at the same time.

Designing an employee tracking application

Let's say you want to build an application similar to the example we have used in this chapter for tracking employee and salary information. The first thing you need is a table for employee information; and the very first thing you need in this table is a key field that ties together all of the tables you create for your application. In employee tracking applications, the key field is usually an employee identification number. If the company doesn't issue employee ID numbers, you can create them or you can use social security numbers. Whichever you choose, the employee ID should be the first field in each table. This will make it easier to see how each table is related.

It isn't imperative that the key field is the first field in each table. However, this does improve the organization of your tables, and you can see at a glance which fields are the key fields.

You might create another table to track the employee payroll checks, such as the PayHist table in Figure 6-1. Because you're using the employee ID as a key field, you don't have to include fields for employee names in the PayHist table. This payroll table has to store only the information from paychecks, such as check number, amount, and the various withholding amounts. Yech, taxes!

To make up for the misery of tax withholdings, another table can keep track of paid time off. As in the PayHist table, the employee ID field ties this table to the employee information table. Because you have established a relationship between the two tables, the time-off table doesn't need fields for employee names. Instead, the time-off table can be limited to only those fields that are used in determining how much paid time off is available for each employee.

A salary information table and a date information table will also be useful. When deciding what information goes into the parent table and what should go in a child table, you should try to put information of a specific type, such as payroll information, in a child table. In Figure 6-1 you can see that the Salary table does not contain repeating information. However, it does contain information of a specific type that can be grouped into a separate table. The same is true of the DateInfo table in Figure 6-1.

Although this relational structure doesn't necessarily make your program more efficient, it does help organize the information. In an office with no computers, you could easily put all of the employee information into one huge manila folder. Although this would certainly make filing easier, it wouldn't do much for your information management needs.

Once you set the relationships between the parent and child tables based on the key field you have chosen, you can use all the tables as though they are one large table that contains everything you ever wanted to know about an employee but were afraid to query for.

One big happy table, or so it seems

You relate tables to each other by entering the SET RELATION command in the Command window:

```
SELECT Parent Table
SET RELATION TO Key Field INTO Linked Table
```

For example, if you have a table called Employee that contains the key field EMP_ID, you could relate it to another table called PayHist. The PayHist table must also have EMP_ID as its key field.

The key fields in different tables all must match. They must have the same type and width, and if they are numeric, they must have the same decimal length. ■

The following commands let you link your Employee table to the PayHist table:

```
USE Employee in 1     && Open the employee table in work area 1
USE PayHist in 2      && Open the payhist table in work area 2
SELECT Employee       && Make employee the active table
SET RELATION TO EMP_ID INTO PayHist
```

The EMP_ID field is the same in both tables, and the PayHist table is indexed on EMP_ID. As you move through the Employee table, the record pointer in PayHist moves to match the EMP_ID in the Employee table.

Creating a really big family

You've seen how you can relate two tables to create one virtual table. Now you can go for the gusto. You can add more tables to your relationship by using the keyword ADDITIVE in your SET RELATION command:

```
USE Employee in 1    && Open the employee table in work area 1
USE PayHist in 2     && Open the payhist table in work area 2
Use Salary in 3      && Open the salary table in work area 3
Use Deductn in 4     && Open the deductions table in work area 4
SELECT Employee      && Make employee the active table
SET RELATION TO EMP_ID INTO PayHist
SELECT PayHist
SET RELATION TO CHECK_NUM INTO Salary    && Set the 1st relationship
SET RELATION TO CHECK_NUM INTO Deductn ADDITIVE    && then the 2nd
```

If you don't use ADDITIVE, each successive SET RELATION command replaces any existing relations. In the preceding example, each table is opened in a different work area. The Employee table is a parent table. Once the tables are opened, the Employee table is selected as the currently active work area.

This example also shows that child tables can be parents to other child tables. CHECK_NUM becomes the key field that links the salary-related tables. As the record pointer moves in this parent table, all the other related tables move to match it.

When you are setting relationships, make sure the key field in the child table is unique. For example, you shouldn't use names because there are more than a few John Smiths in the world. Try to use a unique number, such as the social security number, driver's license number, or a number that either you or the computer assigns. As you learn more about programming in dBASE for Windows, you will be able to have the computer assign unique numbers. ■

You can see relationships visibly by creating a form that contains several Browse objects. Use the DataLinkage property types to link each Browse object to a different related table. As you use the Browse object to move through the parent table, you can watch the child or related tables move to match the key field in the parent table.

Here's how you can create a form to view this type of relationship:

1. Use the CREATE command to create two tables, Employee and Salary. The tables should share a similar field that can be used as the key field. When creating the table structure, make sure the key fields are the same type and width. You will want to enter some sample data in each table. Make sure that the key field information in the Employee table matches the key field information in the Salary table.

2. Open the two tables in different work areas and set the relationship between the two tables, as shown in the following example:

```
USE Employee IN 1
USE Salary IN 2
SELECT Employee
SET RELATION TO Emp_ID INTO Salary
```

3. Create a new form by issuing the CREATE FORM command in the Command window.

4. Select the Controls window. If it isn't open, click on the form with your right mouse button and select Controls from the pop-up menu.

5. Click the Browse control icon and click back on the new form. This puts a new Browse control on the form. Do this again, so that your form has two Browse controls.

6. Click on one of the Browse controls with your right mouse button and select Object Properties from the pop-up window that's displayed. This opens the Properties window.

7. In the Properties window, look for the DataLinkage property types, which lists two properties, ALIAS and FIELDS.

8. Click the tool icon for the ALIAS property. The two tables you opened in step 2 should be listed. Select one and click the OK button.

9. Click on the other Browse control and repeat steps 6, 7, and 8 to link the Browse control to the other table.

10. Save the form and then run it. As you move through the parent table, the records in the Browse control that displays the child table move to match key fields.

The organizational capabilities of relational databases have simplified infor-mation management. We are overburdened with data, and organizing your information has become essential. By organizing information types into child tables such as payroll information or employee start dates, you can create applications that make it easy to manage all this information.

The next chapter shows you how to create powerful queries using the dBASE for Windows Query Designer. These query files can open your tables, set rela-tionships, and more.

Chapter 7

Query by Example, e.g.

So far in this book, we have concentrated on building tables and creating forms that manage the information in those tables. Putting information in a table and editing it is only part of the fun. There's nothing better than asking questions about your data and getting answers.

This is why most people bother to put information in a computer in the first place. They want to be able to ask sophisticated questions about their information. Executives need to know the bottom line; sales managers need to check sales by region; engineers need to run trigonometric functions on stored data to provide satellite guidance. Being able to query, or ask questions about the data that's stored in tables is an important part of any application. The Query Designer is a powerful dBASE for Windows tool that can help you provide answers to the many questions that life (and users) throw our way.

What Would You Do with a Query Designer if You Had One?

If you've ever tried to get information out of a computer, you might have an idea how Dorothy felt on her quest for the great Wizard of Oz. In fact, if you were working in your office very late at night, you were probably clicking your heels and muttering under your breath, "There's no place like home." With a Query Designer and at least one of the following:

> ✔ a dog named Toto,
>
> ✔ a daughter named Liza, or
>
> ✔ a tendency to hallucinate after being sharply rapped on the noggin,

you too can have the power to create queries that will return the information you need.

Oil those elbows, pack your straw, or primp your mane, because we're off to see the Query Designer. (Refer to your Windows manual to find out how to change your background wallpaper to yellow bricks.)

To start creating a new query:

1. Open the tables you want to query. If you have multiple tables, you can set relationships in the Command window or by using the Query Designer. The preceding chapter showed you how to set relationships in the Command window. You learn how to set relationships using the Query Designer later in this chapter.

2. Type CREATE QUERY in the Command window, or select File | New | Query from the dBASE for Windows menu. As shown in Figure 7-1, dBASE for Windows displays the Query Designer.

May I take your order please?

As shown in Figure 7-1, the Query Designer lists each of the open tables and the fields in each table. If all of the fields aren't visible, you can scroll to the right by pressing the Tab key. As you'll see a little later in this chapter, any relationships you set are graphically represented with lines between the table names.

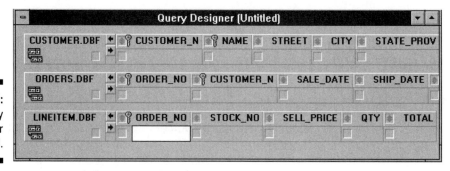

Figure 7-1:
The Query
Designer
knows all.

You can do several things with the Query Designer:

✔ Select which fields you want to use as parts of your query.

✔ Create relationships between tables.

✔ Change the order in which your fields are displayed, both on the screen and in the result of your query.

✔ Set filters on your data. For example, you can filter out all records in which the zip code doesn't equal "90210". Only records with that zip code would be returned in response to your query.

These uses of the Query Designer are described in the following sections.

Selecting the fields that you want to use in your query

You select a field that you want to use in your query by clicking the Check-Box next to the field name. As shown in Figure 7-2, you can select all of the fields in a table by clicking the CheckBox beneath the table name. When you do this, the Query Designer automatically checks the individual field names for you. Giving them a check is like paying them to do your bidding.

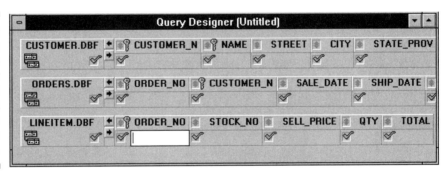

Figure 7-2: Select some or all the fields by placing a check mark next to the appropriate field names.

Changing the field order

You may want your fields displayed in a different order than the structure of the table. To change the order in which your fields are displayed:

1. Click anywhere on the field name and hold down the mouse button. The cursor changes to the shape of a hand.

2. Drag the field to a new position by continuing to hold down the mouse button while moving the mouse to reposition the field.

3. Release the mouse button when your field is in place.

Creating relationships between tables

You can use the Query Designer to create relationships between tables. To start defining a relationship, select Query | Set Relation from the Query Designer menu. As shown in Figure 7-3, dBASE for Windows displays the Define Relation dialog box. If you have a steady hand, you can also use your mouse to bring up the Define Relation dialog box. You can do this in the Query Designer by positioning the mouse pointer on the table icons to the left of the parent table name, and then moving the mouse over the icon for the child table.

The computer world is full of sometimes conflicting acronyms and terminology. Although we have tried to standardize on terms as they are commonly used in the computer industry, you should understand that there may be two ways of saying the same thing. For example, dBASE for Windows uses the terms parent and child to describe the relationship between a controlling table and a table that is being controlled. However, you might also hear this relationship referred to as a master-slave relationship. ∎

Using the drop-down list in the upper-left corner of the Define Relation dialog box, select a parent, or master, table for the relationship. As you saw in Chap-

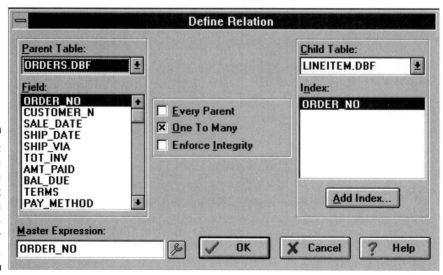

Figure 7-3:
The Define
Relation
dialog box
helps you
play match-
maker for
your tables.

ter 6, the parent table is the one that asks the child table to move its record pointer to a value that matches a key field.

In the Define Relation dialog box, choose a key field from the list of fields in the selected parent table. You are constructing a relationship between a parent table and a child table, just as you did in Chapter 6 with the following command:

```
SET RELATION TO Key Field INTO Child Table
```

The key field in this command is the field in the parent table that ties the parent table to the child table.

The child table should always have an index on the field that matches the parent's key field. Remember, the field in the parent table uses the child table's index to find a match in the child table.

As shown in Figure 7-3, three CheckBoxes in the middle of the Define Relation dialog box allow you to customize the way the tables are related:

- ✔ *Every Parent.* This option specifies that you want the query results to include every record in the parent table, regardless of whether there is a matching record in the child table. Turn off this option if you want the query results to include only those records that match your key field.

- ✔ *One To Many.* This option specifies that the query results should include all of the records in the child table that match the key field. In other words, you expect that the child table contains more than one record that matches the key field in the parent table, and you want to see all of the matching records. Turn off this option if you want to display only the first matching record that's found in a child table.

- ✔ *Enforce Integrity.* This sounds like enforced family values. This option controls whether or not you can have orphaned child records, or illegitimate children. If this option is checked, you can't delete a parent record that has children, and any child records that are created are automatically given the parent key.

The next step in setting the relationship is to select a child table from the list of tables on the right side of the Define Relation dialog box.

When you are being truly creative with the Query Designer, you might suddenly realize that your child table doesn't have an index on the key field. Fortunately, your flow of creativity won't be blocked, because you can create an index on the fly by clicking the Add Index button in the Define Relation dialog box. When you click this button, dBASE for Windows displays the familiar Index Designer. You can refer to Chapter 5 if you need help creating the index.

When you're finished with all the possibilities offered by the Define Relation dialog box, you can close it and return to the Query Designer window by clicking the OK button. As shown in Figure 7-4, lines are added to show the relationships between tables, and child tables are shifted to the right.

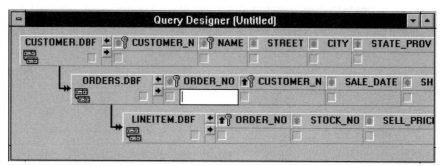

Sorting the results of your query

To select the order for sorting your query results, click the double arrow to the left of the name of the field that you want to use for sorting the table. A pop-up menu of arrows is displayed, giving you the following options for sorting the results of your query:

- ✔ If nothing is selected, the table remains unsorted. This is the order in which data was entered.

- ✔ The up-arrow icon selects ascending order. This option sorts the records from lowest to highest. Uppercase letters come before lowercase letters.

- ✔ The down-arrow icon selects descending order. This option sorts the records from highest to lowest.

- ✔ The double up-arrow icon selects ascending order and ignores case. In other words, this option sorts from lowest to highest, ignoring whether letters are upper- or lowercase.

- ✔ The double down-arrow icon selects descending order and ignores case.

Seeing the world through rose-colored glasses

The heart of the Query Designer is its ability to set filters on the table. A filter is an expression that dBASE for Windows uses to evaluate each of the records in a table or tables. As shown in Figure 7-5, you can set a filter in the Query Designer by entering an expression in the space below a field name. In Figure 7-5, the filter tells dBASE for Windows to find the records in which STOCK_NO equals "13456".

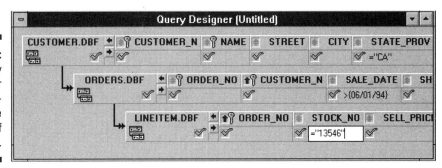

Figure 7-5:
The Query Designer lets you filter the results of your query.

Once a filter is set, dBASE for Windows evaluates each record in a table or tables. If the information in a record doesn't match the expression, dBASE for Windows temporarily makes that record invisible. When dBASE for Windows finishes the filter process, the only visible records are those that match the filter expression.

You can set filters either by using the Query Designer or by entering the SET FILTER command in the Command window:

```
SET FILTER TO LASTNAME = "Smith"
```

With this command, only the records that contain the last name Smith are available for viewing or editing. To remove the filter, issue the SET FILTER TO command with no parameters:

```
SET FILTER TO
```

Tables, commands, and functions behave differently after you set a filter. For example:

- ✔ Records that don't match the filter are temporarily invisible.

- ✔ The COUNT command returns the number of records that are still visible.

- ✔ The RECCOUNT( ) function returns the actual number of records in the table. Records are counted regardless of whether they are visible.

- ✔ The SEEK, FIND, and LOCATE commands cannot find invisible records.

- ✔ Indexes still update correctly for the entire table, regardless of whether the records are visible.

To set a filter in the Query Designer:

1. Click in the space below the field name.

2. Enter a comparison operator from the list in Table 7-1.

3. Enter a value that is to be compared with the value in the selected field.

4. Set additional conditions for your filter, as explained in the following paragraphs.

Query filters can include character information, numeric data, dates, and logical values. Remember to enter character information in quotes, numeric values without quotes, dates in curved brackets ({}), the logical value true as .T., and the logical value false as .F. These are the only field types you can specify in a query filter. ◼

To create a filter that finds the records for all sales orders that were placed after June 1, 1994, you would enter the following comparison expression in the SALE_DATE field of the ORDERS table:

```
>{06/01/94}
```

The braces around the date in this expression are necessary because they tell dBASE for Windows that this value is date type information and not character or numeric data.

Your filter can include more than one condition for the selected field. In such cases, you can specify that the value of the field must satisfy all of the condi-

Table 7-1: Filter comparison operators

Operator	Description
>	Greater than
<	Less than
=	Equals
< > or #	Does not equal
>= or =>	Greater than or equal to
<= or =<	Less than or equal to
$	The field contains the specified value
Like	The value in the field matches a specified pattern. You can use the * and ? wildcards to define the pattern.

tions, or that it must satisfy at least one of the conditions. For example, you might want to limit your query results to the records in which the value in the SALE_DATE field falls between June 1, 1994 and December 31, 1994. In other words, the value in the SALE_DATE field must be greater than one value *and* it must be less than another value.

To specify that a field must satisfy all of the conditions, use commas to separate the comparison expressions that you enter for that field. For example, you would enter the following conditions to find the records in which the SALE_DATE field falls between June 1, 1994 and December 31, 1994:

```
>{06/01/94},<{12/31/94}
```

You can also create a filter to find all the records that meet any of several conditions. For example, instead of finding all the sales orders that were placed during a specific period, you might want to find all the records in which the SALE_DATE field is either before one date or after another date.

To specify that the field must satisfy one of several conditions:

1. Click in the space below the field name, and enter the first comparison expression.

2. Press the down-arrow key to display a new blank line for entering the next comparison expression.

3. Enter the second comparison expression. If you need to enter another comparison expression, press the down-arrow key to display another blank line.

You can also create filters that include conditions for several different fields. As with filters for individual fields, you can specify that a record must satisfy all of the conditions, or you can indicate that it is sufficient for the record to satisfy one or more of the conditions.

For example, you might create a filter to find recent sales transactions that exceed a certain dollar amount. In other words, the value in the SALE_DATE field must be greater than a specified value, *and* the value in the SALE_AMT field must exceed a specified value. You would set this type of filter by simply entering the necessary comparison expressions in the appropriate fields of the Query Designer dialog box.

It's a bit trickier when you want to create a filter in which a record needs only to satisfy one or more of the conditions. For example, instead of creating a filter that finds recent sales transactions that exceed a certain amount, you might want a filter that finds all recent sales (regardless of the amount) as well as all large sales (regardless of the date).

To create this type of filter, click in the space below the first field name, and enter the comparison expression for that field. Then, click in the space beneath the second field name, and press the down-arrow key. An entry space is displayed, and you can enter the comparison expression for the second field.

Saving your query

You don't need lifeguard training to save your query. When you are finished creating the query, press Ctrl-W or choose <u>C</u>lose from the Query Designer System menu. dBASE for Windows asks you to name your query file. The filename is automatically assigned the extension .QBE.

Although it is possible to name your files with extensions other than those used by dBASE for Windows, it isn't a good idea. Many dBASE for Windows functions look for files by their three-letter extension, rather than by file type. If you start fooling around with these extensions, dBASE for Windows could become confused. Stick with the default extensions:

- ✔ .DBF is a dBASE table.
- ✔ .MDX is a production index.
- ✔ .QBE is a query file.
- ✔ .WFM is a form file.

These and other extensions are covered in greater detail in the dBASE for Windows manuals. ▪

Putting the Query to Use

You can use a query or .QBE file from the Command window, or you can attach it to a form. When you issue the command to use a particular query, dBASE for Windows performs the following tasks:

- ✔ Opening all of the tables in the query.
- ✔ Establishing the table relationships.
- ✔ Setting filters.
- ✔ Determining which fields will appear and in what order.

You may want to use the query file from the Command window to open tables, set relations, or set filters. Using the query file to open several tables and set their complex relationships is easier than typing all of the necessary commands in the Command window. You can test your queries by viewing the results in the Browse window. You can also use the lightning bolt (Run) icon and the drafting tools (Designer) icons to test your queries and return to the Query Designer. ▪

Because you are looking at one particular view of the data, using a query file to set up your environment is called setting the view. To use a query file, you enter the SET VIEW command in the Command window:

```
SET VIEW TO MyQuery
```

You can watch the query file do its thing by checking the status bar, which changes as each table in the query is opened.

If you aren't sure whether the query did its job, you can see which tables are open, as well as their relationships, indexes, and filters by typing the following command in the Command window:

```
DISPLAY STATUS
```

This command displays information about your tables, and it lists all of the dBASE for Windows environment settings. It is a good idea to become familiar with these settings. They can give you an overall look at the settings available in dBASE for Windows and how they are set by default. ▪

Placing the results on a form for all to enjoy

One thing you will want to do with your query file is attach it to a form. This causes a query file to run automatically when the form is opened.

You should create buttons that let you skip through the records. A query isn't much fun if you can only see the first record. It's like asking someone to name the colors in the rainbow and then walking away disappointed after they say, "Red." ▪

As described in the following steps, you can link or attach the query file to your form by setting the View property of the form:

1. In the Form Designer, use your right mouse button to click on the form, and select Object Properties from the pop-up menu that's displayed. This opens the Properties window.

2. Select the View property and click its tool icon. As shown in Figure 7-6, dBASE for Windows displays the Choose View dialog box.

3. Choose a query file from the list on the left side of the dialog box. You may have to change directories if your query file isn't in the current directory.

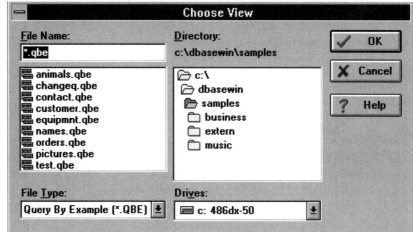

Figure 7-6:
You can choose from a list of query files to attach to your form.

If your query is complex or you are setting filters on very large tables, it may take some time for your form to open while the query file creates the view. Be patient. Whatever you do, don't get annoyed and reboot the computer. This is the worst thing you can do to a dBASE for Windows table. Turning off or rebooting the computer while a table is open can cause loss of data. ▪

What if there's no answer?
Who is John Galt?

There are few things as frustrating as the empty result set. This is what you get if nothing matches the expression in your filter. It's like being at a carnival, buying a ticket to see the Egress, walking through the self-locking door, and finding yourself outside.

When you specify a filter in your query, such as lastname = "Smith", dBASE for Windows issues a SET FILTER command and evaluates the records in the table. You need to be aware that in some cases, no records will match your filter and the result is nada, zip, the big zero, the empty result set. Don't be frightened when this happens. The data is still in your tables, it's just that all the records are invisible.

If the query produces an empty result set and you have controls DataLinked to your tables, the controls will be empty (as though you were adding a new record). ListBoxes won't list. Editors won't edit. All in all, it's a sad state of affairs.

One way out of this bind is to create a button that clears your filter. Remember that all of the tables you specified in the query are open, and any relationships you specified are set. The only problem is that you can't see anything.

You can turn off a filter by:

✔ Closing your tables

✔ Setting a new filter

✔ Issuing the SET FILTER TO command with no expression

You don't have to keep a poker face while typing the command SET FILTER TO with no expression. You can giggle and laugh or cry in your soup if you want. Issuing this command clears any filters that have been set.

Here are the steps for creating a Panic Button to clear your filter:

1. Create a PushButton on your form and label it Clear Filter or Panic Button or something equally as clever.

2. In the Form Designer, click the PushButton with your right mouse button, and select Object Properties from the pop-up menu that's displayed. Select the Events tab at the bottom of the Properties window. In the Events section of the Properties window, click the tool icon for the OnClick event.

3. In the Procedure Editor that appears, type the command SET FILTER TO.

4. Save this procedure by selecting <u>C</u>lose from the control menu in the upper-left corner of the Procedure Editor window.

The Procedure Editor automatically saves whatever you have typed. It doesn't ask you if you want to save the procedure you just created. If you use Ctrl-W to close the Procedure Editor, you can be assured that it has saved the procedure. ▪

Changing filters

You may want to give your application the ability to change filters. There are two basic ways you can do this. You can create another .QBE file and run it in an event of one of the controls on your form, or you can issue a new SET FIL-

TER command in the event. Table 7-2 lists some advantages and disadvantages of each approach.

Table 7-2: Deciding whether to use .QBE files or the SET FILTER command

Approach	Advantages	Disadvantages
.QBE Files	It's easier to create relationships, limit fields, and set filters in a .QBE file. If you need to change the filter statement, you can enter the change in the .QBE file, and the change is automatically implemented everywhere the filter is used.	To change filters using a .QBE file, you must close all of your tables and then reopen them. This takes time.
SET FILTER command	You can issue the SET FILTER command without closing and reopening tables. You can create SET FILTER commands on the fly in your application. This is useful if you don't know your query ahead of time.	It is more difficult to create the SET FILTER expression manually. If you need to modify the filter statement, you must enter the change everywhere the filter is used. This can be time-consuming if the SET FILTER command is used in many places.

There will be times in your application when you want to set or change filters without using a query file. This might seem intimidating, but the graphical approach of the Expression Builder can help you build your expressions. ▮

The Query Designer can unlock the secrets held in your tables. The query file that it creates is a workhorse. It opens files, sets relationships and filters, and it can sort and format results. Linked to a form, the query or .QBE file can help you create easy-to-use and powerful programs. The next chapter shows you how to enhance your programs by doing more with the events and procedures in your objects.

Part III

Doing More with Events and Procedures

The 5th Wave   By Rich Tennant

In This Part...

In the first two parts of the book, you've experienced the fun and creative style of visual programming in dBASE for Windows. In this part, you learn how to do much more with the procedures you've been writing. You find out how to use variables, and you learn how to give your procedures some decision-making capabilities. In Chapter 10, you write a complete application. Then, when those unavoidable problems arise, we show you how to find and correct them.

Chapter 8

Creating and Using Variables

. . . .

. . . .

*d*BASE for Windows has many tools and features that allow you to build applications without having to type in hundreds of lines of program code. You've already learned how to create powerful programs by putting simple commands and functions into object events. However, there will be times when your procedures need to do even more. This chapter shows you how to store information in *variables*, which are sort of like a scratch pad in your computer. To put those variables to work, you also need to understand *operators*. Finally, this chapter shows you how to put variables and operators together to form statements called *expressions*.

Change Is Good, So Use a Variable

One of the most important things in life is having a good place to store stuff. Where would we be without closets, pockets, cupboards, garages, and junk drawers? Fortunately, dBASE for Windows doesn't let you down in this regard. A variable is an excellent place for storing temporary information.

This storage place in memory is called a variable because the information you store in it can change. Fields are useful for storing information that you need to save for relatively longer periods of time. However, some information needs to be in memory only while your program is running. A variable is the perfect place for this type of information.

Variables are sort of like videotapes. You can save information on them, replay them over and over again, edit them, and erase them. You can also save them for later use.

Variables are similar to fields in a table, except that fields are more permanent places for storing data. Like fields, variables have names, types, and lengths. However, variables are a bit more selective than fields. When a table is open, any procedure can reference it. Variables, on the other hand, are a bit more selective about who or what gets to peek inside for a look at their values.

You need to follow a few rules and regulations when naming your variables:

- ✔ Variable names must start with a letter.

- ✔ A variable name can be up to 32 characters long.

- ✔ Variable names that contain spaces must begin and end with colons— for example, :variable name:. When characters such as colons are used in this way to mark the beginning and the end of something, they are referred to as delimiters.

- ✔ You can avoid using colons as delimiters by separating words with an underscore—for example, variable_name.

- ✔ To avoid confusion, a variable should not have the same name as a field in a table.

- ✔ Variable names should be meaningful and they should relate to the data that is stored in the variable.

Many styles are used for naming variables. Don't worry, we won't bore you with all of them. However, we do have a couple of suggestions.

Instead of underscores, we use upper- and lowercase letters to separate words in a variable name—for example, VariableName. This style keeps the length of variable names reasonable, which is important because typing is a big part of any programming effort. Long variable names are burdensome, especially after midnight. If someone did some research on the subject, they'd probably find that variable names get shorter as the day progresses.

Another useful convention is to precede the name of the variable with a letter that designates its type. For example, nVariableName would be a numeric variable. Technically, it is possible to precede your variable name with M–>, which officially identifies it as a variable name. However, this style gets a little hard to read.

Make sure you don't give your variable the name of a dBASE for Windows command or function. If you're in doubt, look up the variable name in <u>H</u>elp. In addition, some variable names are already used by dBASE for Windows. These variables and the names of commands and functions are known as *reserved words*. You can refer to the dBASE for Windows manual for a list of these words. ■

Once you have a name for a variable, you can use it to store a value. As shown in the following examples, there's more than one way to assign a value to a variable:

```
cFirstName = "Al"
Store "Al" to cFirstName
```

Both of these statements assign a character value to a variable named cFirstName.

Choosing a variable type you can live with

As you learned in Chapter 3, each field in a table has a type. Fields can be character, numeric, date, and so on. Each variable also has a type. As shown in Table 8-1, the type is determined by what you store in the variable.

Objects are variable types. However, as you know, they are more than variables. They also contain properties, graphic images, and values. When you name an object, you are really naming a huge memory variable. ■

Variables choose their type automatically when they're created. However, you need to keep track of a variable's type. If you don't know what's in a variable, you won't know how to use the variable in your program. Refer to Table 8-1 if you've created a variable and need to find out what type it is.

Table 8-1: The most common dBASE for Windows variable types

Type	Description	Example
Character	Text information	cFirstName = "Mary"
Numeric	Integers	nCounter = 3
Float	Decimal numbers	nValue = 3.56
Date	Date information	dDOB = {06/19/54}
Logical	True or false	lHappy = .T.

One potato, two potato, three potato, four

What if you wanted to store the name of each state in a variable? You could create 50 variables and name them state1, state2, and so on. Or, you could store the names in one variable that has 50 places to store things. This special type of variable is called an *array*, and the storage places in the array are called *elements*. An array is sort of like a drawer with many little compartments.

An array is actually an object. So far, most of the objects you've used have been visual controls. Unlike PushButtons, arrays do not have graphical displays. Like controls, however, arrays have properties and methods.

The following statement creates a 50-element array called MyArray:

```
aMyArray = NEW ARRAY (50)
```

Now you have a place to store the names of all 50 states.

To understand how arrays work, think of a compact disc by your favorite musician. Each CD usually has 10 or more tracks, and each track contains one song. Your CD player knows how many tracks are on the CD and it can find the track you want by referring to the track number.

Arrays operate in a similar fashion. You can store information in an array element by referring to its element number:

```
aMyArray[1] = "Alabama"
aMyArray[2] = "Alaska"
aMyArray[3] = "Arkansas"
```

Similarly, when you want to see what's in a particular element, you refer to the element by its number. You can use the question mark command (?) to take a peek at what is stored in each element of the array. The following statements tell dBASE for Windows to display the values of these array elements in the Results window:

```
? aMyArray[1]
? aMyArray[2]
? aMyArray[3]
```

As you might expect, dBASE for Windows responds by displaying the following information in the Results window:

```
Alabama
Alaska
Arkansas
```

Some CD players can hold several CDs at the same time. To access a particular track, you must select the CD and then the track. You can create something similar with a special type of array called a *multi-dimensional* array. In a multi-dimensional array, each element has sub-elements. To picture this, a simple array is like the squares in a sidewalk: one square after another in a single row. A multi-dimensional array is more like a checkerboard or the spaces in a tic-tac-toe game. A tic-tac-toe game would represent a 3-by-3 array.

You create a multi-dimensional array by entering both dimensions separated by a comma. For example, the following statement creates a 5-by-3 array:

```
aMultiArray = NEW ARRAY (5,3)
```

In other words, each of the five elements in the array has three elements of its own. This means the array contains a total of 15 elements.

To continue our example of storing states, you might want to store the area in square miles and the state capital along with each state name. With the additional information, you now need a 50-by-3 array. The first statement in the following example creates this array, and the subsequent statements store information in the first few elements of this multi-dimensional array:

```
aStates = NEW ARRAY (50,3)       && state names, capitals, and area
aStates[1,1] = "Alabama"
aStates[1,2] = "Montgomery"
aStates[1,3] = "51,609"
aStates[2,1] = "Alaska"
aStates[2,2] = "Juneau"
aStates[2,3] = "586,400"
aStates[3,1] = "Arkansas"
aStates[3,2] = "Little Rock"
aStates[3,3] = "53,103"
```

We could continue until we have entered the information for all 50 states, but our fingers are getting tired, so let's stop here.

You refer to specific information in a multi-dimensional array by using both element numbers. You can think of a multi-dimensional array as being like a data table. Each first element is like a record, and the second element is like a field in that record. In the preceding example, the table would have 50 records and 3 fields in each record.

You can use a one-dimensional array as the DataSource for a ListBox or a ComboBox control. (You can't use a multi-dimensional array as the DataSource because ListBoxes and ComboBoxes are one-dimensional controls.) This approach is useful if the information in the ListBox or ComboBox doesn't change. For example, you might want to create a ComboBox that allows a user to fill in a state field by selecting from a list of the 50 abbreviations of state names. We now relinquish control of your television set and return you to your own dimension. ■

Dial 0 for Operator

What would life be like without operators? Who else can we rely on to be there, 24 hours a day, 7 days a week, ready and eager to help us? When you call an operator, you usually need some information, or you need the operator to perform some action. Sometimes it's fun to call the operator just to say, "Hi!," though many of them have a tough time accepting this.

Just like the phone company, dBASE for Windows has lots of operators, and they're always willing to carry on a conversation with you. Each operator performs some action on the values it is given, and many operators return a value after their operation is complete.

There are four main types of operators:

- *Numeric.* Remember math class?
- *Relational.* How do you compare?
- *String.* These operators let you manipulate text.
- *Logical.* This will make sense, trust us.

These types of operators are described in the following sections.

One plus one is two (tell that to our government)

The numeric operators allow you to perform mathematical operations. They are listed in Table 8-2.

Table 8-2: Numeric operators in dBASE for Windows

Operator	Description
+	Addition
−	Subtraction
*	Multiplication
/	Division
** or ^	Exponentiation

Certain numeric operators take precedence over others. In other words, when dBASE for Windows is asked to perform a series of mathematical operations, it does so in the following order:

1. Exponentiation

2. Multiplication and division

3. Addition and subtraction

In the following example, dBASE for Windows performs the multiplication operations first and then adds the results:

```
? 4 * 6 + 5 * 3
```

The result of this statement is 39.

By using parentheses, you can force dBASE for Windows to perform mathematical operations in a different order. In the following example, the parentheses force dBASE for Windows to perform addition before multiplication:

```
? ((3 + 4) * (7 + 4))
```

The result of this statement is 77 (7 times 11).

Are you keeping up with the Joneses?

All things being equal, some things aren't. People use comparisons as incentive to achieve more, to push themselves farther, and to try harder. Comparisons are also important in programming. Although they won't instill in your programs a desire to function properly, they are helpful if you need your program to make decisions.

A comparison in dBASE for Windows is a question that can be answered with yes or no, or true or false (.T. or .F.). You can ask questions such as, Do you like my new shoes?, Will you lend me twenty dollars?, or Does God exist?; however, these questions won't help your programming.

In programming, comparisons ask about the relationship between two items. As shown in the following examples, comparisons can involve variables and values:

✔ Is variable A equal to variable B?

✔ Is variable C less than variable D?

✔ Is variable E equal to the word "supercalifragelisticexpialidocious"?

✔ Is variable F greater than 13?

To use comparisons in your programs, you need to construct a question using one of the relational operators listed in Table 8-3.

Table 8-3: Relational operators in dBASE for Windows

Operator	Description
=	Equals
==	Exactly equals
<	Less than
>	Greater than
<> or #	Does not equal
<=	Less than or equal to
>=	Greater than or equal to
$	String is contained within

Using relational operators, the previous example questions would look like this:

```
A == B
C < D
E == "supercalifragelisticexpialidocious"
F > 13
```

To display the results of a comparison question, you can enter the ? command in the Command window. To see this work, type the following statement in the Command window:

```
? 1 = 1
```

Because this comparison is true—that is, 1 does equal 1—dBASE for Windows displays .T. in the Results window.

You can use the ? command to evaluate any expression. For example, the following statement tells dBASE for Windows to display the result of a mathematical expression:

```
? 5 * 8
```

This statement causes dBASE for Windows to display the number 40 in the Results window. ∎

Two of the operators in Table 8-3 deserve more attention. The == and $ operators are special operators. You can use the == operator, which means exactly equals, to compare any type of information. When comparing strings, this operator forces dBASE for Windows to make an exact match regardless of any other environment settings that would allow a partial match.

Strings seem to have an innate desire for equality. When you use the = operator to compare strings, it returns .T. (true) if the string to the right of the operator equals the beginning of the string on the left. For example, the following comparison returns .T.:

```
"There is nothing to fear" = "There is nothing"
```

Sometimes, this is really handy; other times, it's really annoying. To ask whether an entire string exactly equals another entire string, use the == operator. For example, the following comparison returns .F. (false):

```
"There is nothing to fear" == "There is nothing"
```

When you've had enough of chasing bugs caused by the = operator's strange concept of string equality, you can force it to behave like the == operator. To do this, issue the following command:

```
SET EXACT ON
```

You can use the $ operator only when you are comparing strings. You use the $ operator to determine whether one string is contained within another string. This operator returns a true value (.T.) if the string to the left of the operator is found in the string on the right, and false (.F.) if it isn't. Because this comparison is case-sensitive, the following example returns a false value (.F.):

```
"GRENADE!" $ "The Holy Hand Grenade!"
```

If you have the courage, you can use the ? command in the Command window to display the results of this example:

```
? "GRENADE!" $ "The Holy Hand Grenade!"
```

Lucky for you, it was a dud. The Result window returns .F. (false). ▪

When to use logical operators (.AND. when .NOT. to)

Asking simple comparison questions is fun; you could go on for hours asking all sorts of them. You might even ask whether you wouldn't enjoy surfing more than sitting in front of your computer screen. The comparison Surfing > BeingAChairWeight would probably be true.

Sometimes you need to ask more complex questions, such as, Would I rather be surfing or would I rather be SCUBA diving? In such cases, you need to use a logical operator.

Logical operators let you combine short, simple comparison questions to create long, overly confusing comparison questions. These operators come in three flavors:

- ✔ .AND.
- ✔ .OR.
- ✔ .NOT.

Each logical operator combines comparisons differently. You might say that each one follows its own logic.

The .AND. operator returns a true value (.T.) only if both of the comparisons it combines are also true. For example, the following comparison is true, because the comparisons on both sides of the logical operator are true:

```
? 1 = 1 .AND. 2 = 2
```

However, the following .AND. operation returns a false value because the first comparison is false:

```
? 1 <> 1 .AND. 2 = 2
```

The .OR. operator returns a true value (.T.) if one or both of the comparisons is true. For example, the following operation is true because at least one of the comparisons is true:

```
? 1 <> 1 .OR. 2 = 2
```

The .NOT. operator returns the opposite of the answer to the question it precedes. In other words, it reverses the answer to any comparison question. The following example returns false because the comparison question following the .NOT. operator returns true:

```
? .NOT. 1 = 1
```

Unlike .AND. and .OR., the .NOT. operator doesn't actually combine two comparison questions. However, as shown in the following example, you can use .NOT. in conjunction with the other two logical operators:

```
? 1 = 1 .OR. .NOT. 2 = 2
```

Now you know why these logical operators can become overly confusing. You can make logical operations easier to understand by using parentheses to separate each comparison question. The preceding example can be rewritten like this:

```
? (1 = 1) .OR. (.NOT. 2 = 2)
```

Smile When You Create That Expression

When you think of expressions, you probably think of smiling, frowning, and screwing up your face in a look of exasperation. As you've probably noticed, dBASE for Windows can cause all of these expressions and more. Now you can give dBASE for Windows some expressions of its own. No matter how complex they are, these expressions always result in a single value. Just like it takes more than 64 facial muscles to frown, the result is still just a frown.

As shown in the following example, expressions don't have to involve numeric information:

```
? "Bill " + " likes " + "candy."
```

The preceding example tells dBASE for Windows to add three character strings together and display the result in the Results window. The result from this expression is: Bill likes candy.

You can build expressions using any combination of the following:

- Variables
- Constants
- Field names
- Operators
- Functions

As shown in Figure 8-1, the Expression Builder is a visual tool for creating expressions. You use the Expression Builder throughout dBASE for Windows whenever you need to create an expression. You can also access the Expression Builder by choosing Build Expression from the Edit menu, or by pressing Ctrl-E.

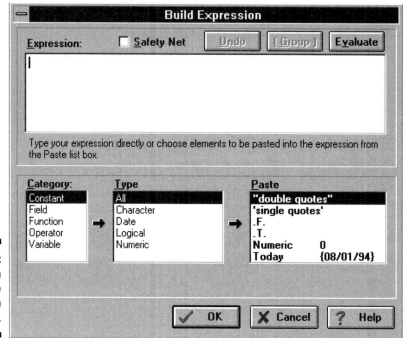

Figure 8-1:
Smile when
you use the
Expression
Builder.

To see helpful prompts and instructions throughout the process of creating
an expression, click the Safety Net CheckBox. ■

The Expression Builder contains a blank workspace and several ListBoxes.
You use the Category and Type ListBoxes to change the contents of the Paste
ListBox. To insert an item into the Expression workspace, double click that
item in the Paste ListBox.

To better understand how you create expressions, let's take a tour through
the Expression Builder. However, before we can put the Expression Builder
to work, we need a couple of sample variables. To create them, type the following statements in the Command window:

```
MyVar = 6
YourVar = 9
```

You have created two numeric variables called MyVar and YourVar. Now
let's create an expression that evaluates whether the values stored in MyVar

and YourVar are equal. Of course, you already know they aren't. But what if one of the values changes? Variables change all the time in programs. That's why they're called variables.

It's time to call in the Expression Builder. Press Ctrl-E to display the Expression Builder.

Select Variable from the Category ListBox in the lower-left corner of the Expression Builder. This tells dBASE for Windows that the first part of our expression is going to be a variable.

The Type ListBox now has two choices, System and User. This ListBox lets you choose between variables created by dBASE for Windows (system variables) and variables that you have created. Select User from this list.

The Paste ListBox now lists any variables you have created during your session in dBASE for Windows. Look through this list for the variables we just created, MyVar and YourVar. Use your left mouse button to double click MyVar in the Paste ListBox. MyVar is pasted into the Expression workspace near the top of the Expression Builder.

This example uses the automated method of expression building in which everything is accomplished with clicks and double clicks in the three List-Boxes at the bottom of the Expression Builder. If all this mouse clicking makes your hand tired, you can type any of your choices directly into the Expression workspace. ■

Our expression so far is:

```
M->MYVAR
```

This is already a valid expression because its result is a single value. The result of this expression is the number 6. You can test this by clicking the Evaluate button. The result appears in the middle of the Expression Builder.

Notice that MYVAR is preceded by M–>. This is how dBASE for Windows denotes variables. The M stands for memory, as in memory variables. Although it isn't required, this notation is helpful because it allows dBASE for Windows to distinguish between a variable and a field that might have the same name.

The next step is to choose an operator. Select Operator from the Category list. The Type list now allows you to select which type of operators you want listed. For the equal sign, you can select either All or Relational. The Paste window lists the operators of the selected type. Double click the equal sign (=) in the Paste window, and the Expression Builder pastes an equal sign in the Expression workspace, which now looks like this:

```
M->MYVAR =
```

To create a valid expression, you need something to the right of the equal sign. In this example, you want to enter the name of the other variable, YourVar. As mentioned, you can add YourVar to the expression by clicking on the appropriate selections in the Category, Type, and Paste ListBoxes, or you can simply type YourVar in the Expression workspace.

The complete expression should now read:

```
M->MYVAR = YourVar
```

If you use the Category, Type, and Paste ListBoxes, it looks like this:

```
M->MYVAR = M->YOURVAR
```

This is a true-false expression. In other words, the values of the two variables are either equal (True) or they are not equal (False). Yes, you already know the answer, but click the Evaluate button anyway. The result, .F., is displayed in the middle of the Expression Builder.

When you finish building an expression, click the OK button and dBASE for Windows pastes the expression into whatever tool you happen to be using. If you are in the Procedure Editor, the expression is pasted into the current cursor position in the procedure you are editing. If you are using the Command window, as we are in this example, the expression is pasted into the Command window. Don't try to run the expression in the Command window without putting the ? command in front of it. Without the ? command, you won't see the result in the Results window.

Entire volumes have been written on what we've covered in chapter. It is wise to supplement your knowledge with other sources. The dBASE for Windows User's Guide and on-line help are good places to start.

Chapter 9

Directing Traffic with Branches and Loops

- -

In This Chapter

▶ Making decisions

▶ Handling lots of choices

▶ Doing something over and over again

▶ Doing it a certain number of times

▶ Stopping when you don't want to do it anymore

▶ Making it stop when it doesn't want to

- -

*Y*ou make decisions every second of your life. You decide whether to sit, stand, lean, talk, or smile. You also decided to learn dBASE for Windows. Computer programs make decisions too. By using the statements that are introduced in this chapter, you can tell your program to decide between different courses of action, depending on many possible things. For example, your program might cause a form to turn blue if the user enters correct information, or red if the user makes a mistake. You can use IF statements or DO CASE statements to give a program this type of decision-making, or branching, capability. You can also make your program go in loops, processing the same commands over and over. Depending on your requirements, you might create a loop using the DO WHILE, DO UNTIL, FOR NEXT, or SCAN statements.

Changing Direction with the IF Statement

The IF statement causes a program to make a decision based on the value of an expression. We've been doing this all our lives. When we were kids, we evaluated our parents' expressions to determine whether or not it was a good time to ask for our allowance.

An IF statement has the following general form:

```
IF expression
  One or more programming statements
ENDIF
```

When dBASE for Windows evaluates an expression, the result is either true or false. The result of the expression in an IF statement determines whether dBASE for Windows executes the programming statements immediately following the IF statement. If the expression is true, dBASE for Windows executes the programming statements following the IF statement. If the expression is false, dBASE for Windows skips those commands or program statements and continues execution with the first statement after ENDIF.

The following example shows how the IF statement works:

```
cSky = "BLUE"

IF cSky = "BLUE"
  Do this
  Do that
  Do something else
ENDIF
```

In this example, we create a character variable called Sky and set it equal to the text BLUE. In our IF statement, the expression cSky = "BLUE" is true. As a result, dBASE for Windows executes the fake commands, Do this, Do that, Do something else.

If we set cSky equal to "Red", the expression following the IF statement would be false, and dBASE for Windows would ignore our fake commands. In this case, execution of the program would continue with the next statement after ENDIF.

As shown in the preceding example, you use the IF statement to make a simple decision: Should dBASE for Windows perform the following task (or tasks)? We make this type of decision every morning. "Should I get up and drag myself to the office, or not?" To put this decision in the form of an expression, we might add some criteria for making the decision: "If the sun is shining and the coffee is already brewing, I'll get up and go to work." If the two statements are true, your work gets done. Otherwise, you get several more hours of sleep.

You can use the logical .NOT. operator to do things if the statement is false. However, the .NOT. operator can be a little tricky. For example, how would you answer if someone asked you, "Is the ocean NOT full of water?" Because it is true that the ocean is indeed full of water, the correct answer would be, "That is false." Using the .NOT. operator, our blue sky example would look like this:

```
cSky = "GREEN"

IF .NOT. cSky = "BLUE"
  Do this
  Do that
ENDIF
```

In this example, the expression cSky = "BLUE" is false because the variable cSky contains the text "GREEN". The .NOT. operator creates an IF statement that says, "If it is not true that the sky equals blue." Because this expression is true, dBASE for Windows executes the Do this and Do that commands. ■

Creating an IF statement

Like life, an IF statement has a beginning and an end. We begin with the keyword IF and the expression that is to be evaluated. Next comes the work that is to be performed if the expression is true. As shown in the following example, the IF statement ends with the keyword ENDIF:

```
cSky = "Blue"
IF cSky = "Blue"
  cDay = "Wonderful"
ENDIF
```

In this example, the first statement stores the string "Blue" in a variable named cSky. The IF statement evaluates the expression cSky = "Blue". In other words, the IF statement determines whether or not the string "Blue" is stored in the variable cSky. In this case, the answer is yes, or true. As a result, the character string "Wonderful" is stored in the variable cDay.

If the variable cSky contained anything other than "Blue", the expression in the IF statement would be evaluated as false. If the expression is false, the program skips the contents of the IF statement and continues processing with any statements immediately after the ENDIF.

In the preceding example, you might notice that the program statement inside the IF statement is indented. Indenting related lines of code makes a program easier to read. For example, it's much easier to see where an IF statement begins and where it ends. How much you indent is a matter of personal taste. Many people use a single tab. ■

Creating complex IF statements

The previous chapter introduced the different types of comparison and logical operators. As shown in the following example, you can use these operators to build complex IF statements:

```
cSky = "Blue"
nTemperature = 75
Summer_Plans =  "Undecided"
IF cSky = "Blue" .AND. nTemperature >= 75
  Summer_Plans = "Spend vacation at home"
ENDIF
```

The first three statements in this example create variables and store values in those variables. The .AND. operator is used to create an IF statement that evaluates two different expressions. Specifically, the IF statement determines whether the variable cSKY contains the character string "Blue", as well as whether the variable nTemperature contains the value 75. Because both of those expressions are true, the character string "Spend vacation at home" is stored in the variable Summer_Plans.

If either of the expressions in the IF statement was false, the program would skip the statement in which "Spend vacation at home" is stored in the variable Summer_Plans. In this case, the program would continue with the statements (if any) immediately after ENDIF.

Let's say that's just what happened. The weather turned cool and cloudy, and you need some different summer plans. How do you tell your program what to put in the Summer_Plans variable if the expression in the IF statement isn't true?

It's simple; you use an ELSE statement. If the expression in the IF statement is false, dBASE for Windows executes the statements that follow ELSE. If you want to see how the ELSE statement is used, check out this example, else skip it:

```
cSky = "Cloudy"
nTemperature = 65
Summer_Plans = "Undecided"
IF cSky = "Blue" .AND. nTemperature >= 75
  Summer_Plans = "Spend vacation at home"
ELSE
  Summer_Plans = "Extended vacation in Tahiti"
ENDIF
```

In this example, we store values in three variables: cSky, nTemperature, and Summer_Plans. Then two of those variables are evaluated to see if our

Summer plans involve staying at home. If not, our Summer plans are deter-mined by the statement following the ELSE statement. Because the tempera-ture is not greater than or equal to 75, we get to spend an extended vacation in Tahiti.

If this isn't enough decision making for you, there's more. With ELSEIF, you can make lots of choices within the IF statement. The ELSEIF statement con-tains an expression that is evaluated if the initial IF expression is false. In other words, when the expression in the IF statement is false, dBASE for Win-dows evaluates the expression in the ELSEIF statement.

An IF statement can be followed by as many ELSEIF statements as you want. When your program includes a series of ELSEIF statements, dBASE for Win-dows works through them in succession until it finds an expression that is true. No choices here, you have to read this example:

```
cSky = "Cloudy"
nTemperature = 65
dToday = {06/15/97}
Summer_Plans = "Undecided"
IF cSky = "Blue" .AND. nTemperature >= 75
  Summer_Plans = "Spend vacation at home"
ELSEIF cSky = "Blue" .AND. nTemperature > 62 .AND.;
    dToday > {05/05/97}
  Summer_Plans = "Go to the beach and have a good time"
ELSEIF cSky = "Cloudy" .AND. nTemperature < 62 .AND. ;
    dToday < {05/05/97}
  Summer_Plans = "Stay in bed"
ELSE && When all else fails
  Summer_Plans = "Extended vacation in Tahiti"
ENDIF
```

One of the first things you might notice in this example are the semicolons at the end of several lines. When program lines get so long that they run off the page, you can continue them on the next line by placing a semicolon in the program code and continuing the line on the next line. Although dBASE for Windows has no problem reading long lines of code, you may find that using semicolons to break up long lines of code makes your programs easier to read. ■

In the preceding example, the first IF statement is false because cSky is Cloudy, not Blue. The first ELSEIF statement is evaluated as false because it too has the sky as Blue. The next ELSEIF is false because the temperature is 65 and the expression calls for a temperature less than 62. Because none of these expressions are true, we fall back on the catchall ELSE statement. Yes, another extended vacation in Tahiti.

In the preceding examples, each decision results in execution of a single statement. Specifically, each decision causes a different value to be stored in the variable Summer_Plans. However, you don't have to limit the result of each decision to a single statement. In fact, each choice in an IF...ELSEIF structure can actually include as many statements as you need. You can also place parentheses around certain logical statements to have them evaluated before other parts of the expression.

Branches, Limbs, Twigs, and Leaves

If you've ever cooked dinner for more than two people, you know that sometimes decisions are complex and there can be decisions within decisions. If I start the pie before I get in the shower, I should be able to take the pie out before it burns. The guests might arrive while I'm in the shower, so I'll leave the refreshments out and put a note on the door. If the dog is in the house, he'll eat the refreshments, so I'd better put the dog out. Oh no! The pie is burning and I'm not even in the shower. The avocado is turning brown, the dog is eating the bean dip, and the guests are early. Put the bean dip in the backyard so the dog will go out. Throw the pie at the guests and tell them to take a shower so they will be entertained, and then eat the avocado before it gets worse. Then join the guests in the shower.

Believe it or not, there is a point to all this. There are very few situations in life where one decision is enough. The same is true in programming. As shown in the following example, the result of one IF statement might lead to a decision that must be evaluated with another IF statement:

```
cSky = "Blue"

IF cSky = "Blue"
  WaterTemp = 70
  IF WaterTemp > 65
    Summer_Plans = "Go to the beach."
  ENDIF
ENDIF
```

The second IF statement in this example is called an *embedded* IF. That is, the second IF statement is embedded, or nested, inside the first IF statement. The cSky is Blue, so the expression in the first IF statement is true. As a result, the program creates a new variable called WaterTemp and sets it equal to 70. The embedded IF statement evaluates the WaterTemp variable to see if it is greater than 65. Luck seems to be running in our favor. Summer_Plans now equals "Go to the beach."

All programs have a flow. In other words, they must start somewhere and they must end somewhere. The two main types of programming flow are:

- ✔ *Procedural.* This type of program begins with the first line of code and, although it may contain branches, it generally continues in a linear fashion to the last line of code.

- ✔ *Object-oriented.* An object-oriented program begins by creating objects. The objects then interact, completely free of any line of flow, until the program is terminated by the object that is responsible for that task.

Using dBASE for Windows, you can write both procedural and object-oriented programs. Programs with a Windows user interface are object oriented by design. Because object-oriented programs usually have fewer branches and loops than procedural programs, they tend to be less complex, easier to write, and simpler to maintain. ▪

Taking responsibility for your decisions

The human brain is a remarkable piece of machinery. As you know, the more complex machinery gets, the more likely it is to get muddled. Compared to the human brain, computers—even big ones—are relatively simple. So, they are less likely to get muddled.

When creating the logic for your branching statements, it's always best to keep things as simple as possible. Unfortunately, you will encounter situations where this is impossible. In these situations, the Expression Builder can help you define and evaluate your logic.

It's much simpler to take precautions while you are writing programs than it is to find the flaws in your logic after the program is complete. To help you find the error of your ways, dBASE for Windows provides numerous debugging tools. Chapter 11 shows you how to use these tools. ▪

Trimming the logic tree

ELSEIF is kind of a strange term. As you've seen, it can also produce some fairly complicated programs. If your program needs to cover a lot of choices, a series of CASE statements is probably a simpler solution.

Here's how a CASE statement operates: If you make a case for something being true, dBASE for Windows carries out the instructions that follow immediately after that CASE statement. In other words, the logic of the CASE statement is similar to that of the ELSEIF statement.

Each series of CASE statements begins with a DO CASE statement and ends with ENDCASE. The CASE statements are evaluated in succession. If a CASE is true, dBASE for Windows executes the statements that follow that CASE, and then continues execution with the statements following ENDCASE. If the CASE is false, dBASE for Windows evaluates the next CASE statement. This process continues until dBASE for Windows encounters either an OTHERWISE statement or the ENDCASE statement, which indicates that there are no more choices. The OTHERWISE statement works exactly like the ELSE statement. When all else is false, dBASE for Windows executes the code following this optional statement.

The following example shows how CASE statements work:

```
DO CASE
CASE cSky = "Blue"
  cSummerPlans = "Go to the beach"
CASE cSky = "Cloudy"
  cSummerPlans = "Stay home and build models"
CASE cSky = "Dark"
  cSummerPlans = "Stay home with a model"
OTHERWISE
  cSummerPlans = "Undecided"
ENDCASE
```

Each of the CASE statements is evaluated in succession. The value that is assigned to the variable cSummerPlans depends on the value of cSky.

As shown in this example, you can include an OTHERWISE statement at the end of the DO CASE statements. Similar to the last ELSE in a series of ELSEIF statements, the statements that follow OTHERWISE are executed if the expressions in all of the preceding CASE statements are false. The OTHERWISE statement is optional.

Although DO CASE statements are a little easier to read, there is no functional difference between the DO CASE and ELSEIF statements. Which statement you use is a matter of personal taste. However, to preserve your sanity when you start embedding IF statements in each case, we recommend using DO CASE statements. Even the best indenter in the world gets confused after a while.

Look at the difference between the following examples. The first example uses lots of IF and ELSE statements:

```
IF cSky = "Blue"
  IF nTemp > 75
    cSummerPlans = "Go to the beach"
  ELSE
```

```
        cSummerPlans = "Stay home with a book"
      ENDIF
   ELSEIF cSky = "Cloudy"
     IF nPrecipitation > 0.5
        cSummerPlans = "Stay home and build models"
     ELSE
        cSummerPlans = "Motocross racing"
     ENDIF
   ELSEIF cSky = "Dark"
     IF lGoodHairDay
        cSummerPlans = "Stay home with a model"
     ELSE
        cSummerPlans = "Stay home and dream about models"
     ENDIF
   ELSE
     cSummerPlans = "Undecided"
   ENDIF
```

The second example does exactly the same thing as the first, but it's much easier to read:

```
   DO CASE
   CASE cSky = "Blue"
     IF nTemp > 75
        cSummerPlans = "Go to the beach"
     ELSE
        cSummerPlans = "Stay home with a book"
     ENDIF
   CASE cSky = "Cloudy"
     IF nPrecipitation > 0.5
        cSummerPlans = "Stay home and build models"
     ELSE
        cSummerPlans = "Motocross racing"
     ENDIF
   CASE cSky = "Dark"
     IF lGoodHairDay
        cSummerPlans = "Stay home with a model"
     ELSE
        cSummerPlans = "Stay home and dream about models"
     ENDIF
   OTHERWISE
     cSummerPlans = "Undecided"
   ENDCASE
```

You can embed as many IF statements as you need. You can also embed DO CASE statements within other DO CASE statements.

Round and Round We Go

A hula hoop wouldn't be much fun if it only spun around once. Slot machines would be pretty boring if they simply flashed a Won-Lost sign after you put your money in the slot. The Indianapolis 500 would be tough to watch if it started in Indianapolis and ended somewhere near Pittsburgh. Do you get the idea that going around and around can be fun?

In programming, a loop provides a way to execute the same statements over and over. Each time a program loops, dBASE for Windows evaluates an expression to see if the program should continue looping.

When you need to perform repetitive tasks in dBASE for Windows, you can use one of several types of loops in your program. DO WHILE and DO UNTIL loops let you execute a series of statements over and over, as long as an expression continues to be true. A FOR loop lets you execute a series of statements a specific number of times. To be helpful, the FOR loop keeps count for you. Another type of loop scans through records in a table until its expression is true and it can stop. These different types of loops are described in the following sections.

Using the DO WHILE loop

In programming as in life, it's important to know when to stop and when to keep on going. This is the key to creating a DO WHILE loop that works.

A common programming problem involves a loop that won't stop. In other words, the program just keeps executing the same statements over and over again. This is known as an endless loop. If an endless loop ever happens to you, we're betting that you'll come up with some other names for it too.

To avoid the aggravation of an endless loop, you need to spend some time figuring out how to tell the DO WHILE loop to begin and, more important, how to tell it to stop.

A DO WHILE loop has three main parts:

- ✔ The beginning expression.
- ✔ Statements that are executed as long as the beginning expression is true.
- ✔ An ENDDO statement.

To start a DO WHILE loop, dBASE for Windows evaluates the beginning expression. If the expression is false, dBASE for Windows skips the statements in the loop and continues with the next statement after ENDDO. Case closed, end of story.

If the beginning expression is true, dBASE for Windows executes the statements in the loop. After executing the last statement in the loop, dBASE for Windows goes back and re-evaluates the beginning expression. If the expression is still true, dBASE for Windows executes the statements in the loop a second time, and then goes back to re-check the beginning expression. This process continues until dBASE for Windows evaluates the beginning expression as false. When that happens, dBASE for Windows leaves the loop and moves on to the statement immediately after ENDDO.

Here's a simple example of a DO WHILE loop:

```
FarmsAreCool = .T.
USE Animals

DO WHILE FarmsAreCool
  cAnimal = Animals->Name
  lDangerous = Animals->Danger
  IF lDangerous
      FarmsAreCool = .F.
  ENDIF
  SKIP
ENDDO
```

In this example, you see that FarmsAreCool evaluates to .T. (true), so the program enters the loop and starts processing the records in the table called Animals. Each time the program comes to the ENDDO statement, it loops back to the DO WHILE statement and re-evaluates the expression. In other words, it determines whether FarmsAreCool is still true. If so, the program goes back through the loop and processes the next record from the Animals table. (Remember, the SKIP statement at the end of the loop moves the record pointer to the next record in the table.)

When a dangerous animal is encountered while skipping through the table, the DO WHILE expression is evaluated as .F. (false). At that point, the program leaves the loop and continues with any statements after ENDDO.

Skipping through tables is one of the most common uses of the DO WHILE loop. The following example uses a dBASE for Windows function to create a DO WHILE loop that skips through each record in a table:

```
USE Animals

DO WHILE .NOT. EOF()
  IF Animals->Name = "Kangaroo"
```

```
       ? "I found a kangaroo at record "
       ?? RECNO()
   ENDIF
   SKIP
ENDDO

CLOSE DATABASES
```

EOF( ) is a dBASE for Windows function that indicates whether the record pointer is at the end of the file. The EOF( ) function returns .T. (true) when the record pointer reaches the last record in the table.

In this example, the statement DO WHILE .NOT. EOF( ) tells the program to keep looping until the record pointer reaches the end of the file—that is, the last record in the Animals table. Whenever the program finds a record for a kangaroo, a message is printed in the Results window. The program uses the RECNO( ) function to include the current record number in this message. Each time the program encounters the SKIP command, the record pointer advances to the next record in the table. As mentioned, this process continues until the program has checked all the records in the Animals table. The last statement in the example closes all open tables.

ENDDO isn't the only statement that can cause the program to loop back to the DO WHILE. The LOOP command is like being able to cut in on a long line at the movies:

```
cJelly = "Grape"
cSpread = "Peanut Butter"

DO WHILE cSpread = "Peanut Butter"

  DO CASE
  CASE cJelly = "Grape"
     cJelly = "Strawberry"
     cSpread = "Peanut Butter"    && This goes with strawberry
  CASE cJelly = "Strawberry"
     cJelly = "Mixed Fruit"
     cSpread = "Mayonnaise"
     LOOP
  CASE cJelly = "Mixed Fruit"
     cJelly = "Orange Marmalade"
     cSpread = "Nothing"            && Nothing goes with marmalade
  ENDCASE

  ? cJelly + " and " + cSpread + ", mmmmm yummy!"
ENDDO
```

In this example, the jellies keep changing. If the result is a tasty combination, the program prints a yummy message. Here's what happens:

1. The program enters the loop because cSpread is Peanut Butter.

2. cSpread continues to be Peanut Butter with the first change in cJelly.

3. When cJelly is changed to Mixed Fruit, cSpread becomes mayonnaise and the program encounters a LOOP statement.

4. The program immediately loops back to the DO WHILE and the expression is now false.

5. The program leaves the loop and continues after the ENDDO.

Because the LOOP command causes the program to loop before it reaches the ENDDO, we are spared the result of "Mixed Fruit and Mayonnaise, mmmmm yummy!"

Using the DO UNTIL loop

The DO UNTIL loop is similar to the DO WHILE loop. The difference is that the expression is evaluated at the end of the loop instead of at the beginning. As a result, the loop always executes at least once, the first time through. The following example shows how the DO UNTIL loop works:

```
MyCounter = 0

DO
   MyCounter = MyCounter + 1
UNTIL MyCounter = 5
```

In this example, MyCounter is a numeric variable that adds one to itself each time through the loop. Because there is no expression in the DO statement, dBASE for Windows enters the loop. The UNTIL expression is evaluated at the end of the loop. When the value of MyCounter reaches 5, the loop stops and the program continues with any statements after the UNTIL statement. If you want to do something at least once, this is the loop to use.

Scanning for intelligent life

In an earlier section of this chapter, we used a DO WHILE loop to go hunting for kangaroos in our data tables. There's a slicker way to find those pesky varmints. It's called the kangaroo hunting loop. Actually, it's called SCAN.

The SCAN statement accomplishes the same thing as the following DO WHILE loop:

```
DO WHILE .NOT. EOF()
  IF MyField = MyVariable
     Do Something
     EXIT
  ENDIF
  SKIP
ENDDO
```

However, the SCAN statement is much simpler:

```
SCAN FOR MyField = MyVariable
  Do Something
ENDSCAN
```

As shown in this example, SCAN requires fewer lines of code than DO WHILE. SCAN evaluates each record as it automatically skips through the table. When the expression is true, the statements between SCAN and ENDSCAN are executed. The following example shows how you could use SCAN to go kangaroo hunting:

```
USE Animals

SCAN FOR Animals->Name = "Kangaroo"
     ? "I found a kangaroo at record "
     ?? RECNO()
ENDSCAN

CLOSE DATABASES
```

The SCAN statement also has a few more features than DO WHILE. Here is the entire SCAN statement:

```
SCAN scope FOR condition1 WHILE condition2
  statements
  LOOP
  statements
  EXIT
  statements
ENDSCAN
```

The *scope* tells SCAN how many records to scan. You can give SCAN a specific record number, or you can use keywords such as ALL or NEXT, which tells SCAN to scan the NEXT so many records. You can also use REST to specify the rest of the records from the current record position.

FOR *condition1* tells SCAN what to scan for. For example, you might want to scan the table for a field that equals the value of a variable:

```
SCAN FOR MyField = MyVariable
```

Although WHILE *condition2* might sound like a hair conditioner, it actually tells SCAN how long to keep scanning. The program keeps scanning as long as condition2 is true.

Statements are the commands and functions that are executed if SCAN finds what it is looking for.

LOOP operates the same as it does in a DO WHILE loop. This command advances the record pointer to the next record and then loops back to the SCAN statement.

The EXIT command is a quick way out of the loop. Use this command in your statements if you want to stop looping before the FOR *condition1* or WHILE *condition2* statements stop the SCAN.

For your next trick

When was the last time you ran laps around a track? Did you count the number of laps? Of course you did, it's only natural. Like all you track stars, the FOR loop counts the number of times it goes through a loop. As its coach, you get to tell the FOR loop how many loops to run.

Like the DO WHILE loop, the FOR loop has three parts:

> ✔ The FOR statement, which specifies how many times the program should go through the loop. It also keeps track of how many times the program has gone through the loop.
>
> ✔ The statements that are to be executed a certain number of times.
>
> ✔ The NEXT command, which sends the loop back to FOR.

The beginning of the FOR loop can be a little tricky the first time you see it. The general form of this statement is:

```
FOR CounterVariable = StartingNumber TO EndingNumber
```

CounterVariable represents the variable that counts how many times the program has gone through the loop. As you might have guessed, *StartingNumber* and *EndingNumber* are the first and last values that are assigned to your counter variable. For example, if you want your program to go through the loop five times, the beginning of the loop would look like this:

```
FOR nVar = 1 to 5
```

Here's the entire FOR loop, which displays the value of the counter variable in the Results window each time the program goes through the loop:

```
FOR nVar = 1 to 5
  ? nVar
NEXT
```

First, nVar is set to 1. Then, the statement in the loop displays this value in the Results window. When the program reaches the NEXT command, it loops back to FOR, which increases the value of nVar (the counter variable) to 2. The program goes back through the loop and displays the new value of nVar in the Results window. This looping continues until nVar reaches 5 and this value is displayed in the Results window. When the program loops back to FOR, nVar exceeds its ending value, so the program leaves the loop and continues with the statement after NEXT.

You don't have to start at one. In a calendar application, you might create a loop to limit the output to days 15 through 30:

```
FOR nDay = 15 to 30
  ? "I am real busy on day: "
  ?? nDay
NEXT
```

If there's something you don't want executed, you can use the LOOP command as a shortcut back to FOR. It works the same way it does in a DO WHILE loop.

This is all well and good, but what if you want to count backward? Or, you might want to count by twos. If you're playing hide and seek, you might even want to count by tens. Don't worry, you can count by anything you want, either forward or backward. You tell the FOR loop how to count by adding the word STEP followed by a positive or negative number. The following example counts by tens from 1 to 1,000:

```
FOR nVar = 1 to 1000 STEP 10
  ? nVar
NEXT
```

The following FOR loop counts backward:

```
FOR nVar = 1000 to 1 STEP -10
  ? nVar
NEXT
```

As shown in this FOR loop, the first number after nVar is always the starting value. In this case, it is the number you want to count down from. The second number is always the ending value. The third value tells the program how to change the counter each time the loop comes around.

As you can see, the FOR loop is something you can really count on!

Stop the world, I want to exit

According to an old story, P.T. Barnum once changed all the EXIT signs in his sideshow to EGRESS and charged people money to see what was beyond the curtain. Curious people would find themselves standing outside. In dBASE for Windows, the EXIT command isn't quite so tricky.

The EXIT command takes you out of a loop, regardless of the expression in a DO WHILE loop or the counter in a FOR loop. The following example uses the EXIT command to jump out of a DO WHILE loop:

```
USE Animals

DO WHILE .NOT. EOF()
  IF Animals->Name = "Porcupine"
     ? "I got stuck on the Porcupine."
     EXIT
  ELSE
     ? Animals->Name
  ENDIF
  SKIP
ENDDO
USE IN Animals  && Another way to close this file
```

This sticky example shows us the way out. When the name field in the animals table is "Porcupine" the IF statement becomes true. As a result, the string, "I got stuck on the Porcupine." is printed in the Results window. Then the program sees the EXIT statement and jumps all the way out of the loop. The program continues after the ENDDO statement and closes the Animals table.

Sometimes you need to force a program to enter a loop despite the fact that several expressions could immediately cause the program to stop looping. If so, you can make the program enter the loop by using an expression that is always true. Then, you can use the EXIT command to allow the program to stop looping. Here is how you do it:

```
USE Animals

DO WHILE .T.  && It's True no matter what
  DO CASE
```

```
      CASE Animals->Name = "Armadillo"
         REPLACE Animals->Name with "Road Chicken"
      CASE Animals->Name = "Tarantula"
         EXIT
      CASE EOF()
         EXIT
      ENDCASE
      ? Animals->Name
   SKIP
ENDDO
USE IN Animals
```

In this example, .T. is used as the expression in the DO WHILE loop. This seems like cheating doesn't it? However, it meets all the criteria for a logical expression; it evaluates to a single true or false value.

As we skip through the Animals table, the CASE statements are evaluated. Different things happen depending on the animals we encounter. Two cases end our loop. The first case is finding a Tarantula. This CASE has a sure ticket right out of the loop. The second case is the end of the file. When EOF() is true, the EXIT command takes us out of the loop.

You can have loops inside loops. I guess that would make them loop-d-loops. Which brings us to carnival rides...

Carnival rides, motion sickness, and endless loops

Remember how dizzy some carnival rides made you feel? Well, nothing in a program really moves, but it can sure make your head spin when you realize that your program has been looping for 20 minutes and has no intention of stopping.

Use every available means to test loops before you send them off on their own. Loops that won't stop are frustrating, a waste of time, and can, in some situations, ruin your tables. ■

If a loop never evaluates to false, it will never stop. Of course, never means until you reboot, the machine wears out, you move out of state, or the world comes to an end. This situation is known as an endless loop. By taking the following simple precautions, you can protect yourself from this very frustrating occurrence:

- ✔ SET ESCAPE ON. This command lets you stop your program by pressing Esc. This is perhaps the simplest and most useful precaution.

- ✔ Add an OTHERWISE with an EXIT command to your DO CASE statements.

- ✔ Make sure you have a SKIP command if you are looking through a table. This is the number one cause of endless loops, looking at the same record over and over and over...

Do not reboot if you can avoid it. We know; sometimes, there's just no other way. If you have to reboot, you should be aware of what could happen. If a table is open when you reboot, the computer might put an End of File marker somewhere in the table where it doesn't belong. This is known as an embedded End of File marker. Your data is still there, but the computer can't reach it because the End of File marker keeps getting in the way. The status bar will probably list the correct number of records. ▨

Being careful with loops will keep you from making the same mistake over and over the same mistake over and over the same mistake...[machine reboot at 01:14:15]

Chapter 10

Writing Really Useful Programs

. . . .

In This Chapter

▶ Getting ready to program

▶ Creating a rough draft of your program

▶ Using the rough draft to build a complete application

. . . .

Creating useful applications takes practice. To complete a programming job, you need to remember the various tools, techniques, and tricks of the trade that you've acquired. More important, you need to figure out how to put them all together to create programs that do what they're supposed to. In this chapter, you get to apply everything you've learned so far in this book to the creation of a sample application.

"To Boldly Go Where No One Has Gone Before"

Each application you write will be a unique adventure. There's no right way or wrong way to build an application, only ways that work and ways that don't. Creating our sample application involves the following steps:

1. Summarizing the program's requirements and planning its structure.

2. Creating a rough draft, or prototype, of the user interface.

3. Creating the database tables and completing the user interface.

4. Writing code to handle data processing and applying finishing touches to the application.

The approach we use in this chapter works well for simple programs. With experience, you'll develop your own programming style. As long as your programming style gets the job done, you're on the right track.

This Is the Way Programming Begins, Not with a Bang...

Every program begins with a need, or a reason to write a program. The motivation for developing our sample application involves an imaginary challenge in an imaginary enterprise:

> The employees in our firm are spending far too much time working, and not enough time surfing in the corporate wave pool, using the corporate tennis courts, or exercising in the corporate gym. We must immediately do something about this situation. We need a program that tracks the number of hours each employee spends using these facilities daily.

Now that we have a reason to program, it's time to develop a plan. For our sample application, planning means two things:

✔ Deciding what our application should do.

✔ Figuring out how it should do it.

Out of habit, and for superstitious reasons, the first thing we do is create a form. A blank form is like a scratch pad that you can doodle on while planning the structure of your application. Besides, creating a form gives the reassuring impression that you've started programming. Sometimes this helps you get through the beginning of the planning process with less agony.

To create a new form, enter the following command in the Command window:

```
CREATE FORM
```

After some thought and a bit of doodling on the blank form (see Figure 10-1), we decide that users of our program need to do three things:

✔ Add new employees to a database table.

✔ Add daily time reports for employees, indicating how many hours are spent using the wave pool, tennis courts, and gym.

✔ Print a report showing the total number of hours each employee uses the three facilities.

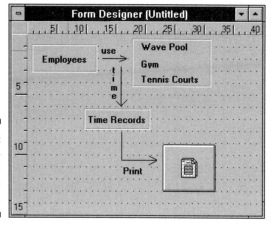

Figure 10-1:
Doodle +
Divine
Intervention
= Plan.

Employees never quit and the company makes so much money that nobody is ever fired, so the user of our program won't need to remove employees.

Because we've made a few assumptions about our application, the planning is complete. Anything that hasn't been planned yet will be worked out while we program. The assumptions we've made are:

- ✔ This application will use database tables to store information.
- ✔ The table structures will include relationships that are based on the needs of the program.

The next step is creating a rough draft of our application. Because we assume the existence of database tables, we can start designing the part of our application that requires the most creativity: the user interface. After sketching out a complete user interface, we can focus on building a working application.

A Rough Draft Is More than a Harsh Wind

A rough draft of an application is known as a *prototype*. To build a prototype, you begin programming as though you're developing a complete application. However, instead of filling in every detail, you concentrate on major parts that demonstrate the most important features of the application. Building a prototype gives you a bird's-eye view of your project and simplifies the development process.

You might be inclined to design database tables as part of your prototype. After all, tables are a major part of your application, right? Well, tables are important, but they aren't necessary in most prototypes. With a good prototype, you can leave this level of detail for later.

When creating a prototype, you should concentrate on those elements of an application that help you determine what information will be required in your tables. It's better to create a prototype application that needs imaginary database tables than it is to create database tables that need an imaginary application. ▤

From the plan we developed in the preceding section, we can see that the prototype should include the following major elements of our application:

✔ A form for adding employees
✔ A form for adding time reports
✔ A main menu for good luck

It's time to start building our prototype application. Throughout this process, remember that the decisions we make while creating this program are based on our experience and the needs of our imaginary application. Most of our decisions aren't the only answer to the challenge at hand. At each step, you should try to think of other ways to approach this application.

Roughing Out Our Sample Application

To create the rough draft of our application, we'll start by building prototypes of the two forms and a menu that lets us use the forms. Then, we can assemble the pieces of our prototype. When the prototype is complete, we'll be able to see how the three primary components of our application work together.

Creating a prototype of the employee data entry form

To get started, let's build a prototype of the form for adding employees. Open the Form Designer and create a blank form named EMPLOYEE by entering the following command in the Command window:

```
CREATE FORM EMPLOYEE
```

Next, we need to ask ourselves what information the user of our program will want to enter when adding a new employee. For each employee, the user needs to enter the following information in the employee data entry form:

✔ First and last name

✔ Employee number

Your form should include EntryField controls for the first and last names because this information will be entered as text. To add EntryField controls and descriptive labels to our EMPLOYEE form:

1. Open the Controls window (if it's not already open) by clicking on the form using your right mouse button and then checking the Controls option on the pop-up menu that's displayed.

2. Click the EntryField icon in the Controls Palette, and then click on the EMPLOYEE form in the location where an EntryField should appear for the employee's first name.

3. Click the Text icon in the Controls Palette.

4. Place a Text control to the left of the EntryField on the EMPLOYEE form. This Text control will contain a descriptive label for the EntryField.

5. The descriptive label that will appear in this Text control should be "First". To enter this text, click the Text property in the Properties window and type over the default value. (If the Properties window isn't displayed, remember that you can open this window by clicking the Text control in the Form Designer with your right mouse button, and then selecting Object Properties from the pop-up menu that's displayed.)

6. The EMPLOYEE form also needs an EntryField and a Text control for the employee's last name. Place these controls to the right of the EntryField for first name. Use "Last" as the Text property for the new Text control.

Because the employee number will be entered as a number, we'll use a SpinBox control instead of an EntryField. Although an EntryField would work, the scroll arrows in a SpinBox give the user a visual cue that a number is required. To add a SpinBox control with an informative label to our EMPLOYEE form:

1. Click the SpinBox icon in the Controls Palette.

2. Click on the EMPLOYEE form in the location you've chosen for the SpinBox. For this example, place the SpinBox below the EntryFields that you've created for first name and last name.

3. Click the Text icon in the Controls palette.

4. Click on the EMPLOYEE form to place a Text control to the left of the SpinBox.

5. In the Properties window, change the Text property of this Text control to "Employee Number".

6. Finally, let's add a label to our EMPLOYEE form. Place a Text control at the top of the form and change its Text property to "Employee".

Now you can sit back and admire what you've created. Figure 10-2 shows our first draft of the employee data entry form. It doesn't do anything yet. It's like an old, beat-up sailboat—a simple shell that's full of potential, if you use your imagination.

When you're satisfied that you've thought of everything, save the employee data entry form by pressing Ctrl-W.

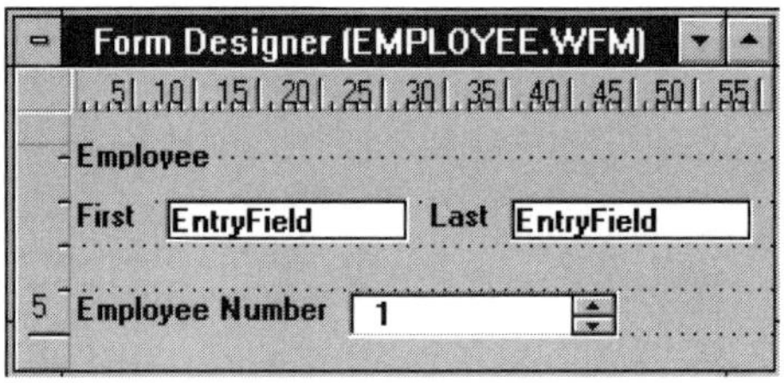

Figure 10-2:
Our
Employee
data entry
form.

Creating a prototype of the time report form

Now we can turn our attention to employee time reports. The application needs another data entry form, so you should create a blank form by entering the following command in the Command window:

```
CREATE FORM TIMEREP
```

Before you can add controls to this form, you need to make a basic decision about how your program is going to work. There are two possible approaches for adding time reports:

✔ The user could select an employee and add a time report.

✔ The program could prompt the user to enter a time report for each employee.

The first approach makes more sense because daily time reports aren't always required for every employee. For example, daily time reports aren't necessary for employees who are on vacation. The second approach forces the user to enter a daily time report for each employee.

The employee time report data entry form needs the following elements:

  ✔ A list that lets users select the employee for whom they're entering a time report.
  ✔ A SpinBox for entering time spent using the wave pool.
  ✔ A SpinBox for entering time spent using the tennis courts.
  ✔ A SpinBox for entering time spent using the gym.

Because the user is entering numbers, the SpinBox is an easy choice for the three controls that let the user record how much time an employee spends using each facility. However, you need to decide how the user is going to select an employee. Three types of controls let a user choose something from a list:

  ✔ Browse controls
  ✔ ListBoxes
  ✔ ComboBoxes

Each of these control types requires a slightly different programming approach. Although any of them would work, a Browse control requires less code than a ListBox or a ComboBox.

Determining which employee is selected from the list is easier with a Browse control because the record pointer is positioned on that employee's record in the table. Whenever a user clicks a row in a Browse control, the record pointer moves to the corresponding record in the table to which the control is linked. For this reason alone, we'll use the Browse control.

Figure 10-3 shows our first draft of the employee time report data entry form. You already know how to place controls on a form, and you know which controls to use for this form. You also know how to change the Text properties of the Text controls that we are using as descriptive labels on our data entry forms. As a result, we won't bore you with step-by-step instructions for completing this prototype form.

Although we are still assuming the existence of database tables, you can see how their structures will emerge. It's clear from the decisions we just made that we'll want a separate table for the employees and one for time reports.

Save the employee time report data entry form by pressing Ctrl-W. You now have prototypes of your two user interface forms! You don't have any tables and you haven't written any code for the controls yet, but you have illustrated the basic elements of your application. When you can open these forms using a menu, you'll be able to demonstrate the structure and operation of your entire application.

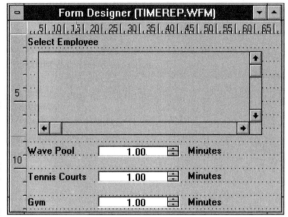

Figure 10-3:
The
employee
time report
data entry
form.

Creating a prototype menu

Drafting a menu is simple if you know what's cooking. You start by creating a list of options for the menu. Our menu needs to include the following options:

- ✔ Exit the program
- ✔ Add a new employee
- ✔ Add a time report for an employee
- ✔ Print a report summarizing facility use

Most menus list several high-level categories directly on the menu bar, with each menu option listed under a category. In keeping with this standard, let's separate the four menu items into three categories:

- ✔ File
- ✔ Employees
- ✔ Time Tracking

To create a menu that contains these three categories:

1. Open the Menu Designer and create a new menu called APPMENU by entering the following command in the Command window:

```
CREATE MENU APPMENU
```

2. The Menu Designer is displayed and you can enter the first item in your menu bar. When you are using the Menu Designer, remember that you

can use an ampersand to identify a hot key for each menu item. The letter immediately after the ampersand is the keyboard equivalent for the menu option. The first category in your menu bar is File, so you should type &File. The ampersand specifies that the letter F is the hot key for this menu item. In other words, a user can open the File menu by pressing Alt-F.

3. For now, Exit will be the only option in the File menu. Press the down-arrow and type E&xit. The ampersand specifies that the user can select the Exit option when the File menu is open by pressing x.

4. Because the File menu contains only one option, you are ready to move back to the menu bar and create the next menu category. Press the up-arrow key to return to the &File menu category, and then press Tab to move the cursor into position for entering the next menu category. Type &Employees.

5. The Employees menu should include an option for adding an employee. Press the down-arrow and type &Add Employee.

6. You are ready to return to the menu bar and enter the name of the last menu category. Press the up-arrow key to return to the &Employees menu category, press Tab, and type &Time Tracking.

7. The Time Tracking menu will include two options. To create the first menu option, press the down-arrow key and type &Add Time Report.

8. Create the last menu item by pressing the down-arrow key and typing &Print Summary.

9. Save the menu by pressing Ctrl-S.

Figure 10-4 shows the menu categories we've created, and the menu option for exiting the program.

We put the option for exiting the program under the File menu because that's where Windows programmers usually put the Exit option. There will be many situations when you do things simply because other Windows programmers do them. However, if you see a Windows programmer climb out

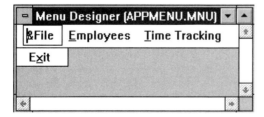

Figure 10-4: A menu provides a simple, easily understood user interface.

onto a window ledge, you can break with Windows programming tradition and stay inside.

You may wonder why our Print option isn't under the File menu. After all, most Windows programs have a Print option under the File menu. Well, those programs are typically used to create documents of some kind, such as word processing documents, spreadsheets, and so on. In addition, most of them allow you to open more than one document at a time. When you want to print a document, you choose the Print option, and the program figures out what you're working on at the moment and prints that document.

Our application doesn't create those types of documents. The only printing in our program is the generation and display of a summary report. Therefore, it doesn't really make sense to include a Print option in our File menu. In general, you should follow Windows programming traditions only if they make sense for your application.

Writing event procedures for the menu

Now that we have a menu, we can give it the ability to open our prototype forms. To open a form from the menu, we need an event procedure that is activated when the user chooses one of the menu items. Use the following steps in the Menu Designer to create an event procedure that is executed when the user selects the Add Employee menu item:

1. Click the Employees category in your menu bar to display the Add Employee menu item.
2. Click the Add Employee menu item.
3. Find the Properties window and click the Events tab to display the events for the Add Employee menu item.
4. Click the OnClick row to display the tool icon for the OnClick event.
5. Click the tool icon to access the Procedures window.

Although you haven't entered any commands yet, you now have an event procedure that is executed when the user selects the Add Employee menu item. However, this procedure isn't very useful yet. As shown in Figure 10-5, you should type the following command in the Procedures window:

```
DO EMPLOYEE.WFM
```

Now the OnClick event procedure really does something. When the user selects the Add Employee menu item, this procedure opens our EMPLOYEE form.

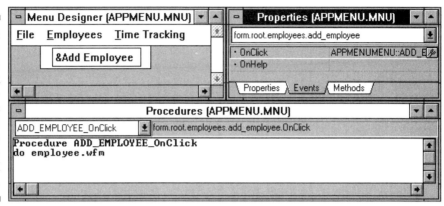

Figure 10-5:
The Add
Employee
OnClick
event pro-
cedure uses
the DO
command to
open the
EMPLOYEE
form.

You can use the DO command to execute form files because forms are built using the dBASE for Windows programming language. Application development tools such as the Form Designer actually write dBASE for Windows code for you!

You also need to create an event procedure for the Add Time Report menu item. With the exception of the command that you enter in the Procedures window, you should follow the same basic steps that you just used for the Add Employee menu item. As shown in Figure 10-6, you should use the following command in the event procedure for the Add Time Report menu item:

```
DO TIMEREP.WFM
```

Figure 10-6:
The Add
Time Report
OnClick
event pro-
cedure uses
the DO
command to
open the
TIMEREP
form.

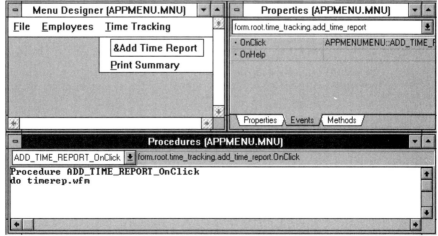

To complete our prototype menu, the Exit menu option should close all open forms and exit our application. The following command closes all open forms:

```
CLOSE FORMS
```

Using the CLOSE FORMS command in the Exit option of the menu is an easy way to exit our application. As shown in Figure 10-7, you should put this command in the OnClick event procedure for the Exit menu option. Using Ctrl-W to exit the Menu Designer.

CLOSE FORMS closes every open form, even those that have nothing to do with the application you're running. Don't use CLOSE FORMS to exit your program if there are forms that you want to leave open. ▪

Figure 10-7:
The Exit
OnClick
event pro-
cedure uses
the CLOSE
FORMS
command to
exit our
application.

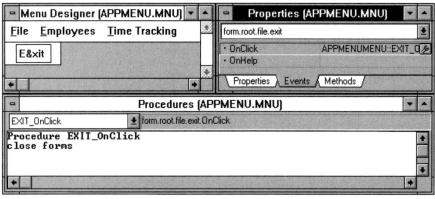

Attaching menus to forms

Now that we have a prototype menu, it's time to use the menu with our two prototype forms. The easiest way to use a menu in an application is to attach the same menu to each of the forms. You do this so that every form in the application displays the same menu.

To attach our menu to both forms:

1. Specify that you want to modify the EMPLOYEE form by entering the following command in the Command window:

```
MODIFY FORM EMPLOYEE
```

2. Find the Properties window and click the Properties tab.

3. Click the MenuFile property.

4. Click the tool icon to open the Choose Menu window.

5. Select APPMENU.MNU from the list of menus and click OK.

6. Press Ctrl-W.

7. Repeat the preceding steps for the TIMEREP form.

Most applications begin with some type of main window, and ours is no exception. Create a new form called FUNMAIN.WFM and use Figure 10-8 as a model for the text that you add to this form. After saving this new form, you can attach your prototype menu to FUNMAIN as described in steps 2 through 6 in the preceding list.

Finally, our prototype is ready to run.

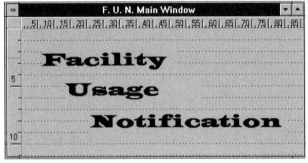

Figure 10-8: The main window for our application.

Run, prototype, run!

To run the prototype program, enter the following command in the Command window:

```
DO FUNMAIN.WFM
```

When you enter this command, dBASE for Windows runs the application by opening the main window and displaying your application's menu in place of the dBASE for Windows menu. To evaluate your design, you can use the menu options to navigate through the application. Choose Exit from the File menu when you're done.

Our next step is to build database tables. Because the application is nearing completion, creating the tables becomes more exciting. You'll get a sense of divine intervention as the rest of the program falls into place.

Stop and Smell the Vaporware

At this point, your application is still mostly vaporware. In other words, you can wave your arms around and show everyone the pretty forms you've created, but the application doesn't really do anything yet. The development style we're using in this example could be described as transforming vaporware into software. This style is one of the easier ways to write programs in dBASE for Windows. If you can wave your arms, point at a few forms you've created, and explain in detail how your application is going to work, several things happen:

> ✔ You can quickly finish the application and avoid major rewrites resulting from oversights in the design of your application.

> ✔ You can impress everyone you work with by visually demonstrating your programming progress.

> ✔ The exercise you get by waving your arms will relieve stress.

Let's dispense with the hand waving and start transforming the vaporware you've created into working software.

Tables Make the World Go 'Round

In previous sections of this chapter, you've created prototypes of your data entry forms. Provided that we haven't missed anything important, you should be able to use these forms as a guide for designing your database tables.

Designing the employee table

The employee date entry form allows the user to enter the following information:

> ✔ Employee number
> ✔ First name
> ✔ Last name

As you might expect, these are the fields that will make up your Employee table. To create the Employee table:

1. Enter the following command in the Command window:

```
CREATE EMPLOYEE
```

2. The Table Structure window is displayed and you can start defining the fields for the Employee table. Type EMPNUMBER in the Name column for field 1.

3. Press Tab and choose Numeric from the list of Types for field 1.

4. Press Tab and set the field width to 6.

5. Press Tab and set the decimal width to 0.

6. Press Tab and choose Ascend for the index.

7. Press Tab and type FNAME in the Name column for field 2.

8. Using the Tab key to move from one column to the next, set Type to Character, Width to 15, and Index to None.

9. Type LNAME in the name column for field 3, and set Type to Character, Width to 15, and Index to None.

10. Figure 10-9 shows the Table Structure window with the information for the Employee table. Verify that your table structure is complete, and save the EMPLOYEE table by pressing Ctrl-W.

Now you can complete your employee data entry form!

Figure 10-9:
The employee data entry form uses this Employee table.

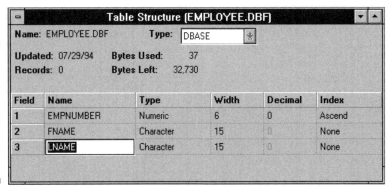

Field	Name	Type	Width	Decimal	Index
1	EMPNUMBER	Numeric	6	0	Ascend
2	FNAME	Character	15	0	None
3	LNAME	Character	15	0	None

Completing the employee data entry form

To compete the employee data entry form, you need to link the controls on this form to fields in your Employee table. You should also add PushButton controls that allow the user to close the form, and you need to write procedures that allow users to add a new record and close the form. To make these changes to the employee data entry form:

1. Open the Form Designer by entering the following command in the Command window:

```
MODIFY FORM EMPLOYEE
```

2. You need to link each control on this form to a field in the Employee table. Remember that you use the Properties window to define the DataLink property for a selected object. Click the EntryField control for Employee Number, find the Properties window, and click the Properties tab. Select the DataLink property, click the tool icon, and select the EMPNUMBER field in the Employee table as the DataLink for this control. Repeat this process, linking the First Name EntryField to the FNAME field, and the Last Name EntryField to the LNAME field.

3. Next, you need to add two PushButtons to the form. A PushButton labeled OK will allow users to close the form and confirm the addition of a new employee. A Cancel PushButton will allow users to close the form and leave the Employee table unchanged. Find the Controls Palette, click the PushButton icon, and place a PushButton control near the bottom of the form. In the Properties window for the new PushButton, select the Text property and change it to OK. Then you can add a second PushButton control to the bottom of the form and change its Text property to CANCEL.

4. When a user opens the employee data entry form, your program should add a new record to the Employee table. To add this capability to your application, you need to create an OnOpen event procedure for your employee data entry form. Click on a blank area of the form in the Form Designer. Find the Properties window, click the Events tab, select the OnOpen event, and click the tool icon to access the Procedures window. Type the following commands in the OnOpen event procedure for your employee data entry form:

```
SELECT EMPLOYEE
APPEND BLANK
```

5. The OK button will allow users to confirm the addition of a new employee. Click the OK button in the Form Designer. Find the Properties window, click the Events tab, and open the Procedures window by clicking the tool icon for the OnClick event. Enter the following command in the Procedures window:

```
form.close()   && close the form, the new employee record is ok
```

6. The CANCEL button will allow users to cancel the addition of a new employee and leave the EMPLOYEE table unchanged. Add the following commands to the CANCEL button's OnClick event procedure:

```
DELETE         && mark the new employee record for deletion
form.close()   && close the form
```

You might want to PACK tables when you delete records. To keep the example as simple as possible, we've left out this step. Leaving deleted records in the table shouldn't cause problems, as long as your program ignores them. By default, dBASE for Windows ignores deleted records. If you want to PACK the Employee table in the OnClick event procedure of the CANCEL PushButton, you need to insert the PACK command after DELETE and before FORM.CLOSE(). ■

Our employee data entry form is shown in Figure 10-10.

Designing the time report table

The employee time report data entry form allows the user to enter the following information:

- ✔ Employee number
- ✔ Time spent using the wave pool
- ✔ Time spent using the tennis courts
- ✔ Time spent using the gym

As shown in Figure 10-11, you need to create a corresponding time report table. To open the Table Structure window, enter the command CREATE TIMEREP in the Command window. Define the structure of this table by entering the field names, types, lengths, and indexes as listed in Figure 10-11.

Note that in place of the Browse control, we've created an employee number field named EMPNUMBER. This field is identical to the EMPNUMBER field in the Employee table. This key field is necessary for creating our summary report because it lets us set the relationships between the Employee table and the Time Report table. When our application is used, each EMPNUMBER value in the Time Report table will match a single EMPNUMBER value in the

Figure 10-10:
The completed employee data entry form.

```
┌─────────────────────────────────────────────┐
│ -  Form Designer [EMPLOYEE.WFM]      ▼  ▲    │
├─────────────────────────────────────────────┤
│    ..5l.10l.15l.20l.25l.30l.35l.40l.45l.50l.55l│
│   ┌Employee··································  │
│   ┌First·┌──────────┐ Last·┌──────────┐     │
│ 5 │ Employee Number    0        ▲▼      │    │
│      ┌──────────┐    ┌──────────┐           │
│      │    OK    │    │  CANCEL  │           │
│      └──────────┘    └──────────┘           │
└─────────────────────────────────────────────┘
```

Figure 10-11:
The
employee
time report
data entry
form will
use this
time report
table.

Field	Name	Type	Width	Decimal	Index
		Table Structure [TIMEREP.DBF]			
	Name: TIMEREP.DBF	Type: DBASE			
	Updated: 07/29/94	Bytes Used: 25			
	Records: 0	Bytes Left: 32,742			
1	EMPNUMBER	Numeric	6	0	Ascend
2	WAVEPOOL	Numeric	6	2	None
3	TENNIS	Numeric	6	2	None
4	GYM	Numeric	6	2	None

Employee table. This one-to-many relationship between the Employee and
Time Report tables allows us to identify the employees for whom time
reports are entered.

Because the EMPNUMBER field is used as a unique employee identifier, you
would normally force the values in this field to be unique among employees in
the Employee table. For example, you could use a SEEK command to ensure
that a value you are adding to the table isn't a duplicate. To keep the example
simple, our application doesn't do this. We're assuming that the user will keep
track of employee numbers and avoid entering duplicates. In the real world,
you wouldn't usually make this kind of assumption. Sometimes users accidentally enter the wrong value, and a well-designed program should account for
this possibility. If duplicate employee numbers are entered in our application,
the summary report will show incorrect summaries. ■

Completing the time report data entry form

The steps for completing the time report data entry form are similar to those
you used for completing the employee data entry form:

1. Open the Form Designer by entering the following command in the Command Window:

```
MODIFY FORM TIMEREP
```

2. DataLink the three SpinBox controls on form to the appropriate fields in the Time Report table. To define the DataLink property for a control, click the control in the Form Designer, find the Properties window, click the Properties tab, select the DataLink property, click the tool icon, and choose the appropriate field in the Time Report table. You should link the Wave Pool SpinBox to the WAVEPOOL field, the Tennis Courts Spin-Box to the TENNIS field, and the Gym SpinBox to the GYM field.

3. Add OK and CANCEL PushButtons to the time report data entry form. To add the OK button, open the Controls Palette, click the PushButton icon, and click to place a PushButton control near the bottom of the form. In the Properties window, change the Text property for this PushButton to OK. Then, add another PushButton to the bottom of the form and change the second PushButton's Text property to CANCEL.

4. Create an event procedure that automatically creates a new record when a user opens the time report data entry form. To access the Procedures window, click on a blank area of the TIMEREP form, find the Properties window, click the Events tab, select the OnOpen event, and click the tool icon. dBASE for Windows displays the Procedures window, and you can type the following commands in the form's OnOpen event procedure:

```
SELECT TIMEREP
APPEND BLANK
```

5. Write an event procedure for the OK button to allow the user to confirm the addition of a new time report. To add this capability to the OK button, click the OK button in the Form Designer and find the Properties window. Next, click the Events tab, and open the Procedures window by clicking the tool icon for the OnClick event. Enter the following commands:

```
REPLACE timerep->empnumber WITH employee->empnumber
form.close() && close the form, the new time report record is ok
```

The REPLACE command is used to set the EMPNUMBER field in the time report table equal to the EMPNUMBER of the employee that was selected in the Browse control. Remember that the record pointer in the Employee table moves whenever the user selects a row in the Browse control.

The CANCEL button allows the user to cancel the addition of a new time report, and leaves the TIMEREP table unchanged. Add the following commands to the CANCEL button's OnClick event procedure, following the steps described for the OK button:

```
DELETE        && mark the new time report record for deletion
form.close()  && close the form
```

Our time report data entry form is shown in Figure 10-12.

We're almost done! Our menu and data entry forms are complete, and the application only needs two more pieces.

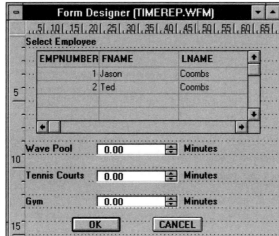

Figure 10-12:
The com-
pleted
employee
time report
data entry
form.

Using Query Files to Open Your Tables

Your application needs to know which database tables it should access. To allow the application to access both the Employee and Time Report tables, you need to create a query by example (.QBE) file by entering the following commands in the Command window:

```
USE EMPLOYEE IN 1
SET ORDER TO TAG EMPNUMBER
USE TIMEREP IN 2
CREATE QUERY
```

After you enter these commands, dBASE for Windows displays the Query Designer, and you can save the .QBE file by pressing Ctrl-W. When you save the file, dBASE for Windows prompts you for a filename. For this example, call the file FUNMAIN.QBE. This query file opens the Employee and Time Report tables and activates the EMPNUMBER index.

Figure 10-13 shows the Query Designer for our query. After saving this query as a .QBE file, you can attach it to the main window, FUNMAIN.WFM, by changing the form's View property.

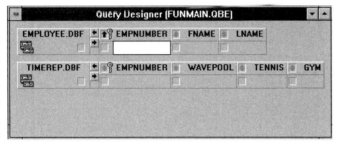

Figure 10-13:
The Query Designer for our .QBE file.

To change the View property of the form:

1. Open the Form Designer by entering the following command in the Command Window:

```
MODIFY FORM FUNMAIN
```

2. Click on the form with your right mouse button and select Object Properties from the pop-up menu that appears.

3. In the Properties window, click the tool icon for the View property.

4. Select FUNMAIN.QBE from the list of views that appear in the selection list and click the OK button.

When a user opens FUNMAIN.WFM, the Employee and Time Report tables will be opened in work areas 1 and 2, respectively.

Creating a Summary Report

The final piece of the application is a summary report that lists the amount of time each employee has spent in each facility. This report is created using the dBASE for Windows Command Language. Because the report requires a little more code than you are used to seeing, this section includes a line-by-line explanation. In addition to the detailed explanation that follows the procedure, you'll notice that comments appear throughout the code to help you understand what's happening. Remember that comments are always preceded by an asterisk (*) or a double ampersand (&&).

The application should generate a summary report when the user selects the Print Summary option from the application's menu. In other words, you need to create an OnClick event procedure for one of the options on the application's menu. To open the Menu Designer and create the event procedure that generates the summary report:

1. Enter the following command in the Command window:

   ```
   MODIFY MENU APPMENU
   ```

2. In the Menu Designer, click the Time Tracking menu category to reveal its menu options.

3. Click the Print Summary menu option, find the Properties window, and click the Events tab.

4. In the Properties window, click the OnClick event, and open the Procedures window by clicking the tool icon for the OnClick event.

5. Type the following code in the Procedures window:

   ```
   * Usage Report
   * This report lists Wave Pool, Tennis, and Gym use by employee

   SET TALK OFF              && No chit chat

   SELECT EMPLOYEE
   SET ORDER TO EMPNUMBER       && Activate Employee Number index
   SELECT TIMEREP
   SET RELATION TO EMPNUMBER INTO EMPLOYEE && Set table relationship

   STORE 0 TO nWavePool, nTennis, nGym   && Set up total variables
   nEmp = EMPNUMBER             && Store current employee id
   GO TOP                       && Go to the top of TIMEREP table

   CLEAR                        && Clear the Results window

   && Print report headings
   ? "Employee Name          Pool        Tennis        Gym"

   DO WHILE .NOT. EOF()       && Loop until the end of the file
      IF nEmp # EMPNUMBER     && If the employee has changed
         ? EMPLOYEE->LNAME    && Print the employee name and totals
         ?? " "
         ?? nWavePool
         ?? nTennis
         ?? nGym
         STORE 0 TO nWavePool, nTennis, nGym && Reset variables to 0
         nEmp = EMPNUMBER      && Reset employee number variable
      ELSE                    && If it is still the same empnumber
         nWavePool = nWavePool + WAVEPOOL && Add Wavepool time
   ```

```
        nTennis = nTennis + TENNIS       && Add Tennis time
     nGym = nGym + GYM      && Add Gym time
      SKIP                   && Skip to the next record
   ENDIF
ENDDO                        && Fnd of the loop

SELECT TIMEREP              && Make sure timerep is selected
SET RELATION TO            && Unset the relationship
SELECT EMPLOYEE            && Select Employee for luck
```

Although it might seem like a lot of code, there's nothing here that you haven't seen before. To be on the safe side, let's walk through this event procedure and make sure that everything makes sense.

The procedure starts by telling dBASE for Windows to keep what it is doing to itself. The SET TALK OFF command tells dBASE for Windows that it should not display the result of every single command in the Results window.

The next four lines activate the production index for the Employee table and establish a relationship between the two tables, using EMPNUMBER as the key field:

```
SELECT EMPLOYEE
SET ORDER TO EMPNUMBER              && Activate Employee Number index
SELECT TIMEREP
SET RELATION TO EMPNUMBER INTO EMPLOYEE && Set table relationship
```

Next, the procedure creates three memory variables—nWavepool, nTennis, and nGym—and sets them to zero. These memory variables are used to store running totals as the procedure adds up the number of hours each employee spent using the three facilities. By using the STORE command, we can create these variables in one step rather than entering three statements, as follows:

```
nWavepool = 0
nTennis = 0
nGym = 0
```

The next line in the procedure creates a new memory variable called nEmp and sets it equal to the value stored in the EMPNUMBER field of the TIMEREP table. Although you could use the STORE command to create a single variable, it seems like too much work in this case:

```
STORE EmpNumber TO nEmp
```

The nEmp value lets the procedure figure out when it should print subtotals for each employee. As long as nEmp matches EMPNUMBER, the procedure is still looping through the records for an employee. Because the TIMEREP table is indexed in EMPNUMBER order, all of the records for each employee are grouped together. When nEmp doesn't match EMPNUMBER, it means that the procedure has reached the records for a different employee. When this happens, the procedure performs the following tasks:

- Using the ?? operator to print the subtotals that are stored in the memory variables to the Results window:

```
? EMPLOYEE->LNAME   && Print their name and totals
?? " "
?? nWavePool
?? nTennis
?? nGym
```

- Clearing the counter variables by resetting them to zero:

```
STORE 0 TO nWavePool, nTennis, nGym
```

- Resetting the nEmp variable so that it matches the employee ID number for the current employee:

```
nEmp = EMPNUMBER
```

Because TIMEREP is the currently selected work area, it isn't absolutely necessary to precede the field name, EMPNUMBER, with the name of the table. However, this approach is recommended if you are writing long, complex programs.

The GO TOP command moves the record pointer to the top of TIMEREP, which is the currently selected table.

The CLEAR command clears any text from the Results window to make room for the first line of our output. The question mark command (?) sends the output of our expression, in this case a text string, to the Results window. The following statement prints the header of our report, which contains the column titles:

```
? "Employee Name           Pool      Tennis          Gym"
```

A DO WHILE statement starts a loop in which the procedure skips through the records in the TIMEREP table, adds up the hours, and stores them in the memory variables we've created:

```
DO WHILE .NOT. EOF()
```

The EOF() function returns a value of .T. (true) when the procedure reaches the end of the table. The expression in the DO WHILE statement tells the procedure to keep looping until it reaches the end of the table.

The first thing we encounter in the loop is an IF statement:

```
IF nEmp # EMPNUMBER
```

This IF statement determines whether the value stored in the variable nEmp matches the employee ID number in the current record. The # operator means not equal. In other words, the IF statement determines whether the nEmp variable is not equal to the EMPNUMBER field. If these values don't match, the procedure has totaled all the records for an employee, and the record pointer has moved to the first record for the next employee in the TIMEREP table. In this case, the procedure prints the totals for the employee it has just completed.

If nEmp equals EMPNUMBER, the procedure is still looping through the records for the current employee. In this case, the procedure executes the statements immediately after ELSE. This code adds the hours in the different facilities to the counter variables:

```
nWavePool = nWavePool + WAVEPOOL
nTennis = nTennis + TENNIS
nGym = nGym + GYM
```

The procedure calculates these running totals by adding the value already stored in the variable to the hours found in the table.

When the procedure skips to a new employee number, it prints the values that have been accumulating in the memory variables. The ? command provides simple, streaming output to the Results window.

Once the totals for an employee are printed in the Results window, the procedure resets the memory variables to 0 and the employee number variable to the new employee number:

```
STORE 0 TO nWavePool, nTennis, nGym
nEmp = EMPNUMBER
```

The process continues until the procedure reaches the end of the TIMEREP table. When the EOF() function returns .T. (true), the procedure stops looping. This is the end of our summary report.

To continue with the rest of the application, the procedure must return the tables to their original state. To do this, the procedure unsets the relationship between the tables by using the SET RELATION TO command with no parameters. Then, the SELECT command makes the Employee table the currently selected table.

To test the report, run the application by entering the command DO
FUNMAIN.WFM in the Command window, and then select the Print Summary
menu option. Results of the summary report are shown in Figure 10-14.

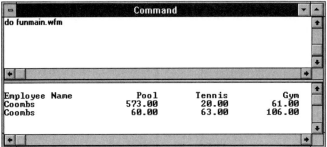

With a simple application development style that's easy to follow, you can
develop complete applications in no time. There are many ways to apply
dBASE for Windows tools and concepts to produce the desired results. Be
patient and don't be afraid to experiment, and your programming skills will
quickly increase.

Chapter 11

Let's Play Doctor

In This Chapter

▶ Manually finding and fixing problems in your programs

▶ Letting dBASE for Windows help you

▶ Recovering from a fatal error

*E*veryone makes programming mistakes. You might make a simple spelling error, forget something, or use the wrong syntax when entering a command. These programming mistakes can cause problems in your application. These problems are known as *bugs*. Bugs show up in many ways, including incorrect data, strange behavior, or an error message when you're demonstrating your new program in front of 15,000 people.

This chapter shows you how to find those bugs, how to catch them automatically, and what to do when a bug is so significant that it causes your program to crash. As an added bonus, this chapter provides a clever error-handling system that will help your programs gracefully handle errors.

Healing the Sick Program

To cure a program that catches a bug, you need the tools and skills of a dBASE for Windows doctor. Fortunately, you can acquire these skills without attending medical school for four years. There are two approaches for fixing bugs, or *debugging* your program. One approach involves debugging techniques that use concepts you're already familiar with, variables and printing. The other approach is to use the debugging utilities provided with dBASE for Windows.

Finding bugs is like solving a mystery. Detective work and bug tracking have a lot in common...

"The night fog curled around the pilings as though it was the breath of the pier itself. I heard the scrape of metal against metal that only a stiletto can make against an empty 50-gallon drum. I knew it was him, the informant. He rose up out of darkness and whispered, 'It was the loop counter.' When I turned to ask him what he meant, he was gone. Fog swirled where he had stood, as though he was only a phantasm."

Using spies and informants to find your bugs

Even the greatest detectives use spies and informants to uncover clues. If we believe what we see on television, crime would run rampant if criminals didn't tell on each other. When debugging a dBASE for Windows program, one of your simplest options is to insert spies and informants into the program.

When you are debugging a program, variables make good spies, and printing is a reliable informant. You can insert temporary variables to monitor the activities of your program, and use the question mark command (?) to print the values of those temporary variables in the Results window. Using variable names that start with Debug—or something equally as odd—makes it easier to find and remove these temporary variables after you've debugged the program.

Let's look at an example that shows how you can use variables as spies and printing as an informant. Suppose one of your programs includes the following procedure (Please humor us if you see the problem right away):

```
SET TALK OFF
cName = "Wally"
nIncome = 0

IF cName == "wally"
  nIncome = 50000
ENDIF

? "Wally's income is: "
?? nIncome
```

As shown in Figure 11-1, the procedure always shows Wally's income as zero, but we want it to be 50,000.

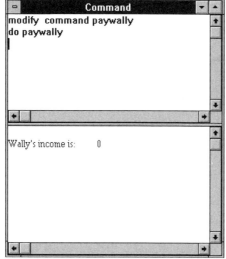

Figure 11-1:
According to our procedure, Wally's income is zero, but it should be 50,000.

The procedure should work like this:

1. Set TALK to OFF.

2. Set cName to Wally.

3. Set nIncome to zero.

4. Set Wally's income to 50000.

5. Print Wally's income in the Results window.

The program doesn't print the value we expect for Wally's income, so it must have a bug. To determine whether the program is properly setting the variables cName and nIncome, we can add the following lines to the program:

```
Debug_cName = cName
Debug_nIncome = nIncome
? "cName = "
?? Debug_cName
? "nIncome = "
?? Debug_nIncome
```

As shown in the following procedure, these new lines are inserted immediately after the statements that set the initial values for cName and nIncome:

```
SET TALK OFF
cName = "Wally"
nIncome = 0
```

```
Debug_cName = cName
Debug_nIncome = nIncome
? "cName = "
?? Debug_cName
? "nIncome = "
?? Debug_nIncome

IF cName == "wally"
  nIncome = 50000
ENDIF

? "Wally's income is: "
?? nIncome
```

Figure 11-2 shows the results that are displayed when we run the modified procedure. The Results window shows that cName is Wally, and nIncome is zero. These are the correct initial values for the two variables. In other words, our spies and informant tell us that the error isn't in the first three lines of the procedure.

To check the value of nIncome after it is set to 50000, we can add the following lines immediately after ENDIF:

```
Debug_nIncome = nIncome
? "After the IF statement, nIncome = "
?? Debug_nIncome
```

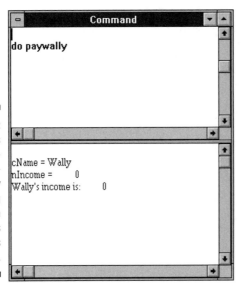

Figure 11-2:
The results of our modified procedure display debugging information as well as Wally's income.

The revised procedure is as follows:

```
SET TALK OFF
cName = "Wally"
nIncome = 0
Debug_cName = cName
Debug_nIncome = nIncome
? "cName = "
?? Debug_cName
? "nIncome = "
?? Debug_nIncome

IF cName == "wally"
  nIncome = 50000
ENDIF

Debug_nIncome = nIncome
? "After the IF statement, nIncome = "
?? Debug_nIncome

? "Wally's income is: "
?? nIncome
```

Figure 11-3 shows the results of this revised procedure. The new print statement reveals that nIncome is still zero after the IF statement. This means that the comparison used in the IF statement is false. If the comparison was true, Wally's income would be set to 50000 and there wouldn't be a problem.

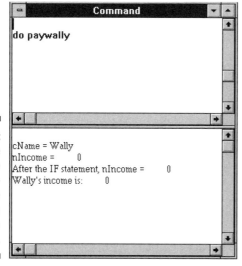

Figure 11-3: These results give an important clue regarding the location of the bug.

Let's examine this comparison in more detail:

```
cName == "wally"
```

Of course! We know from the previous print statements that cName is equal to "Wally", so comparing it to lowercase "wally" won't work. We've just discovered the bug. To fix it, we replace the comparison with:

```
cName == "Wally"
```

Because the bug is fixed, we can remove the Debug variables and print statements to produce the following debugged procedure:

```
SET TALK OFF
cName = "Wally"
nIncome = 0

IF cName == "Wally"
  nIncome = 50000
ENDIF

? "Wally's income is: "
?? nIncome
```

Figure 11-4 shows the output of our debugged procedure. We've successfully used spies and informants to fix our first bug! Don't worry, you'll get plenty of

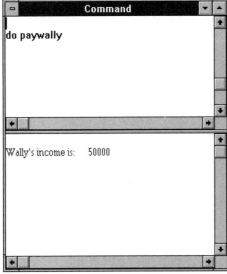

Figure 11-4:
Finally, the results of our debugged procedure show Wally's correct income!

practice debugging your programs. In fact, as you gain programming experience, you'll start making really nasty mistakes that create really interesting bugs.

"It was cold the night that Wally came into the precinct. His overcoat hadn't been cleaned in a long time. It was obvious that the poor bloke hadn't been paid in a while. We had the facts for him. He had been done in by a nefarious computer bug down at the plant. We sat him down in front of a PC with some steaming java while we spilled the story to him. We showed him how our operatives had located the problem and iced it. It was another case of a missing uppercase letter, solved. He left a happy man."

Finding and using the right tools has helped us debug this program for poor Wally. Using variables as informants can offer valuable clues that help you quickly solving these frustrating problems.

Our favorite counter-intelligence equipment

Have you ever wished you could stop time and walk around doing anything you want while everyone was frozen? The SUSPEND command allows you to do this in dBASE for Windows. Of course, SUSPEND only stops time in your program.

After entering the SUSPEND command in the Command window, you can view and change the contents of variables, check the values of fields, and even modify the structure of your table. SUSPEND lets you do anything you want, as though the program wasn't actually running.

As described in the preceding section, you can use the question mark command to check the values of variables that are being used in your program. For example, after entering the SUSPEND command, you could check the value of a 10-element array by entering the following code in the Command window:

```
FOR i = 1 to 10; ? MyArray[i]; NEXT
```

You can't enter programs in the Command window, but we sneak this one in by typing it all on one line. As shown in this example, you do this by separating the statements with semicolons. Semicolons allow you to type in several commands on the same line in the Command window. This is a handy debugging trick. You use a similar technique when writing codeblocks.

This FOR loop uses i as its counter variable. After the first semicolon, the question mark command is used to display the value of an element of

MyArray in the Results window. In addition to counting the number of times the program has looped, the variable i is also used as the index variable for the array. Each time the program loops, the variable i changes, and we see the contents of the next array element. To complete the loop, a NEXT statement follows the second semicolon.

After viewing the contents of the array, we need to restart our program. Right now, it is in a state of suspended animation. Although it might be fun to walk around in a world that's frozen in time, you would get bored if you couldn't start it again.

To restart the program from the point at which it was suspended, enter the RESUME command in the Command window.

The RESUME command doesn't always get your program running again. In some cases, the SUSPEND command is more like an autopsy than corrective surgery, and the RESUME command won't always bring the patient back to life. When you are done poking around, it is safer to issue the CANCEL command and then start the program over again from the beginning. The CANCEL command lets you quit the program and remove it from memory. ■

With your program suspended, it could take a long time to check each value by using the question mark command. It's also possible that a variable you've forgotten is causing the problem. To see all the variables and their values in the Results window at the same time, enter the following command in the Command window:

```
DISPLAY MEMORY
```

As shown in Figure 11-5, this command lists all of the user-defined variables and their values in the Results window. It also lists the system variables. There are usually about 30 variables listed, so you may have to scroll through them.

The Results window lists each variable's scope, type, and current value. A variable's scope can be either public, local, private, or static. A one-letter abbreviation identifies the variable's type. The third column in this Results window lists the values stored in the variables.

Displaying the values of variables isn't the only thing you can do to debug your program. The cure for your bug might be in the answer to one of the following questions:

- ✔ Which tables are open?
- ✔ Which indexes are active?
- ✔ Are any relationships set?

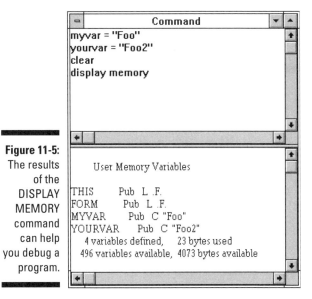

Figure 11-5:
The results
of the
DISPLAY
MEMORY
command
can help
you debug a
program.

✔ Are any filters set?

✔ What are the settings of the dBASE for Windows environment variables, such as SET EXACT?

You can find the answers to all of these questions with one command, DISPLAY STATUS. When you enter this command, you'll usually have to scroll through several pages of information in the Results window. The table information is listed first. In most cases, this is where you'll find any errors that are not indicated by the values of variables.

As shown in Figure 11-6, the currently selected table is displayed first. The Results window lists any production index (.MDX) files, but the DISPLAY STATUS command won't tell you whether or not the index tag is active. The index file can be open even though you haven't issued the SET ORDER command. Remember that the SET ORDER command makes an index active.

The DISPLAY STATUS command gives you more information than you really need about the language driver that is being used for each table. However, it quickly gets back to business describing relationships and filters.

After the table information, DISPLAY STATUS provides information that is useful if dBASE for Windows is having problems finding a file or printing. DISPLAY STATUS lists the current drive and search path. It also lists the currently selected printer port. You might need to check the Windows printer information to determine which printer is assigned to the selected port. The default printer port is LPT1.

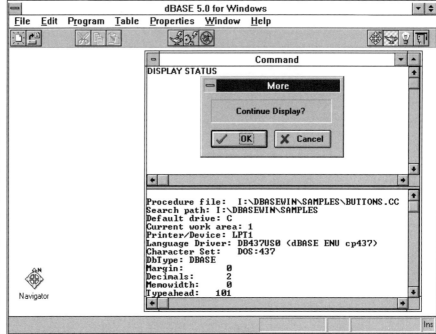

Following the printer information, you can see the numerous dBASE for Windows environment settings. Your dBASE for Windows Command Language reference can help you understand these settings and how they affect your program.

Finally, DISPLAY STATUS lists the settings for the function keys. You can use the function keys as shortcuts to some of the common dBASE for Windows commands. These settings are listed because you can customize the function keys for use in your program.

With the program suspended, DISPLAY MEMORY and DISPLAY STATUS are your two best investigative tools.

If you remember, check the memory

In some cases, you'll find that there is absolutely nothing wrong with your program, but it still won't work. This usually means that you are out of memory. Of course, you don't actually run out of memory; your computer does.

To check the amount of memory your computer has available, select Help | About from the dBASE for Windows menu. As shown in Figure 11-7, dBASE for

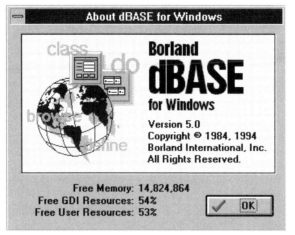

Windows displays a dialog box that tells you a little about the program, and the amount of memory currently in use. By the way, you can see a list of the people who worked on dBASE for Windows by pressing Alt-I while you are in this dialog box.

You may think you have enough RAM to create simulations of global warming on your desktop PC. Although this is probably true in a perfect world, large Windows applications have to contend with something known as memory leaks. Creating an application as large as dBASE for Windows is like building a dam with tinker toys. It's almost impossible to avoid leaks. If you've been using dBASE for Windows for a long time without exiting to Windows, your memory could be pretty low. ■

Do you have enough disk space?

Could anything else possibly be wrong? In a word, yes. If you still haven't found your problem, you can check a few more things. For example, you know you have enough memory, but do you have enough disk space?

After canceling or suspending the program, you can check the amount of available disk space by entering the following command in the Command window:

```
? Diskspace()
```

When you enter this command, dBASE for Windows displays the number of free bytes available on your hard disk in the Results window.

If you are copying or packing a table, your hard disk must have enough space to store two copies of the table at the same time. When packing a table, dBASE for Windows makes a new copy of the table. The original can't be erased until dBASE for Windows creates the new table.

Changing your DOS system file

If you're still having problems with tables that aren't opening, you should check the FILES= setting in your CONFIG.SYS file. As detailed in Chapter 6, this setting specifies how many files your computer can have open at the same time. In addition to dBASE for Windows tables, this setting includes Windows, any files that Windows is using, other programs you might be running, and any network files that your computer needs for operating on a network.

A pretty safe setting is FILES = 100. If the current setting is higher than that, you probably shouldn't change it.

The settings in the CONFIG.SYS file are important to the operation of your computer. If you aren't familiar with a particular command or setting in this file, you shouldn't delete or edit that setting. Getting help from your system administrator or resident technical genius is always a good idea if you are unsure about changing something in this file. ■

After changing the settings in your CONFIG.SYS file, you must reboot your computer. Remember that changes to CONFIG.SYS don't take affect until you reboot.

Building bug traps

The ON ERROR command allows you to define what happens when your program encounters an error. You can use this command to create an ON ERROR routine, which is a bug trap for your program.

An ON ERROR routine is very important—even in a system that has been completely debugged—because there will always be circumstances beyond your control. For example, an ON ERROR routine can help you handle the following situations (to name just a few):

- ✔ The user reboots the computer and corrupts a table or index.
- ✔ The user accidentally erases some files.
- ✔ The user enters something you never anticipated, and the program crashes.
- ✔ Memory leaks finally cause strange problems.

- ✔ The user runs out of disk space.
- ✔ A budding programmer decides to "make it better!"
- ✔ The printer is off.
- ✔ The disk drive door is open.
- ✔ A disk becomes corrupt.

Even if this list filled the rest of the book (we were tempted), it probably wouldn't cover the one situation that was bound to happen to your program. No matter what goes wrong, the ON ERROR routine will be there to catch it.

Although you can put the ON ERROR command anywhere in your program, you usually put it somewhere near the beginning. This allows you to catch any errors that may occur when the program starts.

As shown in the following example, the ON ERROR command is followed by a command or the name of a procedure or function that the program should execute when it encounters an error:

```
* Pass the LINE(), MESSAGE(), and DBMESSAGE() as parameters
ON ERROR DO ErrCatch WITH LINE(), MESSAGE(), DBMESSAGE()
```

If an error is encountered, this ON ERROR command tells your program to execute the following procedure, which is named ErrCatch:

```
PROCEDURE ErrCatch
PARAMETERS Line, Message, dbMessage

? "AN ERROR HAS OCCURRED IN THE PROGRAM!"
? "CALL USER SUPPORT WITH THE FOLLOWING INFORMATION."
? "THE ERROR OCCURRED AT LINE: " + LTRIM(STR(Line))
? "THE ERROR WAS: " + Message
? "THE DATABASE STATUS IS: " + dbMessage
?
? "Turn on the printer to print technical information."
WAIT
LIST STATUS TO PRINT
LIST MEMORY TO PRINT
SET PRINT ON
? "ERROR AT LINE: "+LTRIM(STR(Line))
? Message
? dbMessage
SET PRINT OFF
SET PRINTER TO
CANCEL
RETURN
```

You can use this generic ON ERROR procedure with any of your programs. As you become more familiar with the dBASE for Windows Command Language, you can write more sophisticated procedures. Chapter 16 provides additional details about writing stand-alone procedures.

As mentioned, if your program encounters an error, the following command tells your program that it should execute the ErrCatch procedure:

```
ON ERROR DO ErrCatch WITH LINE(), MESSAGE(), DBMESSAGE()
```

The WITH keyword tells your program to pass the following information to the ErrCatch procedure:

- ✔ LINE(). This function returns the line number on which the error occurred in your program.
- ✔ MESSAGE(). This function returns the text of the error message.
- ✔ DBMESSAGE(). This function returns any error messages having to do with tables or databases.

The ON ERROR procedure begins with the procedure's name, ErrCatch. You can call it anything you like; just don't call it late for dinner.

The PARAMETERS statement on the second line of the ErrCatch procedure has three variables. As mentioned, the ON ERROR command in your program passes three values to the ErrCatch procedure. These values are called parameters. You don't have to use the variable names that we've used in our ErrCatch procedure. For this example, we tried to choose variable names that would be meaningful.

The ErrCatch procedure informs the user that an error has occurred, and displays the line number, the error message, and any table error messages in the Results window. To give the user time to turn on the printer, the WAIT command temporarily halts execution of the procedure and prints the message, "Press any key to continue." in the Results window.

When processing is continued, the ErrCatch procedure prints some of the debugging information we've discussed in the preceding sections of this chapter. LIST STATUS and LIST MEMORY are variations on the DISPLAY STATUS and DISPLAY MEMORY commands. These commands list the status and memory information without stopping for each page. This information is output to the printer. Finally, the line number, the error message, and any table error messages are output to the printer.

To start tracking a bug, you need good information. By adding this procedure to your program, you might prevent a few phone calls from users telling you that the program doesn't work, they don't know what they did, and they turned off the computer because it was beeping at them.

This ON ERROR routine is only an example of the steps you can take to trap bugs in your programs. You can pass other parameters to the procedure, and you might even create a procedure that performs certain recovery functions based on the error message it receives. For example, if a drive door is open, your ON ERROR routine could tell the user to close it, and return to running the program. If an index is corrupt, you could try re-indexing.

 You can have different ON ERROR commands in different parts of a program. Each new ON ERROR command overrides the previously issued command. To cancel all ON ERROR commands, issue the command with no procedures or commands:

```
ON ERROR
```

I've Fallen, and I Can't Get Up

Despite your best efforts with these debugging strategies, there will be times when you just can't find a bug. Even worse is the random bug that happens only when you aren't looking. In some cases, finding a bug requires major surgery.

 Before attempting major surgery, make two extra copies of your program. Put one copy on a back-up diskette, and use the other one as your working copy. Leave the original program alone. ■

Here are some strategies for finding those really sneaky bugs:

- ✔ Using the Command Editor, copy each procedure and paste it into a program file. Test the procedure by passing parameters from the Command window. See Chapter 16 for more information on creating procedures and passing parameters.
- ✔ Use Browse to examine the data your procedure is using.
- ✔ Exit dBASE for Windows and start over again. Gremlins might have taken over.
- ✔ Re-index your tables.

One of the most serious problems you can encounter is the embedded end-of-file (EOF) marker. If an EOF marker becomes embedded within a table, the rest of the table is unusable.

You can purchase utilities for repairing these damaged dBASE for Windows tables. If it's an emergency or you don't care if the table is lost, you can try to repair the table yourself. Although repair utilities will give you a better chance of fixing the table, you might try the following steps:

1. Make a back-up copy of the sick dBASE for Windows table!

2. USE the sick table.

3. Copy the structure to a temporary table by entering the following command in the Command window:

   ```
   COPY STRUCTURE TO Temp
   ```

4. USE Temp.

5. Append the records from the sick table by entering the following command in the Command window (where *OriginalTable* is the name of the sick table):

   ```
   APPEND FROM OriginalTable
   ```

6. Make sure that all the records were appended into the Temp table by checking the record count in the Status Bar at the bottom of the screen.

7. USE the Sick table with the EXCLUSIVE command.

8. Empty the Sick table by entering the ZAP command.

9. Append all the records from the Temp table by entering the following command in the Command window:

   ```
   APPEND FROM Temp
   ```

10. Re-index the restored table by entering the REINDEX command.

If this doesn't work, you might need to write a program that extracts as much good data as possible. Commands such as LIST usually stop at the embedded EOF marker. In some cases, you can use the GOTO command to reach records beyond the embedded EOF marker.

Using the Debugger

The Debugger is a special dBASE for Windows tool that helps you track down those nasty bugs by:

- ✔ Stepping through the execution of your program line by line.

- ✔ Viewing and changing values in variables, arrays, objects, or even in expressions.

✔ Seeing the program branch off to subroutines and functions as it calls them.

✔ Stopping your program whenever you want.

You can activate the Debugger by:

✔ Selecting it from the dBASE for Windows menu.

✔ Entering the DEBUG command in the Command window.

✔ Calling it as a separate program from an icon in Windows.

✔ Issuing the SET STEP ON or SET ECHO ON command in your program.

 The SET STEP and SET ECHO commands are included in dBASE for Windows for backward compatibility with earlier versions of dBASE. Their use is not recommended. The SET STEP OFF and SET ECHO OFF commands are disabled in dBASE for Windows. ■

The Debugger allows to execute your programs in animation mode, which means that you can view lines of code while they are being executed. If you want to hurry up and get to the line with the error, you can choose to run your program at full speed. You can also slow things down and step through the program at a speed you select from the Options menu. To change the animation speed:

1. Select Options from the Debugger menu.

2. Select Animation Speed from the Options menu.

3. You change the animation speed by moving the slide bar that is displayed. Use your left mouse button to click and drag the square tab on the slide bar. Move the tab to the right for faster speeds and to the left to slow down the animation.

There are two primary purposes for stepping through a program with the Debugger:

✔ Watching and possibly changing the values of variables, fields, expressions, or objects.

✔ Setting breakpoints to stop the program at a particular line or when an expression becomes true.

These uses of the Debugger are described in the following sections.

Watch those variables

In the dBASE for Windows Debugger, you can specify that certain variables in your program are *watch* variables. The Debugger pays close attention to these watch variables. Watch variables allow you to see the values of variables or fields displayed in a Watch window as the program runs. If these values change, you see the changes as they happen. It's like CNN for dBASE for Windows.

There are times when variables depend on each other. For example, if you add variables together, or perform other math operations with them, they are dependent on each other. When variables interact in this way, it is helpful to set them up as watch variables so you can see all their values simultaneously. This is one of the most useful features of the Debugger. ■

The Debugger has four main windows. As shown in Figure 11-8, the Watch Window is the upper-right window. To set up variables as watch variables:

1. Select Watch from the Debugger menu.

2. Select Add... from the Watch menu. This opens the Add Watch dialog box.

3. In the EntryField in the Add Watch dialog box, enter the name of the variable that you want to watch.

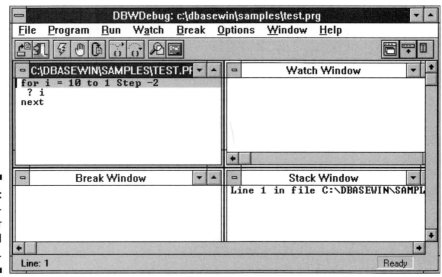

Figure 11-8:
The Debugger is your view behind the scenes.

Fast breaking information

The Debugger also allows you to set breakpoints, which are places where you want the program to stop running. When the program stops, you can check or change values and then restart the program. Figure 11-9 shows an example of adding a breakpoint at a specific location.

Figure 11-9:
Breakpoints can stop or branch the program.

```
┌─────────────────────────────────────────────────────┐
│  ─              Add Breakpoint                        │
│  Location:                                            │
│  ┌──────────────────────────────────────────────┐ ▼ │
│  │C:\DBASEWIN\SAMPLES\TEST.PRG                   │   │
│  Condition:                                          │
│  ┌──────────────────────────────────────────────┐ ▼ │
│  │                                               │   │
│  Action:                                             │
│  ┌──────────────────────────────────────────────┐ ▲ │
│  │                                               │   │
│  │                                               │ ▼ │
│                                                      │
│  Line #:    [  1  ] ▼    □ Global                    │
│  Pass Count: [  1  ] ▼                               │
│                                                      │
│   ✓  OK      ✗  Cancel      ?  Help                  │
└─────────────────────────────────────────────────────┘
```

You can set breakpoints both by line number and by expression. If you specify an expression, the program stops when the expression is true or has changed. Otherwise, the program stops at the specified line number. You can also specify an action that occurs when the program reaches a breakpoint. For example, you might call other programs or set variables.

To specify how many times the program can pass a breakpoint before it stops, you can set a value called a pass count. A pass count is useful when the breakpoint is in a loop. For example, if you are interested in the third loop, you would set the pass count to two. ▪

You can set watch variables and breakpoints in program modules that may not be loaded with the main program. In the Debugger's File menu, you can choose to Load a module. Once a module is loaded, you can set breakpoints. It is possible to set watch variables regardless of whether the module is loaded.

Handling the Debugger

This is the recommended way to use the Debugger:

1. Enter the DEBUG command in the Command window. (You can also start the Debugger by clicking the Debug icon in the SpeedBar.) A list of programs is displayed.

2. Select the program you want to debug.

3. Set up any watch variables using the menu choices in the Debugger.

4. Set any breakpoints.

5. Select Options | Animation Speed from the Debugger menu, and set the animation speed to about half.

6. Select Run | Animate.

This procedure automatically steps through your program line by line. By scrolling through the program in slow motion, you can see the watch variables change as the program continues either to the end or to the first breakpoint.

If a program pauses because it requires user input, you can move the Debugger out of the way, or you can switch to the program by pressing the Alt-Tab key combination. After you supply the necessary input, the Debugger reappears and continues scrolling through the code.

The Debugger also has an emergency brake. You can stop program execution at any time by pressing the hand icon or choosing Run | Stop from the Debugger menu.

Run | Stop is not the same as Run | Terminate. The Run | Terminate menu selection removes the program from memory. With Run | Stop, you can continue running the program and checking variable values. Resetting the program has the same effect as Run | Terminate. Reset terminates the program and then reloads it from the start.

What to do when the whole thing goes "Kaplooey!"

Some things happen that dBASE for Windows just can't handle. It might not know how to handle a particular error, it might suffer a gradual loss of perspective, or perhaps it's just being cranky. If this happens, you'll see a message that says dBASE for Windows has become unstable. The message asks if you would like to try and save your work before exiting.

This invitation to save your work isn't always honored. In other words, you might not be able to save your work if dBASE for Windows becomes unstable. Besides, you should save your work on a regular basis.

The type of error described in this section is known as a General Protection Fault, or GPF. This is a Windows error that lets you know that the memory being used for dBASE for Windows and its programs has somehow become corrupted. ▪

When dBASE for Windows is unstable, it doesn't always know what it is saying. Sometimes you have to click OK buttons on a series of progressively less friendly error messages. You might want to jot down these messages. If the problem persists, you should call dBASE for Windows Technical Support and tell them what you were doing when the system crashed, and what the error messages say.

When you exit dBASE for Windows after it crashes, you should also exit Windows. In many cases, the Windows environment for dBASE for Windows has been corrupted. Restarting Windows generally corrects any of these problems. ▪

Don't Panic

This chapter explains some of the strategies and tools you can use for debugging a program. It is by no means an exhaustive or complete list. Here is a little added advice:

- ✔ Don't panic. This always makes things worse and usually leads to bigger problems.

- ✔ Be methodical. The computer is not out to get you. If you take notes and follow a strategy, you can usually find the problem.

- ✔ Try to create strategies that don't involve rebooting or turning off the computer. Doing so can corrupt files.

- ✔ Include the SET ESCAPE ON command in your programs to enable you to stop your program by pressing the Esc key.

Try to have fun. Debugging programs can be frustrating. If you have a positive outlook, and you treat the problem as a puzzle or a game, you will enjoy programming more and solve problems faster.

Part IV
Creating Awesome Reports

The 5th Wave — By Rich Tennant

THAT'S RIGHT, THE UPPER CASE BUTTON WORKS ON SCREEN, BUT THEY'RE NOT COMING OUT ON THE DANG PRINTER! HOLD? SURE, I'LL HOLD.

Poet e.e. cummings makes his last service call.

In This Part...

Throughout history, philosophers have debated the worth of an idea that isn't communicated to others. Modern-day computer philosophers debate the worth of information in a table if it isn't communicated to others. If a character field is filled with the word "FOREST" and nobody sees it, does it make a sound?

Reports are used in most dBASE for Windows programs to give meaning and value to the information stored in tables. Reports that show people exactly what they need to see are often the most important part of a dBASE for Windows application. The chapters in this part show you how to create reports in dBASE for Windows.

Chapter 12

Printing from Your Application

● ●

In This Chapter

▶ Creating simple reports

▶ Sending your reports to the screen or the printer

▶ Printing to a file

▶ Positioning printed material

▶ Using the dBASE for Windows print variables

● ●

*A*lthough computers were supposed to take us into the paperless age, most of us now use more paper than ever before. Most computer programs print some type of report or document, and an important part of writing applications is teaching your program to print.

Printing Reports the Easy Way

You can create a simple report by listing the contents of a database table, and letting dBASE for Windows format the display for you. To display the contents of a table in the Results window, select a table and enter the following command in the Command window:

```
LIST
```

You can also use the LIST command to display a subset of the records in your table. To do this, include a scope modifier from Table 12-1 following the LIST command:

```
LIST ScopeModifier
```

Table 12-1: Scope modifiers that tell the LIST command to display only selected records from your table

Scope Modifier	Description
RECORD x	Displays the contents of a specified record; x represents the record number of the record you want to list
NEXT x	Displays the next x number of records in the table, beginning with the current record
ALL	Displays all records. Because this is the default for the LIST command, the ALL scope modifier is optional
REST	Displays the rest of the records in the table, beginning with the current record

For example, you can display the next 13 records in the table by entering the following command:

```
LIST NEXT 13
```

If you don't know which records you want to list, dBASE for Windows can decide for you. Simply use the LIST command with a FOR *Condition* modifier instead of a scope modifier:

```
LIST FOR Condition
```

For example, if your employee table contains a lastname field, you could list all records for employees with the last name "Smith" by entering the following command:

```
LIST FOR lastname = "Smith"
```

The LIST command is the simplest way to create a report that lists information from a table. When you enter the LIST command, the contents of the table are displayed in the Results window in a column-and-row format. The field names appear at the tops of the columns.

If the list is several pages long, the pages will scroll by very quickly until dBASE for Windows reaches the end of the report. This makes your report difficult to read, because most of it won't stay on the screen for more than a nanosecond. To create a simple report that lists information one page at a time, use the DISPLAY command instead of LIST.

The DISPLAY command lets you display the contents of a table one page at a time in the Results window. The only difference between the DISPLAY command and the LIST command is that DISPLAY breaks the output into single pages. When DISPLAY encounters the end of a page, it pauses and asks if you'd like to continue the display. Click the OK button to continue, or CANCEL to stop.

To list only certain fields from a table, you can use the FIELDS *FieldList* modifier:

```
LIST FIELDS FieldList
```

FieldList represents a list of the fields that you want listed in the Results window. You use commas to separate the field names in a FIELDS *FieldList* modifier. For example, the following command tells dBASE for Windows to list the contents of only two fields, FNAME and LASTNAME, from a table:

```
LIST FIELDS FNAME, LASTNAME
```

To direct the output of the LIST command to the printer, use the TO PRINTER modifier:

```
LIST TO PRINTER
```

To direct the output of the LIST command to a file, use the TO FILE *FileName* modifier:

```
LIST TO FILE FileName
```

For example, the following LIST command tells dBASE for Windows to output the information to a file called OUTPUT.TXT:

```
LIST TO FILE OUTPUT.TXT
```

To top it all off, you can combine any or all of the LIST or DISPLAY modifiers to tailor your output exactly as you'd like it. The following example lists the FNAME and LASTNAME fields for all records in which the LASTNAME field contains "Smith", and directs the output to the printer:

```
LIST FOR lastname = "Smith" FIELDS FNAME, LASTNAME TO PRINTER
```

Printing a Form

You can also create a simple report by printing a form. When you print a form, everything on the form is printed, graphics and all.

Forms have a special print function called PRINT(). The easiest way to allow users to print a form is to create a Print PushButton, and then use the

PRINT( ) function in the OnClick event procedure for this PushButton. Here are the steps for creating a PushButton that lets the user print a form:

1. Open the Form Designer and your form by entering the MODIFY FORM command in the Command window. Don't forget to tell dBASE for Windows which form you want to modify.

2. Find the Controls Palette, click the PushButton icon, and click on the form in the desired location for the new PushButton control.

3. Select the PushButton by clicking it in the Form Designer. Find the Properties window, click the Properties tab, click the Text property, and change this property to "Print".

4. Click the Events tab in the Properties window, click the OnClick event, and open the Procedures window by clicking the tool icon for the OnClick event.

5. Enter the following statement in the Procedures window:

```
FORM.PRINT( )
```

6. Save the form by pressing Ctrl-W or Ctrl-S.

Figure 12-1 shows an example of the printed output of a form.

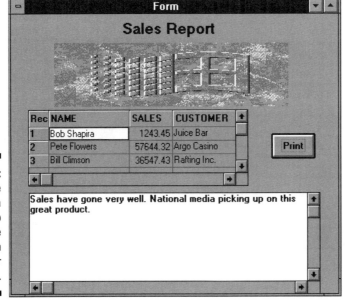

Figure 12-1:
Printing the
form is a
great way to
include
graphics in
your
reports.

Because forms are large graphic images, you may experience problems when printing your form. For example, some printers can't handle graphics, and others might not have enough memory to handle the entire image. If you run into problems when printing a form, you should check the manual for your printer. ■

The two approaches to printing that you've just seen are versatile, yet easy to use. Printing a form is more interesting, because you aren't limited to simple text. However, printing a form takes much longer because Windows must process the form's graphics and communicate them to your printer. If you've ever tried to talk sense to your printer when it wasn't cooperating, you can surely understand what Windows must be going through.

Telling It Where to Go

We can tell you about three places where you can send the output of your program:

- ✔ The screen
- ✔ The printer
- ✔ A file

Sending output to the screen saves paper and makes you a hero with environmentalists. Printing reports can be time consuming, particularly if the program goes into an endless loop and prints the same record over and over. (It happens!) By giving your applications the capability to print reports to the screen, you can allow users to preview reports before sending them to a printer or a file.

You open up a can of worms when you decide to send a report to the printer. For example, do you know which port your printer is attached to? If you are on a network, do you know which printer you want to use?

The SET PRINTER command allows you to direct your output to a specific printer or printer port. Generally, you can choose from three possible parallel ports and no more than two serial ports. However, printers typically aren't attached to serial ports. The default is LPT1, or parallel port one. You can tell dBASE for Windows to use parallel port two by entering the following command:

```
SET PRINTER TO LPT2
```

You can direct the output to the default printer by entering the SET PRINTER TO command with no parameters.

With many dBASE for Windows commands, you can send the results to the printer simply by adding a clause to the command. This capability is useful for creating an impromptu report, debugging your program, or producing documentation of the program.

For example, you can add the optional parameter, TO PRINTER to any command that begins with the keyword LIST. When you enter a command with this parameter, output that is usually displayed in the Results window is directed to the printer.

You've already seen how LIST is used to print information contained in tables. The following example shows how you can use the LIST command with the TO PRINTER parameter to print a listing of your table's structure:

```
USE MyTable
LIST STRUCTURE TO PRINTER
EJECT
```

The LIST STRUCTURE TO PRINTER command sends a listing of the table structure to the printer. We've found that every printer has its own distinct personality (printerality?). Some printers like what you send them so much, they keep it in their memory instead of printing it. We use the EJECT command in this example to ensure that the printer prints the table structure and then ejects the paper. Depending on your printer's personality, you might not need to use the EJECT command.

Choosing a printer named Al

You may have many different printers defined in Windows. Some of these printers might be attached to your computer; other printers could be available on a network. By using the CHOOSEPRINTER() function in your programs, you can allow users to select which printer they want to use. As shown in Figure 12-2, the CHOOSEPRINTER() function displays the Print Setup dialog box, which allows users to select a printer as well as set the following print parameters:

✔ Page orientation

✔ Paper size and source

✔ Print quality options, such as dithering, intensity, and printing of True-Type fonts as graphics

You can give your programs a professional quality by using the CHOOSEPRINTER() function whenever the user chooses to print a report.

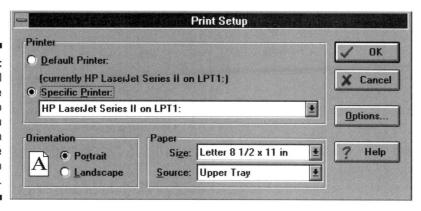

Figure 12-2:
Users will
think you're
a hero
when you
let them
choose
their own
printer.

Simply add CHOOSEPRINTER( ) immediately before printing anything in your program. This function works in the OnClick event procedure of Print Push-Buttons, menu items, and in any other procedure.

The CHOOSEPRINTER( ) function is also commonly used to create a Printer Setup, or Print Setup option in an application's File menu. Many Windows programs include such an option in their File menu.

By including a Printer Setup option in your application's File menu, you allow the user to choose and set up a printer only when they need to, instead of every time they print from your program. To add this option to your program's menu, simply create a new menu item called Printer Setup and enter the CHOOSEPRINTER( ) function in the OnClick event procedure for this menu item.

Printing to a file

Sending output to a printer isn't always an option. You might need to e-mail a report to a colleague. Or, maybe you need to save a report so you can print it or display it at a later time. In such cases, you can send your report to a file instead of the printer.

When you issue the SET PRINTER command, you can designate a filename instead of a printer port such as LPT1. The following example shows how you would send the output to a file named MyFile.PRT:

```
SET PRINTER TO FILE MyFile.PRT
```

As shown in this example, you can include the optional keyword FILE. However, it doesn't help or hinder the process. The keyword FILE simply makes it clear that MyFile.PRT is a file, and not a printer. The following example would have the same effect:

```
SET PRINTER TO MyFile.PRT
```

If you don't specify an extension when you output to a file, it's important to remember that dBASE for Windows adds .PRT as the default extension. If you can't find a file even though you're sure it exists, you probably forgot that it has a .PRT extension. ■

After printing to a file, you must close the file by issuing the CLOSE PRINTER command. This important step helps protect the integrity of your file.

If you don't set the printer back to a default printer, any subsequent print jobs will be sent to the file you specified in the last SET PRINTER TO FILE command. ■

Save a tree, read the screen

When creating reports, it's sometimes helpful to be able to view them on the screen. For example, the report output might be a query result that doesn't need to be printed. Or, the output might be a lengthy, detailed report that the user should review before condemning another tree and sending it to the printer.

On the other hand, you might decide that the output in the Results window is ugly and scrolls by too quickly. The Results window might be covered with forms or it may be completely invisible. To avoid these problems, you can send your reports to files and create Editor controls that allow users to view the files. As shown in Figure 12-3, this approach allows the user to see the report before sending it to the printer.

When you allow users to view screen results in an Editor control, you give them a great deal of power over the printing of their reports. For example, the user might edit the information in the report before sending it to the printer. Without the Editor control, the user could only make this type of change by printing the report, modifying the table, and then printing the report again.

No Swimming in the Print Streams

In previous chapters, you've seen how you can send results of your program to the Results window by using the question mark (?) command. Other results, such as error messages, are also sent to the Results window. If you

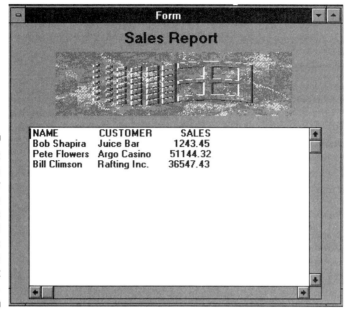

Figure 12-3:
You can use
an Editor
control to
allow users
to view and
edit results
that have
been output
to a text file.

SET TALK ON, you can be entertained for hours with all of the information that is sent to the Results window. This output is said to be streaming out of the program. If you SET TALK ON, you'll know exactly what we mean by streaming.

To send all of this output to the printer instead of the Results window, enter the following command in the Command window:

```
SET PRINTER ON
```

When you issue this command, anything that would normally appear in the Results window is directed to the printer you have chosen. To stop streaming output to the printer, issue the following command:

```
SET PRINTER OFF
```

Don't forget to SET PRINTER OFF. If you forget to issue this command, dBASE for Windows will send many pages of unwanted gibberish to your printer. If it's a network printer, your coworkers will be waiting impatiently while the printer cranks out pages full of things like MyVariable = "FOO".

If you are using an ON ERROR procedure to capture errors, it is a good idea to add a SET PRINTER OFF statement to the ON ERROR procedure. If your program crashes while printing, you want to stop the printed output. ■

What kind of command is a question mark?

Streaming output to the printer might not seem like a very sophisticated approach for formatting reports. However, the ? command is actually a powerful formatting tool. You can use it to send results from your program to the screen, the printer, or a file.

The ? command evaluates expressions and sends the results to the Results window. To send the results to the printer, enter the SET PRINTER ON command. Or, you can send the results to a file by entering SET PRINTER TO FILE *FileName*. ■

As listed in Table 12-2, the expression evaluator—that is, the ? command—gives you several options for controlling the output of your results.

Table 12-2: Using the expression evaluator

Expression	Description
?	Streams results to the designated output device, starting on a new line.
??	Streams results to the designated output device, starting on the row and column where the last output ended. In other words, the output does not start on a new line.
???	Sends output directly to the printer. This is not recommended for use in dBASE for Windows.

The following example shows how the expression evaluator works:

```
cLastName = "Franklin"
cFirstName = "Bennie"

SET PRINTER ON
? "Dear Mr. " + cLastName
?? ":"
? "We understand that you have been experimenting with a new type"
? "of kite tail. "
?? cFirstName + ","
?? " we believe that keys have become"
? "victims to acts of Nature. We ask you to discontinue using"
? "keys for your experimentation. Keys were meant to open and"
? "close locks."
```

```
? ""
? "Sincerely,"
? ""
? "Keys Elevate Your Soul, International"
? "A very non-profit victims rights group"
SET PRINTER OFF
```

The following results would be sent to your printer:

Dear Mr. Franklin:

We understand that you have been experimenting with a new type of kite tail. Bennie, we believe that keys have become victims to acts of Nature. We ask you to discontinue using keys for your experimentation. Keys were meant to open and close locks.

Sincerely,

Keys Elevate Your Soul, International
A very non-profit victims rights group

Beautifying your reports

You can format the output from the ? command by using the PICTURE and FUNCTION keywords. As shown in the following example, you can create PICTURE templates in the same way you create templates for variables:

```
cPhone = "4445551212"
? cPhone PICTURE "@R (999) 999-9999"  && Result: (444) 555-1212
```

The @R formatting function tells dBASE for Windows that the template includes characters that are not to be stored in the field or variable. In the preceding example, the @R function lets us add parentheses and a dash to our phone number without changing the value that's stored in cPhone.

The PICTURE template uses the character 9 to specify how numbers should be displayed. In the preceding example, the template specifies that the first three digits of cPhone should be displayed between the parentheses, the next three digits should appear before the dash, and the last four digits of cPhone should be displayed after the dash.

As shown in the following example, the FUNCTION keyword allows you to format the entire output:

```
cName = "victoria"
? cName FUNCTION "!"
```

The ! function specifies that the results should be output in all uppercase letters. The result from the preceding example would be VICTORIA.

By printing blank lines before your output, you can control where your results appear on the screen or the page. To print blank lines, use the ? command with an empty character string ("").

A single question mark (?) tells dBASE for Windows to skip to the next line before printing your results. To continue printing on the same line as the last output, use the double question mark (??). ▪

As shown in the following example, you can specify the column in which the output is to be printed by entering the keyword AT, followed by the desired column number:

```
? "This has no AT keyword."
? "This will print in column five." AT 5
? "Column 1"
?? "Column 10" AT 10
?? "Column 20" AT 20
```

This example produces the following output:

```
This has no AT keyword.
    This will print in column five.
Column1  Column 10 Column 20
```

In the preceding example, the single question marks specify that the first three lines of the results should be displayed on new lines. The AT keyword indicates that the second line of the results should begin in the fifth column. The double question marks tell dBASE for Windows that the third, fourth, and fifth lines should be printed on the same line. Finally, AT keywords are used to indicate that the fourth and fifth lines of the results should start in columns 10 and 20, respectively.

The importance of the AT keyword depends on the type of font you are using:

- *Non-proportional fonts* have equal widths for all letters in the character set.
- *Proportional fonts* use varying character widths, depending on the character. For example, the character W is wider than the character l.

If you are using a proportional font, it's almost impossible to align columns without the AT keyword. For example, even though they have the same number of letters, the words money and lilac are different widths when printed in a proportional font.

Printing with STYLE

Fonts? Nobody said anything about fonts! Yes, you can format the output of the ? command with any font you own by using the STYLE keyword. Can you see the bumper sticker?

"? users do it with STYLE."

The STYLE keyword is followed by the number of the font, as defined in the dBASE for Windows initialization file. The following fonts are defined in dBASEWIN.INI:

1 = Times New Roman,12,ROMAN

2 = Arial,10,SWISS

3 = Arial,24,SWISS

4 = Ariston,24,SCRIPT

The definitions contain the following information, separated by commas:

- ✔ Font name
- ✔ Font size
- ✔ Font family

You can modify or add to this list by editing the dBASEWIN.INI file, which is usually located in the \dBASEWIN\BIN directory. If this is where the file is located, you can start editing dBASEWIN.INI by entering the following commands in the Command window:

```
cd \DBASEWIN\BIN
MODIFY FILE DBASEWIN.INI
```

Any font that's already set up in your Windows system can be added to the DBASEWIN.INI file; you can even add the same font more than once! As shown in the following example, you can add to this file by defining an existing font and giving it a number:

```
1=Times New Roman,12,ROMAN
2=Arial,10,SWISS
3=Arial,24,SWISS
4=Ariston,24,SCRIPT
5=Small Fonts,8,SWISS OEM
```

In this example, we've added a tiny font called Small Fonts. It is an 8-point font from the SWISS OEM family of fonts (OEM stands for original equipment manufacturer). Swiss family fonts? Is there a book in there somewhere?

To use the Small Fonts that we just defined, you need to use the STYLE keyword:

```
cStatement = "This is a test of the Small Font."
? cStatement STYLE 5  && This prints very small on the printer.
```

You'll see the result of the STYLE keyword only on the printer, not on the screen.

When you print to a file and then send the file to the printer, the fonts will appear correctly. The font changes are embedded in the file that you create when you print to a file. ▧

Chewing Gum and Printing at the Same Time

Before Windows programming, results were sent to the screen (and usually to the printer) as non-streaming output. This type of output is also known as coordinate printing or absolute addressing, because it allows you to direct your output to a specific location on the screen or the printed page. Coordinate printing uses the @ SAY (pronounced *at say*) command to print output at a specific row and column. You can direct the output to the screen, a printer, or a file.

Although coordinate printing was once the preferred method for printing your results, streaming output has been enhanced to include fonts and formatting. As a result, coordinate printing is usually a less-desirable option. However, even though you can't change fonts, coordinate printing is still superior when you need to print to specific coordinates on pre-printed forms.

The @ SAY command in dBASE for Windows lets you print results to specific row and column locations in the Results window or the printer. The capability to send text to the Results window in this way is provided to make dBASE for Windows backward compatible with earlier DOS versions of dBASE.

Just say it

The @ SAY command has two parameters, row and column. The output of this command can be directed to the screen, the printer, or a file. The following example sends text to a specific position in the Results window:

```
SET DEVICE TO SCREEN
CLEAR
@ 2,4 SAY "This is old technology."
```

The first command in this example tells dBASE for Windows to send all output to the Results window. The next command clears the Results window. You don't want any leftover information in the Results window when you start printing. The @ SAY command tells dBASE for Windows to print the string, "This is old technology." on the second row, starting in the fourth column.

By specifying a different output device, you can use the same @ SAY command to send information to a printed page:

```
SET DEVICE TO PRINT

@ 2,4 SAY "This is old technology."
EJECT
SET DEVICE TO SCREEN
```

In this example, the output of the @ SAY command is sent directly to the printer. The text, "This is old technology." is printed on the second row of the printed page, starting in the fourth column.

The EJECT command ejects the paper from the printer. Although some printers and networks do this automatically, it's better to be safe and tell the printer yourself. If you want a job done right...

The example ends with the command, SET DEVICE TO SCREEN. When you are using dBASE for Windows, the output device is usually the screen. (In the first example, we set the device to the screen just for the fun of it.) In this example, we set the printer as the output device, so it's important to set it back to the screen when we're done. If your program stops for some reason before it gets to the SET DEVICE TO SCREEN command, you may have to do it manually in the Command window. Otherwise, all subsequent output will go to the printer. In other words, anything that would appear in the Results window will be sent to the printer.

You can format printed output using the PICTURE and FUNCTION templates. The following example prints a phone number in the fifth row of the output, starting in the fifth column:

```
@ 5,5 SAY cPhone PICTURE "@R (999) 999-9999"
```

Relative positioning doesn't mean throwing your kids out

Sometimes, you don't know exactly which row or column you want to print on next; you just want to continue with the next position. This is known as *relative positioning*. Four functions make relative positioning possible:

🖙 ROW( ) returns the current row in the Results window.

🖙 COL( ) returns the current column in the Results window.

🖙 PROW( ) returns the current row on the printed page.

🖙 PCOL( ) returns the current column on the printed page.

You can use relative positioning when printing to either the screen or the printer. You use the ROW( ) and COL( ) functions when printing to the screen, and the PROW( ) and PCOL( ) functions when printing to the printer. The following program prints names and addresses in a single column down a printed page:

```
USE MyTable
SET DEVICE TO PRINT

DO WHILE .NOT. EOF()
  @ PROW() + 2,5 SAY Name
  @ PROW() + 1,5 SAY Address
  @ PROW() + 1,5 SAY TRIM(City) + ", " + State + " " + Zip
  SKIP
  IF PROW() > 55
     EJECT
  ENDIF
ENDDO
EJECT
SET DEVICE TO SCREEN
```

This program tells dBASE for Windows to perform the following tasks:

1. Open a table named MyTable.

2. Use the printer as the output device.

3. Start a loop that continues until dBASE for Windows reaches the end of MyTable.

4. Print the contents of the Name field in the fifth column of PROW( ) + 2. To determine where to start printing, dBASE for Windows takes the current print row, which is returned by PROW( ), and adds 2. The result is the new print row. As specified in the @ SAY command, the print column is 5.

5. Move to the next line by adding 1 to the current print row, and print the contents of the Address field, starting in column 5 of this row.

6. Move to the fifth column in the next line, and print the following: the contents of the City field, with trailing spaces trimmed off; a comma and a space; the contents of the State field; a space; and the contents of the Zip field. The output will look like this:

```
City, State Zip
```

7. Skip to the next record in MyTable.

8. Determine if the current print row is greater than 55.

9. If the current print row is greater than 55, eject the page from the printer. The new page will automatically reset PROW( ) to 1.

10. After processing all the records in MyTable, end the loop, eject the page from the printer, set the screen as the output device, go home, and eat pizza.

The PRINTJOB Is My Friend

Networks have changed the way we think about printing. The days of printing willy-nilly in an application are long gone. Each time printing is required, we have to think in terms of a document or a print job, because other people on the network might already be printing and you don't want your print request to collide with theirs. Bill in the accounting department would be very unhappy if his quarterly report came out of the printer mixed with your dBASE for Windows form. To avoid these collisions, each print request is treated as a separate print job.

A new print document is started each time you issue the SET PRINT ON command. If your computer is on a network that prints banner pages, the SET PRINT ON command results in the printing of a banner page. When you issue this command, data is streamed to a print queue or directly to the printer. The streaming ends when you issue the SET PRINT OFF command. If your network prints separator pages, the SET PRINT OFF command results in the printing of a separator page. ■

You can control each print job by using the PRINTJOB and ENDPRINTJOB commands to specify when each print job begins and ends. As detailed in the next section, these commands also enable you to use all of the dBASE for Windows system print variables to control how each document is printed.

The following example is a simple print job that prints the contents of an array:

```
* Modified Days of the Week
MyArray = NEW ARRAY(8)
MyArray[1] = "Monday"
MyArray[2] = "Tuesday"
MyArray[3] = "Wednesday"
MyArray[4] = "Thursday"
MyArray[5] = "Friday"
MyArray[6] = "Saturday"
```

```
MyArray[7] = "Sunday"
MyArray[8] = "Playday"

IF PRINTSTATUS("LPT1")
  SET PRINTER ON
  PRINTJOB
  FOR i = 1 TO 8
     ? MyArray[i]
  NEXT
  ENDPRINTJOB
  SET PRINTER OFF
ENDIF
```

This example stores the eight days of the week in the elements of an array. The PRINTSTATUS( ) function verifies that the printer is ready. Does it have paper? Is it turned on, plugged in, and on-line? As shown in the example, you enter the name of the printer port in quotation marks. If you aren't sure which port your printer is connected to or you're on a network, you may want to ask the local administrative assistant for some help. They know everything.

After verifying that the printer is ready, the procedure directs output to the printer, and tells dBASE for Windows that a new print job has been started.

The procedure loops eight times and streams the contents of our array to the printer. After printing the contents of the array, the procedure ends the print job, and turns printing off. Of course, if the printer isn't ready at the beginning of the IF statement, none of this will happen.

Using the System Print Variables

The dBASE for Windows system print variables are very much like object properties. They control the appearance and behavior of your print jobs. You can think of each print job as an object and these system print variables as its properties. The system print variables allow you to build sophisticated reports by changing such settings as paper orientation, margins, word wrap, tab settings, and line spacing.

Some of the system print variables have default values. You can view the contents of any of them by using the ? command. To change a system print variable, use the assignment operator (=) just like you would for any other variable. Table 12-3 lists the system print variables. For a detailed explanation of their use, refer to the dBASE for Windows Help file.

Table 12-3: System print variables

Print Variable	Description
_alignment	Aligns streamed output. Can be set to "LEFT", "CENTER", or "RIGHT". To use _alignment, _wrap must = .T.
_box	If set to .T., allows dBASE IV DEFINE BOXES in streamed output.
_indent	Numeric value specifies column indent when _wrap is .T.
_lmargin	Numeric value specifies the left margin when _wrap is .T.
_padvance	Sets printer advance to "FORMFEED" or "LINEFEED".
_pageno	Holds the current page number. It is set automatically and can be changed manually.
_pbpage	Identifies the current page of a PRINTJOB. It can be set like _pageno.
_pcolno	Holds or sets the current column number of streamed ouput.
_pcopies	Specifies the number of copies PRINTJOB will print.
_pdriver	Holds the name of the current print driver. It can be changed manually or with CHOOSEPRINTER().
_peject	Specifies when PRINTJOB ejects paper: "BEFORE", "AFTER", "BOTH", or "NONE".
_pepage	Set manually to end a PRINTJOB on a certain page.
_pform	Holds the filename of a print file.
_plength	Specifies page length in lines for streamed output. It can be changed manually or by changing _porientation.
_plineno	Holds or sets the current line number of streamed output.
_ploffset	Performs the same function as _lmargin. If both are used, they are additive.
_porientation	Defines the page orientation: "PORTRAIT" or "LANDSCAPE".
_ppitch	Sets the number of characters per inch printed on a page.
_pquality	When set to .F., specifies Draft print quality on non-laser printers.
_pspacing	Sets line spacing to 1, 2, or 3.
_rmargin	Sets the right margin for streamed output when _wrap = .T.
_tabs	Specifies the columns of tab stops with a character string list of comma-separated numbers.
_wrap	Finally! When set to .T., specifies that streamed output is word wrapped between the left and right margins.

The following example uses many of the system print variables to control the appearance of a multi-page report. The example prints a management report containing two sections. Section 1 is a list of salespeople with sales over 1 million dollars. Section 2 is a list of sales by customer. Instead of going through the example line-by-line, we've added comments throughout the procedure to help you see what's going on. As you read through the following example, you can refer to Table 12-3 when you need to check the meaning of a particular system print variable:

```
SET TALK OFF

* Set up data files
USE Customer in 1        && Customer list
USE Salesstf in 2        && Sales staff list
USE Sales in 3           && Sales for the month

SELECT Salesstf
SET ORDER TO SALESSTFID
SELECT Sales
SET RELATION TO SALESSTFID INTO Salesstf, TO Custid INTO Customer

* Set up system print variables
_wrap = .T.
_lmargin = 10
_rmargin = 70
_porientation = "PORTRAIT"
_pcopies = 5
_peject = "AFTER"

SET PRINT ON
PRINTJOB

* The Sales table is currently selected
_alignment = "CENTER"
? "SALES STAFF WITH SALES OVER ONE MILLION DOLLARS"
? ""
_alignment = "LEFT"
LIST FIELDS Salesstf->Name, Sales->Amount;
  FOR Sales->Amount >= 1000000
EJECT

* Set up print variables for Section 2
_alignment = "CENTER"
_porientation = "LANDSCAPE"
_tabs = "5,30"

? "CUSTOMER SALES"
```

```
_alignment = "LEFT"

GO TOP
DO WHILE .NOT. EOF()
  IF Amount > 0
     ? CHR(9), Customer->Name,CHR(9), Sales->Amount
  ENDIF
  SKIP
  IF _plineno > 35
     EJECT
     _alignment = "CENTER"
     ? "CUSTOMER SALES"
     _alignment = "LEFT"
  ENDIF
ENDDO
ENDPRINTJOB
CLOSE PRINTER
```

This example shows two ways of streaming output. One approach uses the TO PRINT keyword with the LIST command. The other approach uses the ? command. You have greater control with the ? command, but it takes more programming.

With a little practice using the various dBASE for Windows print tools, you'll be able to create well-formatted reports using either the customizing capabilities of streamed output, or the simplicity of coordinate printing. No other programming language makes printing this easy.

Chapter 13

Creating Reports with Crystal Reports for dBASE

Crystal Reports is a product that is included in dBASE for Windows. With this what-you-see-is-what-you-get (WYSIWYG) tool, you can quickly and easily create reports that would otherwise require weeks of programming. Crystal Reports simplifies the creation of reports by allowing you to:

✔ Place fields and text in your reports by simply dragging and dropping the desired information

✔ Add graphics to your report

✔ Include OLE objects in the report

✔ Create formula fields

Start Your Engines!

Before you can start creating a report, you need to open the tables you are going to use, and define any relationships that are needed for your report. You don't need to create a query (.QBE) file, because Crystal Reports will create its own query file.

To start Crystal Reports, enter the following command in the Command window:

```
CREATE REPORT
```

A new untitled report is created in the main Crystal Reports window. As shown in Figure 13-1, the Insert Database Field window lists the fields in the open tables. You add a field to your report by dragging a field name from this list to the desired position in the report. To do this, hold down the left mouse button when you click a field name in the Insert Database Field window, drag the selected field into the report, and release the mouse button when the field is correctly positioned in the report. Go ahead and add a few fields to your report.

As you can see in Figure 13-1, Crystal Reports divides the pages of a report into three sections: a page header, a details section, and a page footer. You usually place fields in the details section of the report. We cover the page header and the page footer later in this chapter.

You have successfully created a report. It's that easy with Crystal Reports. At this point, you could save and run your report, or you could continue with the rest of this chapter and learn to create powerful, well-formatted reports.

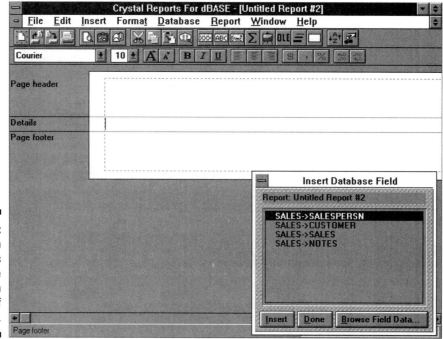

Figure 13-1:
You can drag fields onto the report from the list of fields.

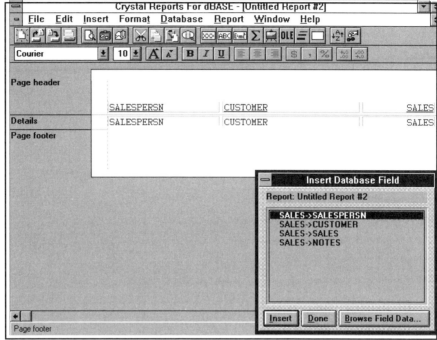

Figure 13-2:
Creating a
simple
columnar
report is
easy with
Crystal
Reports.

Painting Your Report

You can drag fields around your report, dropping them like apple seeds. At this stage in the development of your report, you probably want to place the fields in the details section. Figure 13-2 shows a simple detail report that we created by dragging the fields onto the report.

While you are dragging the fields around your report, Crystal Reports lets you look at the data in those fields. As you can see in Figure 13-2, the Insert Database Field window includes a Browse Field Data... button. If you select a field and click the Browse Field Data... button, Crystal Reports displays another window containing the data in the selected field. Figure 13-3 shows an example of this window.

For some reports, you might need additional room in the details section. For example, you may want to arrange the fields in something other than a columnar format. The three sections of the report are separated by horizontal bars. You can change the height of any section by clicking and dragging these bars with your mouse, or by placing the text cursor in the desired section and pressing the Enter key.

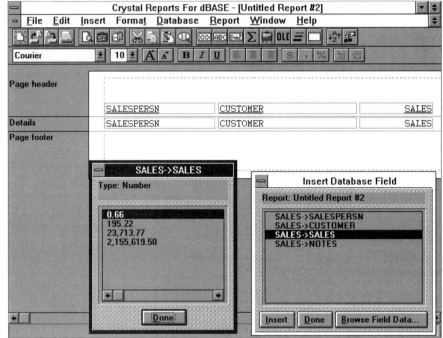

Figure 13-3:
You can
browse
through
your data
while you
are creating
your report.

Adding titles and text

After placing the fields on your report, you need to begin formatting the report with such features as titles, meaningful column headers, comments, and page numbers.

When you are done adding fields, you can close the Insert Database Field window. This window tends to get in the way while you are formatting the report. You can always bring it back by selecting Insert I Database Field from the Crystal Reports menu. ▪

A good report deserves a title. You add a title to your report by adding a text field. To place a text field on the report, select Insert I Text Field from the Crystal Reports menu. As shown in Figure 13-4, Crystal Reports displays a window that allows you to enter and edit text.

When you are finished typing the text in the Edit Text Field window, click the Accept button. The mouse cursor changes shape to show that you are dragging around the outline of a text box. The text box won't appear to contain text until you place it somewhere. Click where you want the text to appear.

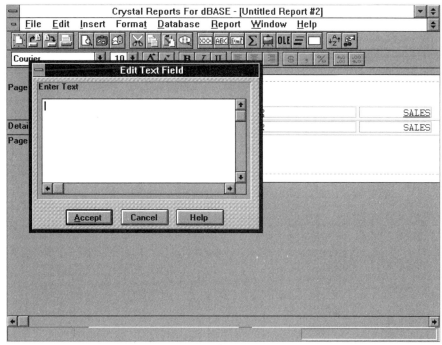

Figure 13-4:
The Edit
Text Field
window lets
you place
text on your
report.

Don't worry about getting it in the wrong place. You can always move the text by clicking and dragging it with your left mouse button.

Editing your text fields

You can go back and edit a text field by clicking on the text field and selecting Edit | Text from the Crystal Reports menu. If you don't click correctly on the text field, you won't be able to choose the Text option from the Edit menu.

Formatting a text field

You can customize the appearance of your Crystal report by formatting text. Crystal Reports lets you format the following characteristics of text fields and character fields from your table:

- The font of the text or character field
- Borders and colors
- Alignment

To customize text and character fields, you can choose formatting options from the Crystal Reports menu, or you can use the SpeedMenu options. To display the SpeedMenu, click the text field or table field name using your right mouse button. You can select the format feature you want from this menu.

To set the font of a selected text or character field:

1. Choose Format | Font from the Crystal Reports menu bar. Crystal Reports displays the Font dialog box.

2. Choose the desired font name from the Font ListBox.

3. Choose a font style from the Font style ListBox.

4. Choose a font size from the Size ListBox.

5. Select any effects such as strikeout or underlining from the Effects List-Box.

6. Set the text color by selecting a color from the Color drop-down ListBox.

7. Click the OK button in the Fonts dialog box to apply these changes.

To set the border and color characteristics of the text or character field:

1. Select the text or character field by clicking it once with your left mouse button.

2. From the Crystal Reports menu, select Format | Border and Colors.

3. The color boxes let you set the color of the text, the fill color, and the color of the border. Click to select a color in each category.

4. Select one of the four border styles displayed.

5. Select which sides you want a border to appear on by clicking the choices. The selected sides will contain check marks. You can also select a Drop Shadow effect for your text field.

6. Set the border to be either the height of the line or the height of the font.

7. Set the border width to be the width of the field or the width of the data. With the latter option, the width of the border changes as the data changes.

To set the alignment of your text and character field:

1. Open the Format String dialog box by double clicking the text or character field.

2. Select the alignment from the drop-down ListBox.

There are other choices available in the Format String dialog box that refer only to data in fields. When formatting text, you can ignore these other settings.

Selecting groups of text fields

You can select more than one field at a time by holding down the shift key and selecting additional fields with your mouse. If you have a color monitor, you will see a blue rectangle appear around each selected field. By selecting several fields at once, you can:

- ✔ Choose a font for the entire group of selected fields.
- ✔ Move the entire group as a single entity with your mouse.
- ✔ Double click on one of the fields in the group and set the format for the entire group.
- ✔ Delete the entire group of fields by pressing the Delete key.

Using text fields

If your Crystal Report Writer is configured to add field titles as default headings, you can turn this feature on and off with the File | Options menu selection. You can also modify the default headings when they appear. Now that you're an expert at adding text to the report and modifying it, this will be a snap.

To edit a default heading:

1. Click the text field that contains the default field name.
2. Select Edit | Text field from the Crystal Reports menu.
3. Modify the text, and click the Accept button to apply your changes.

Column headings are simply text fields. When working with column headings, you can use all the formatting capabilities described in this chapter. You can also move, resize, and delete the default field heading names.

You can move a text or character field by clicking and dragging. In other words, click the field with your left mouse button, and hold down the mouse button while moving the mouse to drag the text field to its new position.

To resize a text or character field, click on the field to select it. Then, click and drag the border until the field is the right size. When you click on the border of the field and hold down your left mouse button, you will notice that the mouse cursor changes to a double arrow, letting you know that you are resizing the field.

To delete a text or character field from your report, click on the field and then press the Delete key.

Be careful when moving fields around the report. You may inadvertently move the field into a different section. Generally, report data appears in the details section, column titles and report titles appear in the header section, and summary information appears in the summary and footer sections. ■

Formatting different field types

The preceding sections showed you how to format text and character fields. You can also format numbers, dates, and logical fields. The following sections introduce the custom formatting options for the different field types.

Making the numbers look good

You can format numeric fields in much the same way that you format text. In fact, numbers have many more formatting possibilities. Figure 13-5 shows the window that Crystal Reports displays when you double click a numeric field.

Figure 13-5:
By double clicking numeric fields, you can open a window of options for customizing those fields.

Format Number
Name: SALES->SALES
☑ Use **W**indows Default Format

☐ **S**uppress if Duplicated	☐ **C**urrency Symbol: [$]
☐ Suppress if **Z**ero	☐ One Symbol Per Page
☐ Hide when **P**rinting	◇ Fixed ◇ Floating
Alignment: [Default ▼]	**P**osition: [-$123 ▼]

Decimals: [1.00 ▼]	**D**ecimal Separator: [.]
Rounding: [0.01 ▼]	☑ **T**housands Separator: [,]
Negatives: [-123 ▼]	☑ **L**eading Zero

Sample:
    -5,555,555.56

[OK]
[Cancel]
[Help]

The Format Number window lets you control the following formatting options for numeric fields:

- ✔ Using the Windows default format for numbers.
- ✔ Suppressing or hiding the number for various reasons.
- ✔ Aligning the number to the left, center, or right.
- ✔ Choosing and formatting a currency symbol, if your number represents money.
- ✔ Setting decimal and rounding accuracy, and the separators for thousands and decimals.
- ✔ Choosing the format for negative numbers.

In the lower-left corner of the Format Number window, a sample shows you how the formatted numeric field will appear in your report.

Making your date look good

The process of formatting a date field is similar to the process you use for formatting text and numeric fields. For example, you can also suppress or hide dates. Double clicking a date field displays the Date Format window, which allows you to choose how your date prints. Changing your date's appearance does not change the contents of the field.

In the Date Format window, you can choose one of the following styles for your date:

- ✔ MDY. The Month Day Year format displays December 25, 1994 as 12/25/94.
- ✔ DMY. The Day Month Year format displays December 25, 1994 as 25/12/94
- ✔ YMD. The Year Month Day format displays December 25, 1994 as 94/12/25

You can also change the separators that are used in the date field. The default is the forward slash (/). You may change this to any character you wish.

When formatting a date, be sure to use a meaningful separator character. Although you are allowed to use numbers and letters as separators, this can be confusing. For example, if you use the number 8 as a separator, Christmas would be 12825894. When choosing a separator, it's best to use non-alphanumeric characters such as / − . * or |. However, the character you choose might cause a date to be confused with a mathematical equation. You could make Christmas look like 12*25/94, which equals 3.1914893. As you may recognize, the resulting number is very close to pi. We call this slight deviation Christmas Pi. ■

Formatting the truth

Fields that contain true or false values are known as Boolean fields. They are named after George Boole, English mathematician and logician, 1815-1864, and that's the truth. In Boole's logic, known as Boolean logic, there are only two possibilities: something is either True or False. This logic has been expanded in today's digital world to mean on or off, yes or no, and 1 or 0.

dBASE for Windows allows you to format your Boolean or logical fields to almost all of those possibilities. You can choose the following formats for a logical field:

- ✔ True or False
- ✔ T or F
- ✔ Yes or No
- ✔ Y or N
- ✔ 1 or 0

When formatting logical fields, remember the words of Confucius:

> "It is man that makes truth great, not truth that makes man great."

Creating Formulas

We aren't talking about the formula that you heat up and then sprinkle on your arm. Parents wonder why their kids throw everything off the high chair, but one of the first things a baby sees is mom or dad shaking formula all over their arm to find out if it's too hot. You can sprinkle your reports with formulas if you want.

Formula fields are created so that you can see more from the information stored in your table. For example, you might have two fields in an inventory table: one for the price of the item; the other for the cost of the item. You can find out how much money you make on this item by creating a formula field called PROFIT. This field is created by simply subtracting the COST field from the PRICE field. The PROFIT field appears in your report as though the information is stored in your table.

This is a fairly simple example. Your formulas can be as complex as you need them to be.

To create a new formula:

1. Select Insert | Formula Field from the Crystal Reports menu. Crystal Reports displays the Insert Formula dialog box.

2. Enter a name for your formula. In our example, we called the formula PROFIT.

3. After you enter a formula name, the Expression Builder is displayed. You can either enter the formula in the Expression Box or use the Expression Builder ListBoxes to help you create the formula. For maximum help, select the Safety Net option at the top of the Expression Builder. Your formula must be a valid dBASE for Windows expression. In our example, we entered PRICE – COST in the Expression Box.

4. Save the formula by clicking the OK button in the Expression Builder.

5. The Expression Builder disappears after you click the OK button. The formula field appears as an outline box on the tip of the mouse cursor. It moves with the mouse cursor until you click the mouse button to place the field. Place the field in the desired column and section and click the left mouse button.

Formula fields can handle many kinds of data. For example, by using formula fields, you can:

- Combine first, middle, and last names in a single field.
- Create mathematical formulas that perform calculations using the data in your table.
- Put different types of data together in a single field by changing their types.
- Count occurrences of something by returning a number each time that particular data is encountered.

Try experimenting with formula fields because they can give you real reporting power. As shown in Figure 13-6, we have added a Commission column to our sample report. This formula field is created by multiplying the Sales field by 0.08. You can easily recognize which fields in your report are formula fields; they all begin with an @ sign. Our commission formula is known as @commission.

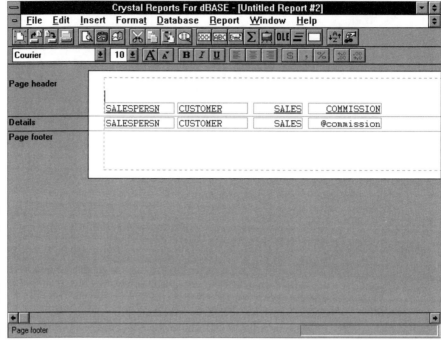

Figure 13-6:
You can use
formula
fields in a
report just
like any
other field.

Building a Summary Report with Formula Fields

Now that you know how to use formulas, you can start building a summary report. Get ready, because it takes some fancy footwork to create this common type of report.

To start building the summary report, we are going to create a formula field that returns the number 1 every time we find something we want to count. The heart of this formula is the IIF() function, which stands for Immediate IF. The IIF() function has the following syntax:

```
IIF(expression, value if True, value if False)
```

As you can see, the first argument in the IIF() function is an expression. The IIF function returns one value if this expression is true, and another value if the expression is false. Our summary report uses the following IIF function:

```
IIF(Customer = "Swan Foods" .AND. Sales > 10000, 1, 0)
```

In this example, the IIF( ) functions returns 1 if the sales for Swan Foods are greater than 10,000. In any other case, the IIF( ) function returns a zero (0). By using this formula in our report, we can create a field that returns a number based on the value of a text field, or an expression based on several fields.

To use this IIF( ) function in a formula field:

1. Select Insert | Formula from the Crystal Reports menu.

2. Enter a name for your formula. Let's call this example BigSales.

3. In the Expression Builder that appears, type the following IIF( ) function in the Expression Box:

```
IIF(Customer = "Swan Foods" .AND. Sales > 10000, 1, 0)
```

4. Click the OK button in the Expression Box to save this formula.

5. The formula field is now attached to the mouse cursor. Place it on the report by clicking in the desired location with the left mouse button. That's all there is to creating a formula field and placing it in a report.

The IIF( ) function is particularly useful for assigning weighting factors to your data. If you want a particular value to have more "points" than another value, simply create an IIF( ) function that returns a higher value.

The next section shows you how to use the values that are returned from our formula field. You may use formula fields in any of the Crystal Reports sections. In our example, we use these values in the summary fields that are built into Crystal Reports.

 You can edit an existing formula by clicking on the formula field and selecting Edit | Formula. If you don't click correctly on the formula field, you won't be able to choose the Formula option from the Edit menu. ■

When You Run Out of Fingers and Toes

Summary fields are built-in formula fields. The summary fields provided in Crystal Reports include:

✔ Summary. The sum of a numeric value, the maximum value of the different field types, or a count of a particular expression or value.

✔ Subtotal. The sum of the values in à numeric field for a group. Groups are created when you specify the criteria for subtotals.

✔ Grandtotal. The sum of the values in a numeric field for all records that appear in your report.

To create a summary field for a field on the report, click on the field you want to summarize, and select Insert | Summary Field from the Crystal Reports menu. When you select this menu option, Crystal Reports adds a new section to your report. You can add other fields or text to this section to enhance or label the summary information. Figure 13-7 shows a Total Sales summary field.

Our summary report uses the formula field that we created in the previous section. To summarize this field, click on the formula field in the details section of the report, select Insert | Summary Field from the Crystal Reports menu, and choose either a Subtotal or Grand Total summary field from the dialog box that's displayed.

The summary field will appear below the field you are summarizing, in a special summary section created automatically by Crystal Reports. Once the summary field is displayed on the report, you can move it to another location by dragging it with the mouse.

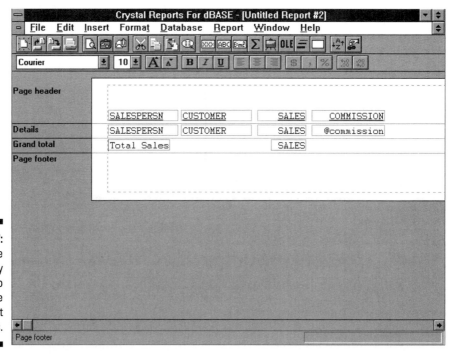

Figure 13-7: You can use summary fields to create report totals.

Two's Company, Three's a Group

Information must be grouped in many of the reports you create. For example, you might want to list employees by department. Some summary choices automatically create groups. Groups are powerful reporting features. If you are a psychotherapist, groups can also be profitable.

To create a group:

1. Select Insert | Group Section from the Crystal Reports menu. Crystal Reports displays the dialog box shown in Figure 13-8.

2. Select the report field or database field on which the report should be sorted and grouped.

3. Select the order in which the fields should be sorted.

When you create a group, a new group section appears in your report. Actually, the new group section appears in two sections of the report. One part of the new report section appears above the details section to let you add titles or text information describing the group. Another part of the new report

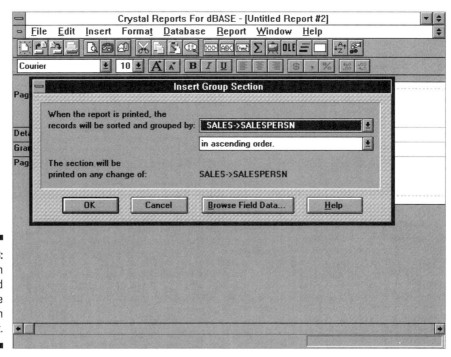

Figure 13-8:
You can group and sort the fields in your report.

section appears below the details section. This part allows you to summarize each group, or enter additional text.

Each group is given a distinct number. This is how you match the two sections above and below the detail section.

Sorting It All Out

Sometimes, records must be in a particular order. Your table may already be in some index order, or it may be sorted in natural order. If not, Crystal Reports can sort the records on the fly.

When you group your records, they are sorted and grouped by the field you select. When you create the group, Crystal Reports informs you that it is going to sort the data and lets you choose ascending or descending order.

You can also create your own sort order. From the Crystal Reports menu, select Report | Record Sort Order. The Record Sort Order dialog box is displayed. To define the sort order:

1. Click on a field in the Report Fields ListBox.

2. Click the Add-> button to move the selected field to the Sort Fields List-Box.

3. Specify the sort order by selecting either Ascending or Descending from the CheckBoxes below the Sort Order ListBox.

4. When you have finished selecting fields for the sort order, click the OK button to apply these changes.

Your report will now be sorted by the fields you have selected. To remove a sort order field, highlight the field in the Sort Order ListBox and then click the <-Remove button. The field is moved back to the Report Fields ListBox.

Playing Hide the Section

When giving someone a tour of your house, have you ever pointed to your closed bedroom door, said, "That's my room," and then continued with the tour? Sometimes, there are things we just don't want other people to see. Crystal Reports gives you the opportunity to hide certain sections of your report from the person running the report.

For example, if you are creating a summary report, as we have been discussing, you will want to hide the details section. What good is a summary report if it includes all of the details?

To show and hide different sections of a report:

1. Select Edit | Show/Hide Sections from the Crystal Reports menu. The Show/Hide Sections dialog box is displayed.

2. Select a section from the list. The S or H next to each section name lets you know whether it is going to be shown or hidden.

3. Click either the Show or Hide CheckBox to specify whether the section should be shown or hidden.

4. Click the OK button in the dialog box to apply these changes to your report.

After you finish choosing sections to hide, the hidden sections appear grayed out in your report.

The Record Jukebox

There are several ways to limit which records appear in your reports:

✔ Setting a filter before you issue the CREATE REPORT command. The filter is added to the .QBE file that Crystal Reports automatically builds.

✔ Creating formula fields that print only if an expression is valid.

✔ Designating a Record Selection Formula from the Crystal Reports menu.

You can set a filter before you begin your report. If this is not practical because of the way your program is designed, you can select Report | Record Selection Formula from the Crystal Reports menu. Enter an expression that must be true, for record information to be printed.

To limit which records will appear on your report:

1. Select Report | Record Selection Formula from the Crystal Reports menu. The Expression Builder is displayed.

2. Use the Expression Builder to enter an expression that will be evaluated against the records in your table. For example, by entering the following record selection formula, you would limit your report to records in which the value in the TOTAL field is greater than 1000:

```
TOTAL > 1000
```

3. Click the OK button to apply this record selection formula to your report.

For help using the Expression Builder, you can select your choices from the Category, Type, and Paste ListBoxes at the bottom of the Expression Builder. For additional help, you can click the Safety Net CheckBox. The Safety Net guides you through the construction of an expression. ▪

Seeing Is Believing

Crystal Reports lets you test your report while you are building it. You don't have to save your report and exit Crystal Reports. Testing your report by running it from within Crystal Reports can save you a lot of time.

Select Report | Refresh Report Data from the Crystal Reports menu, and your report will begin running in a Preview window. When it is done, the icons at the bottom of the Preview window give you the following options:

- ✔ Zooming in and out
- ✔ Refreshing the report data
- ✔ Printing the report
- ✔ Exporting the report to a file
- ✔ Exporting the report to e-mail
- ✔ Closing the Preview window

If your report is printing incorrect information, select Database | Verify Database from the Crystal Reports menu. This option lets you make sure that your database is current. If any changes are made to the structure of your table after the report has been created, Crystal Reports tries to adapt the report to match the new structure. You might also need to check the Record Selection Formula and any formula fields you have created. ▪

Take advantage of the ability to preview your report. Some report writers only let you see what one or two records will look like when the report is run. With Crystal Reports, you can see how the report will look, and you can verify the accuracy of the data.

Creating Labels and Knowing Where to Stick Them

Creating labels is very similar to creating a report:

1. Use the table or tables you need for your label.

2. Enter the following command in the dBASE for Windows Command window:

```
CREATE LABEL
```

3. As shown in Figure 13-9, dBASE for Windows displays the Mailing Labels dialog box. Select the mailing label style you would like for your labels as well as the direction of printing, the number of labels across, and the page layout of the physical page of labels. Your box of labels should contain the information you need for making these choices.

4. Drag fields from the Insert Database Field list onto the label report. You will notice that label reports have only a details section.

5. Add any additional Text or Formula fields. For example, you might want to use a formula field to format names and addresses. You can also use formula fields to create special mailing codes that are printed on your label.

6. If necessary, specify a sort order or record selection criteria. As detailed earlier in this chapter, you access the Record Sort Order dialog box by

Figure 13-9:
You can use predefined label formats or create your own.

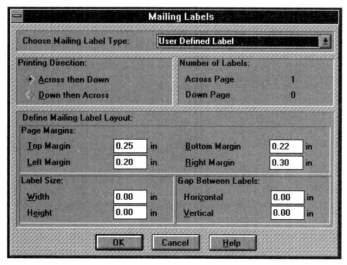

selecting Report | Record Sort Order from the Crystal Reports menu. To open the Expression Builder and create a record selection formula, select Report | Record Selection Formula.

7. Save your label format by selecting File | Save from the Crystal Reports menu. You are prompted for a filename. Crystal Reports saves this file with the default extension .RPL.

If you need to change the label form, enter the MODIFY LABEL command in the dBASE for Windows Command window. This command starts the Crystal Reports Label program.

To use the label form in a program or from the Command window, use the command LABEL FORM *FileName* TO PRINT. The *FileName* part of this command is the name of the Crystal Reports label file you have created. The TO PRINT keyword is optional.

Saving Your Report

You are probably wondering why we would start this section with a Warning. There is only one really confusing thing about using Crystal Reports, and it has to do with saving your report. The Crystal Reports menu includes an option, Save Data with Closed Report. This option saves the data you used when creating the report.

BEWARE! This option can be set by default. If this happens, the users of your report will never see new data!

To make things confusing, this option appears in two different places in the Crystal Reports menu. The File | Options menu selection allows you to set this option for all future reports. IT WILL NOT CHANGE THE CURRENT REPORT. The second place to find this setting is in the Report | Save Data with Closed Report selection.

To change this option in future reports, you set (or unset) this default option by choosing File | Options from the Crystal Reports menu. When you choose this menu option, Crystal Reports displays a dialog box with a radio button that lets you Save data with closed report. Be aware that changing this option will not affect your current report, only future reports.

To set or unset this option in the current report, you must change it using the Report | Save Data with Closed Report menu choice. ■

Sorry to start this section with such a dire warning. The option described in the warning can be particularly nasty if you don't know about it, or happen to forget. On the other hand, the option does serve a purpose. With this option, you can create a report and distribute it to other people who might not have the data. They can run the report with the data you used to create the report. In such cases, you can change the data by selecting Report | Refresh Report Data from the Crystal Reports menu.

To save a Crystal report, choose File | Save from the Crystal Reports menu. You will be prompted for a filename. Reports are saved with the default extension .RPT.

When the file is saved, Crystal Reports also creates its own .QBE file. This is important to know because when you run a Crystal report, all of your files are closed and the report files are opened in the .QBE file. After running the report, you need to restore any files, filters, and relationships that were set before you ran your Crystal report. You can't fool Crystal Reports by emptying the .QBE file. You will either get an error or no report, depending on the barometric pressure multiplied by the likelihood of being hit by a commuter train.

If you're on a network or you use several disk drives, you need to be aware that when you save a report, Crystal Reports creates a .QBE file and saves the directory path for finding that .QBE file. If you are going to distribute this report, everyone must have the same path as the person who created the report. The drive letter isn't important. The path is! ▪

When you save a report, the .QBE file that Crystal Reports creates has the same name as the report. If a .QBE file already exists by that name, Crystal Reports creates a different filename by adding a number to the end of the filename. Your existing .QBE files are safe.

Using the Report in Your Application

This is the easy part. To use the report you have created, enter the following command:

```
REPORT FORM FileName TO PRINT
```

If you issue the REPORT FORM command without the TO PRINT option, your report appears in a window on the screen. When you send the report to the printer, a status window is displayed to let you know how many records have been printed. You won't see the results on the screen if you send them to the printer.

Using label reports is the same as using reports. You can view them on the screen or send them to the printer. Make sure you have labels in the printer before you issue the REPORT FORM command, because it won't wait and Murphy's law says that any person trying to get to the printer before a print job will trip on their own shoelaces. ■

Using the Report as Kindling

Somehow, the idea of the paperless society seems to have been forgotten. We think it's possible that printer manufacturers hate trees because they don't like to rake leaves.

You should test your report on the printer before you distribute it. Testing your report on the screen is very eco-conscious, but this shouldn't be the only way you test your report. In most cases, the printed report looks just like it did on the screen. However, the output might be affected by those odd printer configurations, printer drivers, Windows, memory, networks, weather, and the cyclic pull of the moon in conjunction with how long the coffee has been sitting on the burner. Smelly coffee can sometimes mean a rotten report. Seriously, testing the report on the printer is a good idea.

Whether your reports are simple or complex, Crystal Reports will save you time. Its simple "paint the report" interface makes it almost as much fun as creating forms. As you continue to gain experience with Crystal Reports, you should check out such advanced features as including OLE fields and graphics in your report. You'll have a lot of fun with this report writer and you'll be able to create very impressive reports.

Part V
Your Honor, I Object

The 5th Wave   By Rich Tennant

THE LONG-RANGE EFFECTS OF THE "LOOK AND FEEL" COPYRIGHT LAWSUITS WERE LOST ON NO ONE – LEAST OF ALL CLARABELLE AND BOZO THE CLOWN.

In This Part...

There's more to objects than meets the eye. Have you ever wondered where objects really come from? Your parents probably told you the stork brought them. Well, prepare yourself for a shock, because this part of the book tells you the truth about objects. Then you get to apply your new understanding of objects. The chapters in this part also offer some really neat tips for building better programs and making dBASE for Windows more useful.

Chapter 14

Oh, Oh! There's More To Learn!

*O*bjects may be the building blocks of dBASE for Windows programs, but did you know that objects have building blocks too? Objects are made from a special programming component called a class, or class definition. A class is like an object recipe; it describes exactly what dBASE for Windows must do in order to create a particular type of object.

The Birth of an Object

Each class has a unique class name. Fortunately, most class names are shorter than the names you'd give to recipes. You probably won't find a class with the following name:

```
Grilled_Salmon_With_Dill_Sauce_In_A_Spicy_Remoulade
```

dBASE for Windows has several built-in class definitions. Table 14-1 lists the names of the built-in class definitions, along with the type of object each class describes.

As you can see from Table 14-1, dBASE for Windows provides built-in class definitions for each of the objects you can use in the Form Designer. When you create a new form using the Form Designer or add controls to a form using the Controls Palette, you're actually telling dBASE for Windows to create objects from classes.

Table 14-1: Built-in class definitions make it easy to create the most common objects

Class Name	Object Type
ARRAY	Arrays
BROWSE	Browse controls
CHECKBOX	CheckBox controls
COMBOBOX	ComboBox controls
DDELINK	DDE links to DDE servers
DDETOPIC	DDE links to DDE clients
EDITOR	Editor controls
ENTRYFIELD	EntryField controls
FORM	Forms
IMAGE	Image controls
LINE	Line controls
LISTBOX	ListBox controls
MENU	Menus
OBJECT	Custom objects
OLE	OLE controls
PUSHBUTTON	PushButton controls
RADIOBUTTON	RadioButton controls
RECTANGLE	Rectangle controls
SCROLLBAR	ScrollBar controls
SPINBOX	SpinBox controls
TEXT	Text controls

So far in this book, whenever you needed to create an object or change an object's properties, you had to open the Form Designer, maybe open the Controls Palette, find the Properties window, find the right property, make your changes, save your changes, and hope you didn't make a mistake or you'd have to do it all over again. As detailed in the following sections, a class definition allows you to work with objects in a more straightforward manner, once you understand how class definitions work.

Creating objects from classes

Two commands allow you to create an object from a class. As you'll see later in this chapter, the Form Designer and the Controls Palette also use both of these commands to create objects. Whether you issue the command or let dBASE for Windows create the object for you, one of the following commands is used:

- DEFINE
- NEW

 There is one exception. (Wouldn't life be dull without exceptions?) You can't use the DEFINE command to create ARRAY objects. You use the DECLARE command to create an array. You can't use the DECLARE command with any other class type. DECLARE is a special command just for array objects. ▪

There are a few differences between DEFINE and NEW. Essentially, NEW is used as a "quick and dirty" way to create an object. NEW isn't as powerful as DEFINE, but it's simpler. Also, NEW can't be used in as many places as DEFINE. You'll see more differences emerge as this chapter progresses.

All objects need unique names. The name you give an object is called a *reference*, just like your name is a reference to you. When you use the DEFINE command, this reference is part of the command:

```
DEFINE ClassName ObjectReference
```

ClassName is the name of the class definition that you want to use to create an object. *ObjectReference* is the name you want to assign to the new object.

For example, to create a new form object with the reference Perfection, you would enter the following command, either in the Command window or in a procedure:

```
DEFINE FORM Perfection
```

When you use NEW to create a new object, you place the object's reference to the left of an = sign, and you enter the class name as though it is a function:

```
ObjectReference = NEW ClassName()
```

The example used previously for the DEFINE command looks like this using NEW:

```
Perfection = NEW FORM()
```

Some objects exist only within another object. For example, control objects exist only within a form. When you use DEFINE or NEW to create a new control object, you must identify the form to which the new object belongs. When an object needs to know something like this, its class definition is set up to accept parameters.

Passing parameters to a class definition is simple with NEW. As shown in the following example, you include necessary information in the parentheses that follow the class name:

```
PerfectPushButton = NEW PUSHBUTTON(Perfection)
```

This example creates a new PushButton on the form referred to as Perfection. If you try to create a control object without identifying which form it belongs to, dBASE for Windows will complain.

When you use NEW to add a control to a form, you can let dBASE for Windows pick a unique name for the control. The following example adds a List-Box control to the form called Perfection, and lets dBASE for Windows choose a name for the control:

```
NEW LISTBOX(Perfection)
```

You can also tell a control object which form it belongs to when you are using the DEFINE command. To do this, use the following syntax:

```
DEFINE ClassName ObjectReference OF FormObjectReference
```

FormObjectReference is a reference to the form on which you want to create a control.

For example, you can use DEFINE to create the PerfectPushButton by entering the following command:

```
DEFINE PUSHBUTTON PerfectPushButton OF Perfection
```

You can pass additional parameters to a class definition if the class is set up to accept them. To find out which parameters, if any, a class will accept, you should refer to the on-line Help files or the dBASE for Windows manuals.

When using NEW, you can pass additional parameters to a class definition by separating the parameters with commas. For example, the PUSHBUTTON class will accept a name that you want to assign to the PushButton control. The following example creates a PushButton named "HAPPY" on the form referred to as Perfection:

```
HappyPushButton = NEW PUSHBUTTON(Perfection,"HAPPY")
```

One major difference between DEFINE and NEW is that DEFINE can set the properties of an object when it's created, while NEW can only pass a few parameters. The following syntax lets you set the properties of the object you are creating with the DEFINE command:

```
DEFINE ClassName ObjectReference PROPERTY Property Value, Property
                    Value, Property Value, ...
```

Property is the name of an object property you want to set. *Value* is the value you want to assign to the property. Each *Property Value* pair sets the value of one property. To set the values of multiple properties, use commas to separate the various *Property Value* pairs.

For example, the following command creates a new form named MyForm, with the title "Programming Happens" 50 characters wide and 7 characters tall, positioned 2 characters from the top of the screen and 13 characters from the left. Be sure to type this entire command on a single line in the Command window:

```
DEFINE FORM MyForm PROPERTY Text "Programming Happens", Width 50,
                Height 7, Top 2, Left 13
```

 If you need to set a lot of properties, the DEFINE command can become quite long. When you use the DEFINE command in a procedure, you can stretch the command across multiple lines by placing semicolons (;) at the end of each line. For example, the previous command could appear like this in a procedure:

```
DEFINE FORM MyForm;
  PROPERTY;
  Text "Programming Happens",;
  Width 50,;
  Height 7,;
  Top 2,;
  Left 13
```

Now that you know how objects are created from classes, we'll show you several very useful things you can do with this knowledge. First, there's a handy function that accesses the Properties window for an object directly from the Command window! This means you don't have to open the Form Designer every time you need to change an object's properties, events, or methods.

There's also a way to execute any method of an object using the object's name. As a result, all of the capabilities present in every object are now available for use in your programs!

Inspecting an object's properties from the Command window

Working with classes and creating objects will soon become a natural way for you to program. To help you program using classes and objects, dBASE for Windows provides a way to access the Properties window without using the Form Designer. With this capability, you can use the Properties window to modify any object created from any class.

The INSPECT function lets you access the Properties window for an object. You must know the name of the object you want to inspect. Remember from the previous section that an object's name is also called a *reference*. When you're ready to inspect an object, use the following function:

```
INSPECT(ObjectReference)
```

ObjectReference is the name, or reference, of the object you want to inspect.

For example, assume that you created a new form by entering the following command:

```
FlipperForm = NEW FORM()
```

As shown in Figure 14-1, you could immediately access the Properties window for FlipperForm by entering the following command:

```
INSPECT(FlipperForm)
```

Figure 14-1:
The
INSPECT
function lets
you access
the Proper-
ties window
for any
object.

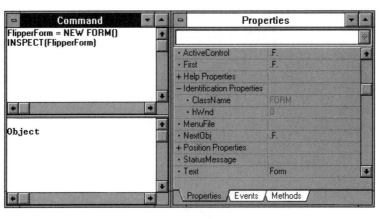

Let's add a control to FlipperForm so we can use INSPECT to access the Properties window for the control. We can add a Browse control to FlipperForm by entering the following command:

```
FlipperControl = NEW BROWSE(FlipperForm)
```

Now we can use INSPECT to access the Properties window for the Browse control we've just added:

```
INSPECT(FlipperControl)
```

As you start to do more with classes and objects, the INSPECT function will become very important. It also comes in handy when you are debugging an application, testing programs, and experimenting with ideas for a prototype.

Getting to the point with your objects

By now, you've seen the dot (.) used several times with objects. In chapter 2, you saw how it is used to access the properties of an object:

```
FORM.DESIRE.Text
```

In Chapter 10, you used it to close a form:

```
FORM.close()
```

Now that you're familiar with object references, we can go into more detail about the dot. The dot is actually an operator, called, appropriately enough, the *dot operator*. You use the dot operator along with an object reference to access properties or methods of an object.

To use the dot operator, create an object reference (in other words, create and name an object) and figure out what you want to access in the object. Then, use the dot operator like this:

```
ObjectReference.WhatYouWantToAccess
```

ObjectReference is a reference to the object from which you want to access something. *WhatYouWantToAccess* is the property or method that you'd like to access. If you want to access a method of the object, you must include parentheses ( ) to tell dBASE for Windows that you're calling a function.

For example, let's create a form using the DEFINE command:

```
DEFINE FORM NiceForm
```

Now we can use the form's reference with the dot operator to access the form's OPEN method:

```
NiceForm.OPEN()
```

As shown in Figure 14-2, the new form is opened on your screen!

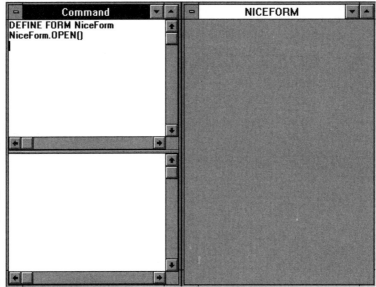

Figure 14-2:
You can use
the dot
operator to
access, or
execute, an
object's
methods.

When you access a property of an object, you have the option of reading and using the property's value, or changing it using the assignment operator (=). As shown in the following example, you can read the value of an object's property by using the dot operator followed by the name of the property:

```
NiceForm.Text
```

To do something with this value—for example, print it in the Results window—you need to treat NiceForm.Text as a variable. The following example displays "NICEFORM" in the Results window because that's the current value of the form's Text property:

```
? NiceForm.Text
```

As shown in Figure 14-3, the following statement changes the contents of the Text property to "BADFORM":

```
NiceForm.Text = "BADFORM"
```

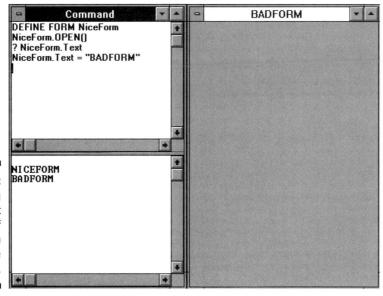

Figure 14-3:
Changing
the Text
property of
a form
changes the
form's title.

When using the dot operator, you need to know about two special object references. First, all objects in dBASE for Windows have a built-in object reference called *this*, which refers to the object itself, without using its proper name. *This* can be used only from within the object; otherwise, dBASE for Windows won't know what *this* refers to.

As shown in the following example, you can use *this* in place of the object's name in an object's methods or event procedures:

```
this.Text = "New Text"
```

The other special object reference applies only to forms. Every form has a special reference called *form*. You can use this reference to the form from anywhere within the form or its controls.

For example, you might recall from Chapter 10 that we used form.close() to close a form. In that example, form.close() appears in the OnClick event procedure of a PushButton control. dBASE for Windows knows which form to close because the *form* reference is within one of the form's controls.

It's important to remember that you can use the dot operator to access the properties and methods of any object, not just forms. The dot operator is very common in dBASE for Windows. In a way, its the glue that holds everything together. Without the dot operator, you wouldn't be able to access your objects' properties and methods. This would make programming extremely difficult.

20,000 Leagues under the Form

You don't need a submarine named Nautilus to explore the depths of a form you've created in the Form Designer. When you see the inside of a form for the first time, you may think you're being attacked by a giant squid. To examine a form that you've created using the Form Designer, you enter the following command:

```
MODIFY COMMAND FormFileName
```

FormFileName is the form's filename, which must include the extension .WFM.

To see how this works, let's create a form by issuing the following command:

```
CREATE FORM NiftyFor
```

Now, press Ctrl-W to save the form and exit the Form Designer.

As shown in Figure 14-4, issuing the following command opens the form file and allows us to examine the insides of NiftyFor:

```
MODIFY COMMAND NiftyFor.WFM
```

Are you having visions of large squid yet? The contents of a form's .WFM file can be a bit intimidating. The following sections dispel the mystery, and show you how the Form Designer's form file works.

Figure 14-4:
By entering
MODIFY
COMMAND,
you can
open a
form's
.WFM file.

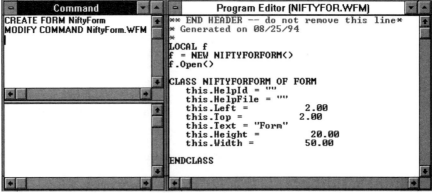

```
                Command              Program Editor (NIFTYFOR.WFM)
CREATE FORM NiftyForm            ** END HEADER -- do not remove this line*
MODIFY COMMAND NiftyForm.WFM     * Generated on 08/25/94
                                 *
                                 LOCAL f
                                 f = NEW NIFTYFORFORM<>
                                 f.Open<>

                                 CLASS NIFTYFORFORM OF FORM
                                     this.HelpId = ""
                                     this.HelpFile = ""
                                     this.Left =           2.00
                                     this.Top =            2.00
                                     this.Text = "Form"
                                     this.Height =         20.00
                                     this.Width =          50.00

                                 ENDCLASS
```

It wasn't the big bang; the first six lines of a .WFM file probably did it!

Everything has to start somewhere. The first six lines of a form's .WFM file take care of starting the form. The first six lines shown in Figure 14-4 are:

```
** END HEADER — do not remove this line*
* Generated on 08/25/94
*
LOCAL f
f = NEW NIFTYFORFORM()
f.Open()
```

The first three lines are comments created by the Form Designer. These comments identify this file as a Form Designer creation. As the comment suggests, you shouldn't remove these lines or you might confuse the Form Designer.

Next, we see:

```
LOCAL f
```

This line creates a new variable called f. There is no particular reason for calling this variable f; that's just what it is. The next line puts something in the f variable:

```
f = NEW NIFTYFORFORM()
```

You should recognize this from the beginning of this chapter. NEW is being used to create a new object, and the object is given an object reference, f. As you can see, the class name is NIFTYFORFORM. The NIFTYFORFORM class is a new type of form created by the Form Designer. This means that the f object reference is actually referring to a form object!

Where did this class name come from? NIFTYFORFORM is a new class, defined at the bottom of the .WFM file. Although Chapter 15 covers creating new classes in detail, we'll skim over this part of the .WFM file in the next section of this chapter.

The sixth line is:

```
f.Open()
```

This line uses the dot operator to access the Open( ) method of the form. This causes the form to appear on the screen.

The first six lines in a .WFM file exist so that you can use the DO command to run a form that you've created in the Form Designer. When you enter the following command, the first six lines of the .WFM file create a new form using the class definition at the bottom of the file:

```
DO NiftyFor.WFM
```

This new form is then opened by accessing the Open( ) method. The rest of the .WFM file simply defines the new class so that dBASE for Windows knows how to create the form object when its class definition is used.

Your first custom class definition

As shown in the following example, the remaining lines in a .WFM file define a new class:

```
CLASS NIFTYFORFORM OF FORM
   this.HelpId = ""
   this.HelpFile = ""
   this.Left =            2.00
   this.Top =          2.00
   this.Text = "Form"
   this.Height =          20.00
   this.Width =          50.00

ENDCLASS
```

The class is called NIFTYFORFORM, and it is based on the existing FORM class. A new class definition is created for every form you create with the Form Designer. The next chapter has more information about creating new class definitions.

You have now seen the inner workings of the Form Designer. The commands, operators, and functions it uses to create and use new objects and new classes are the same ones you can use to write programs in dBASE for Windows. The next two chapters show you how it's done.

Chapter 15

Object Genesis

In This Chapter

▶ Creating the definition of an object

▶ Creating new definitions from existing definitions

▶ Modifying the Form Designer code

*I*n the beginning, there were no objects. Out of the void came dBASE for Windows to still the raging waters and bring forth Forms and objects. New Forms sprung up where there were none before. Objects begat objects. The objects were fruitful and multiplied. Their numbers were many.

You've already experienced the power of creation with dBASE for Windows. However, you don't have to be satisfied with simply creating objects. You can design an object's recipe and then use that recipe to create entirely new objects!

This chapter shows you how to create *classes*, which are the recipes for creating objects. You also learn a shortcut to creating classes in which you use an existing class as a template for the new one. It's a little like creating a masterpiece by tracing a van Gogh and then adding your own variations.

Creation versus Consumption

Throughout this book, you've been using objects to create applications. The nice people at Borland spent years creating classes for all of these objects so you wouldn't have to. However, you aren't limited to the classes that are included in dBASE for Windows. You can build your own.

There are many reasons for building your own classes. The pride of parenthood may even be one of them. Classes allow you to create the same type of object in many programs without building the object from scratch each time. If you change a class definition, the change automatically affects every program you've written that uses the class. This makes it possible to enhance or fix many applications at the same time.

In addition, building your own classes is an excellent way to write large, complex applications. When you've worked on an application for six or seven months, taken two or three vacations, and endured countless distractions due to fires, earthquakes, and irate customers, you're guaranteed to forget the purpose of some pieces of your application. When this happens, it becomes impossible to change pieces of the application without introducing bugs, because some other piece of the application that you've forgotten about usually depends on the piece that you need to change.

With classes, you can divide the requirements of an application into chunks of "responsibility." Each class you build can describe an object that has a specific set of responsibilities. When one object in your application needs to do something for which it isn't responsible, it simply asks the responsible object to please do its thing. With this approach to programming, you can change the way each object handles its area of responsibility as many times as you like without interfering with other objects in your application.

Building applications in this way takes even more practice than normal programming. It may seem strange at first, but once you get the hang of it, this approach offers tremendous benefits. Chapter 16 provides some tips on programming with classes, and helps you understand how to use classes effectively in dBASE for Windows. Even if you don't write applications by creating brand-new classes, learning how classes are created will help you understand what the Form Designer does when it creates a .WFM file. As a result, you will be able to modify the .WFM file directly, without using the Form Designer.

A recipe for objects

Classes are easy to create using dBASE for Windows. You use two commands to create any class. One command marks the beginning of the class definition; the other command marks the end of the class definition. Everything between these two commands defines the new class.

The command that marks the beginning of a class definition is CLASS *ClassName*. *ClassName* is the name that you want to assign to the new class definition. For example, the following command marks the beginning of a class named MyNewClass:

```
CLASS MyNewClass
```

The ENDCLASS command marks the end of a class definition. Here's a simple example using both the CLASS *ClassName* and ENDCLASS commands:

```
CLASS MyNewClass

  the details about the class go here ...

ENDCLASS
```

To start defining a new class, you must create a file for the class definition, and enter the CLASS *ClassName* and ENDCLASS commands in the new file:

1. Type the following command in the Command window, replacing *File-Name* with the name of the file you want to create:

   ```
   MODIFY COMMAND FileName
   ```

2. In the Program Editor that's displayed, type the following command to mark the beginning of the new class, replacing *ClassName* with the name you want to assign to the class:

   ```
   CLASS ClassName
   ```

3. Press Enter a few times to create some blank lines. You'll want to come back later and fill in the details of the class definition.

4. Type the following command to mark the end of the new class:

   ```
   ENDCLASS
   ```

5. Press Ctrl-W to save the new file.

This only creates the shell of a new class. Before you can start adding the details of the new class definition, you need to know a few more things.

Is it soup yet?

No, you haven't made soup quite yet. Your new class isn't ready to eat until you add some details between the CLASS *ClassName* and ENDCLASS commands. There are two parts to the details of a class definition:

- ✔ *Constructor code*, which is program code that is executed when a new object of this type is created, usually to define properties of the object.

- ✔ *Member functions*, or *methods*, which are procedures and functions that define the capabilities of the object.

Constructor code usually comes first in the details of a class definition, immediately following the CLASS *ClassName* command. To define properties using constructor code, you type the special object reference *this* followed by the dot operator and the name of the property you want to define. Then, you use the assignment operator to assign an initial value to the property. For example, the following constructor code creates a property called NumberProperty and assigns a zero to it:

```
this.NumberProperty = 0
```

After defining the properties of a class in the constructor code, you can define the methods. Methods are defined just like any other procedure or function, beginning with the FUNCTION keyword or the PROCEDURE keyword, and ending with the RETURN command if the method needs to return a value.

When you define a function using the FUNCTION command, the function must end by returning a value with the RETURN command. However, a procedure doesn't need to return a value. This is the only difference between a function and a procedure. Methods can be either procedures or functions, depending on whether or not they need to return a value using the RETURN command. ■

The following example adds a method called MyMethod, which returns a value after printing "MyMethod is YourMethod" in the Results window:

```
FUNCTION MyMethod
  ? "MyMethod is YourMethod"
RETURN .T.
```

Without the return value of .T., the same method can be defined as a procedure:

```
PROCEDURE MyMethod
  ? "MyMethod is YourMethod"
```

To see how this all works, let's build a real class definition for an Employee object:

1. Type the following command in the Command Window and press Enter:

```
MODIFY COMMAND EMPCLASS
```

2. Type the following class definition in the Program Editor that's displayed:

```
CLASS Employee
this.FirstName = ""
this.LastName = ""

PROCEDURE PrintFullName
```

```
        ? this.FirstName
        ? this.LastName
    ENDCLASS
```

3. Press Ctrl-W to save the EMPCLASS file.

A class called Employee now exists in the EMPCLASS program file. As you can see from the class definition, the Employee class has two properties. One property is ready to store a character value for the employee's first name. The other property is ready to store the employee's last name. The Employee class also has a single method called PrintFullName, which prints the employee's first and last names in the Results window.

Now, type the following command in the Command window and press Enter:

```
DO EMPCLASS
```

Nothing happens, right? Your screen flashes as the EMPCLASS program is executed, but nothing else happens because a class definition doesn't do anything by itself. Remember, a class is just a recipe. Before anything interesting can occur, an object must be created from the class using DEFINE or NEW.

Let's add a few lines to the EMPCLASS program to create and use an object from the Employee class:

1. Enter the following command in the Command Window:

```
MODIFY COMMAND EMPCLASS
```

2. Insert the following code before the command CLASS Employee:

```
SET TALK OFF

EmployeeObject = NEW Employee()
EmployeeObject.FirstName = "John"
EmployeeObject.LastName = "Galt"

EmployeeObject.PrintFullName()
```

3. Press Ctrl-W to save the modified EMPCLASS program.

Figure 15-1 shows the new EMPCLASS program. The first line, SET TALK OFF, tells dBASE for Windows to keep its chatter to itself. The next line, EmployeeObject = NEW Employee( ), simply creates an object from the class Employee and assigns it an object reference, EmployeeObject. Next, a first and last name are stored in the object's name properties. Finally, the program invokes the PrintFullName method to print the employee object's full name in the Results window.

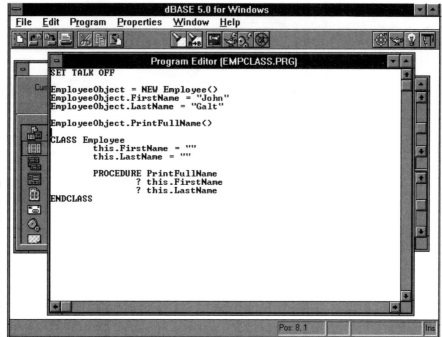

Figure 15-1:
EMPCLASS
combines a
class defini-
tion with
program
code to cre-
ate and use
an object.

Type the command DO EMPCLASS again in the Command window and press Enter. Figure 15-2 shows the results of this command.

Now you've made soup. That's all it takes to create a fully functional class definition in dBASE for Windows. The Employee class you've just created is a recipe for a *non-visual object*. Unlike a Form or a PushButton, a non-visual object can't be displayed on the screen. However, non-visual objects are still objects. When you write complete applications using your own classes, non-visual objects can be more important than the visual ones.

We know this Employee class is overly simplistic. Stay tuned for a more realistic example of how an Employee class can store and retrieve employee data using a table.

Building an object that can access a table

This section walks you, step by step, through the creation of an Employee class that can read from and write to an employee table. If you'd rather not see this right now, you have two options:

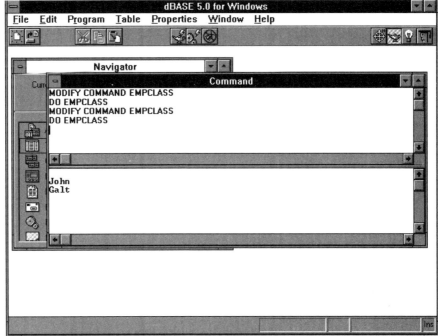

Figure 15-2:
The
results of
EMPCLASS
demon-
strate the
creation
and use
of an
Employee
object.

✔ Close your eyes when you read this section, or

✔ Skip to the section, "Swimming in the Object Gene Pool," to learn more about the power of classes.

Throughout this section, we'll explain why each step is taken, especially when we encounter an important application development concept. However, we're going to breeze through creating the employee table and editing files using MODIFY COMMAND. If you've read the previous 14 chapters, you should be able to follow along. If we do manage to lose you, here are some tips for catching up again:

✔ Re-read any steps that seem confusing. Try to imagine why the steps might be necessary.

✔ Refer to an earlier chapter that covers the steps in question.

✔ If all else fails, just move on to the next step. It's safe to assume that there's a reason for the steps you just took, and you'll probably understand it later if you keep going.

1. Enter the following command in the Command window to open the Table Designer:

```
CREATE EMPTABLE
```

2. Using Figure 15-3 as a guide, create the following three fields to store information about employees:

Field	Type	Width
FIRSTNAME	Character	15
LASTNAME	Character	20
EMPNUMBER	Numeric	5

3. Save EMPTABLE by pressing Ctrl-W. Your Employee objects will access this table.

4. Create a new program file called EMPTEST and enter the following code to define a new Employee class:

```
CLASS Employee
    this.FName = ""
    this.LName = ""
    this.EmpNum = 0

    PROCEDURE Save
        select EMPTABLE
        REPLACE EMPTABLE->FirstName WITH this.FName
        REPLACE EMPTABLE->LastName WITH this.LName
        REPLACE EMPTABLE->EmpNumber WITH this.EmpNum

    PROCEDURE Read(nEmpNumToFind)
        select EMPTABLE
        LOCATE FOR EMPTABLE->EmpNumber = nEmpNumToFind
        this.FName = EMPTABLE->FirstName
        this.LName = EMPTABLE->LastName
        this.EmpNum = EMPTABLE->EmpNumber

    PROCEDURE Print
        ? "My First Name Is: " + this.FName
        ? "My Last Name Is: " + this.LName
        ? "My Employee Number Is: ", this.EmpNum
ENDCLASS
```

This class definition begins by defining three properties for the Employee object: FName, LName, and EmpNum. Then, three methods are defined: Save, Read, and Print. The Save method simply selects EMPTABLE and stores the Employee object's properties in fields of the table. The Read method accepts

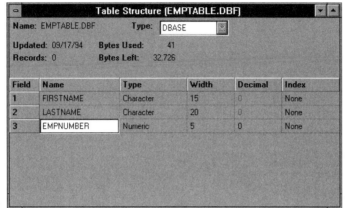

Figure 15-3:
EMPTABLE
will be used
to store
information
about
employees.

one parameter—the employee number to read—finds the right record in the
table, and stores the contents of the table's fields in the Employee object's
properties. The Print method prints the Employee object's properties in the
Results window.

As you know, a class definition doesn't do anything by itself. You need to add
program code to the EMPTEST program to create and use an Employee
object. Using Figure 15-4 as a guide, move to the top of the program file and
insert the following lines:

```
SET TALK OFF
USE EMPTABLE

Bob = NEW Employee()
APPEND BLANK
Bob.FName = "Bob"
Bob.LName = "Jones"
Bob.EmpNum = 1
Bob.Save()

Mary = NEW Employee()
APPEND BLANK
Mary.FName = "Mary"
Mary.LName = "Smith"
Mary.EmpNum = 2
Mary.Save()

EmployeeOfTheMonth = NEW Employee()
EmployeeOfTheMonth.Read(1)
? "Congratulations to our Employee of the Month:"
EmployeeOfTheMonth.Print()
```

Figure 15-4:
Program
code must
appear
before the
class defini-
tion in a
program
file.

The program begins with the SET TALK OFF command, which you've seen before. Next, the program opens the EMPTABLE table. A new Employee object is created, and it is assigned an object reference of Bob. The APPEND BLANK command is used to create a new record in the EMPTABLE table. Then, Bob's first name, last name, and employee number are stored in the Employee object's properties, and Bob is saved in the table using the Employee object's Save( ) method.

This process is repeated for an Employee named Mary Smith. Then, a new Employee object is created called EmployeeOfTheMonth. The Read( ) method is used to read the employee of the month into the Employee object. Then, the text "Congratulations to our Employee of the Month:" is printed in the Results window, and the Print( ) method is used to print the employee's first name, last name, and employee number in the Results window.

Press Ctrl-W to save the EMPTEST program. To run this program, type DO EMPTEST in the Command window and press Enter. Figure 15-5 shows the output from this program.

This example demonstrates how you might use a non-visual object in your application. If a class, such as Employee, is the only class responsible for

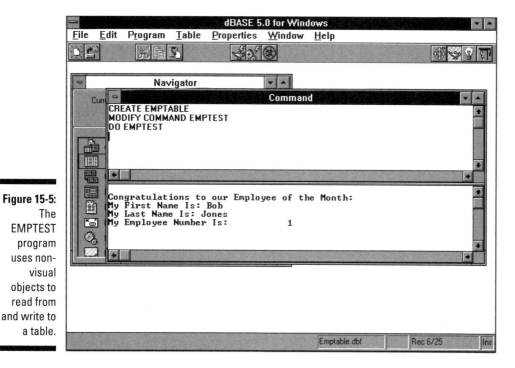

Figure 15-5:
The
EMPTEST
program
uses non-
visual
objects to
read from
and write to
a table.

making changes to an employee table, you will always know where to look if you need to modify the way your application uses the employee table. This is a better approach to application development than having several procedures in your application make changes to the employee table.

Swimming in the Object Gene Pool

The first part of this chapter shows you how to create and use a class definition. This is creation at its highest level, making something from nothing.

dBASE for Windows also gives you the ability to create new classes from existing ones. This is like taking a recipe for meat loaf and adding salsa to create a recipe for taco loaf.

To create new classes from existing ones, dBASE for Windows uses something known as *inheritance*. Inheritance is the process of creating something new by starting with the properties of something old. For example, the taco loaf inherits all of the wonderful features of your meat loaf, and then, with the addition of salsa, it becomes taco loaf. Without the meat loaf to inherit from, the taco loaf would just be salsa.

To create a new class using inheritance, you add the following code to the CLASS *ClassName* command:

```
OF BaseClassName
```

BaseClassName is the name of the class from which you want to inherit. For example, the following command marks the beginning of a new class called NewFormClass, which is inherited from the base class called FORM:

```
CLASS NewFormClass OF FORM
```

To mark the end of an inherited class definition, you use the ENDCLASS command just like you would for a normal class. The following code shows the shell of an inherited class:

```
CLASS NewFormClass OF FORM

... details of the class definition go here ...

ENDCLASS
```

In this example, NewFormClass is inherited from the FORM class. In other words, NewFormClass is a fully functional FORM class that can be used to create Form objects. As shown in the following example, if you add properties and methods to the NewFormClass, the Forms you create using New-FormClass will have all the properties and methods of a normal Form, plus the ones you add:

```
CLASS NewFormClass OF FORM

   this.NewProperty = ""
   this.AnotherProperty = ""

   PROCEDURE NewMethod
      ? "This is a new method"

ENDCLASS
```

Inheritance is an important feature of dBASE for Windows. Used creatively, inheritance can help you build complex applications with minimal effort.

Inheritance helps you create powerful programs without repeating a lot of program code. You can create a base class that fits most of the needs of your objects, and then create additional classes by inheriting from the base class. Not only does this free you from writing lots of duplicate program code, it helps keep your program bug-free. Once the base class is created and debugged, your inherited classes will start out without bugs.

Defining objects as part of a class definition

When you are creating a new class, you can create objects from other classes within your new class! This is like taking all the properties and methods of one class and inserting them as a part of your new class. As shown in the following example, you do this by using the DEFINE command:

```
CLASS NewFormClass OF FORM

   DEFINE PushButton PushMe OF this

ENDCLASS
```

This example creates a PushButton object called PushMe as part of the class called NewFormClass. Let's see how this PushButton works as a part of a NewFormClass object:

1. Create a new program file using MODIFY COMMAND.

2. Enter the following lines in the beginning of the program:

```
NewFormClassObject = NEW NewFormClass()
Inspect(NewFormClassObject)
```

3. Enter the example NewFormClass class definition:

```
CLASS NewFormClass OF FORM

    DEFINE PushButton PushMe OF this

ENDCLASS
```

4. Save the program file, and then execute it using the DO command. When the Properties window appears on the screen, click the Properties tab to see the PUSHME object (see Figure 15-6).

Chapter 14 showed you how to set the properties of an object using the DEFINE command. As you'll see in the following section, this is exactly what the Form Designer does when it creates a new FORM class.

Journey to the center of the form

In Chapter 14, you had the opportunity to dive 20,000 leagues under the Form to see the inner workings of the Form Designer. You saw how new Forms are created with the class definition that's created by the Form Designer, and

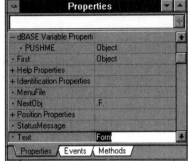

you didn't even have to use SCUBA gear. In this section, we head straight for the heart of the matter and examine the class definition that's created by the Form Designer.

dBASE for Windows uses inheritance when it creates a new Form using the Form Designer. As described in Chapter 14, dBASE for Windows has a built-in class known as the FORM class. When you issue the command CREATE FORM, the Form Designer uses the basic FORM class as a template for creating an entirely new form class.

Let's take another look at the Form Designer code from Chapter 14. The following .WFM file was created by issuing the command CREATE FORM and immediately saving the new Form:

```
** END HEADER - do not remove this line*
* Generated on 08/25/94
*
LOCAL f
f = NEW NIFTYFORFORM()
f.Open()

CLASS NIFTYFORFORM OF FORM
  this.HelpId = ""
  this.HelpFile = ""
  this.Left =            2.00
  this.Top =             2.00
  this.Text = "Form"
  this.Height =          20.00
  this.Width =           50.00

ENDCLASS
```

As you can see, a new class called NIFTYFORFORM is created from the existing FORM class. Inside the class definition, several properties are defined.

Actually, these properties already exist in the FORM class, so they aren't created again, they're just set equal to the indicated values.

Let's take a look at how the Form Designer uses the DEFINE command to create objects within the new Form class:

1. Open the Form Designer by typing the following command in the Command window and pressing Enter:

```
CREATE FORM DefTest
```

2. Using the Controls Palette, place a few PushButtons and a ListBox on the Form.

3. Press Ctrl-W to save the new Form.

4. To see the code that the Form Designer generated, type the following command in the Command window:

```
MODIFY COMMAND DefTest.WFM
```

Figure 15-7 shows the code that's displayed.

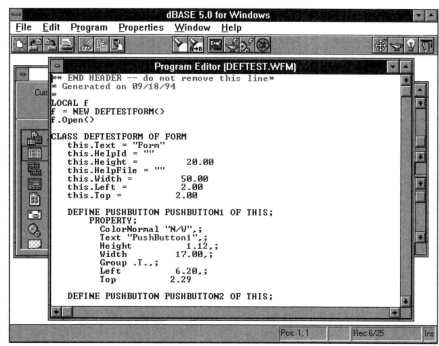

Figure 15-7: The Form Designer uses the DEFINE command to create objects within a new class definition.

Now that you're familiar with class definitions, you can modify the .WFM file to your heart's content. Any changes you make will be reflected the next time you use the Form Designer to modify the .WFM file. If you manage to do something that the Form Designer doesn't understand, it will complain, and allow you to fix the problem.

Kids Are for Mowing the Lawn

Creating new classes from existing classes through inheritance is almost like creating little offspring of the original class. Because we all know what kids are really for, let's put them to work.

When a new class is created from an existing class, the new class is called a *sub-class* of the existing class. From the perspective of the sub-class, the original class is called a *super-class*. This is similar to referring to you as a super-parent.

When the class definition of the super-class includes methods, the sub-class can do one of three things with each method:

- Use the method of the super-class as though it is a method of the sub-class.
- Override the method of the super-class with a new method of the same name in the sub-class.
- Extend the method of the super-class so that the same method in the sub-class can do everything it does in the super-class, and more.

You don't have to do anything to use a method of the super-class as though it is a method of the sub-class. Because the sub-class has inherited the method from the super-class, it can automatically use the method. For example, assume that the following class definitions are a super-class and a sub-class:

```
CLASS ExampleClass
  PROCEDURE ExampleMethod
      ? "This is a method"
ENDCLASS

CLASS ExampleSubClass OF ExampleClass
* sub-class details go here, but they aren't important right now.
ENDCLASS
```

Any objects created from the ExampleSubClass class will have a method called ExampleMethod. The following simple program file illustrates this point. Notice how ExampleObject.ExampleMethod() works just fine:

```
SET TALK OFF

ExampleObject = NEW ExampleSubClass()
ExampleObject.ExampleMethod()

CLASS ExampleClass
  PROCEDURE ExampleMethod
     ? "This is a method"
ENDCLASS

CLASS ExampleSubClass OF ExampleClass
* sub-class details go here, but they aren't important right now.
ENDCLASS
```

The following sections show you how a sub-class can either override or extend the method of a super-class.

I'll do it my own way

Children think they know how to do things better than their parents 100% of the time. Most parents know they're right about 2% of the time. In dBASE for Windows, the class definitions that are created by inheriting from a super-class can override the methods of the super-class. To do this, all you need to do is create a method in the sub-class and give it the same name as a method of the super-class.

Be careful to avoid accidentally overriding the methods of the built-in classes. For example, if you accidentally override the Open() method when creating new Form classes by inheriting from CLASS FORM, the form will not open properly. If you aren't sure, check the dBASE for Windows manual for a list of the built-in methods. ■

There may be cases in which you need to override the member functions of the super-class. The new sub-class may need that member function to behave in a totally different way. For example, two classes might inherit from an Employee class that has a PayMe method. The PayMe method for a Salaried_Employee class is probably quite different from the PayMe method for an Hourly_Employee class. If so, you would need to override the PayMe method of the Employee class to make sure the PayMe method behaves correctly in these new sub-classes.

To see how this example works, you can type the following program in a new program file and execute it using the DO command:

```
SET TALK OFF

NormalEmployee = NEW Employee()
NormalEmployee.PayMe()

SalariedEmployee = NEW Salaried_Employee()
SalariedEmployee.PayMe()

HourlyEmployee = NEW Hourly_Employee()
HourlyEmployee.PayMe()

CLASS Employee
  Procedure PayMe
     ? "Here's $20, now get back to work."
ENDCLASS

CLASS Salaried_Employee OF Employee
  Procedure PayMe
     ? "What?? This company pays you too much already!"
ENDCLASS

CLASS Hourly_Employee OF Employee
  Procedure PayMe
     ? "You only worked 80 hours this week... You're lazy."
ENDCLASS
```

As you can see from Figure 15-8, the PayMe method behaves differently for each type of employee object.

I look like my dad, but act like my friends

There are cases in which the capabilities of a super-class are required in the sub-class, but the sub-class needs to go one step farther. In such cases, you can extend the methods of the super-class.

To do this, you override the method of the super-class. Then, in the first line of the method for the sub-class, you use the *scope resolution operator* to call the method of the super-class. The scope resolution operator tells dBASE for Windows that you want to execute the method of the super-class, not the method of the sub-class. Here's how it's used:

```
SUPER::MethodName()
```

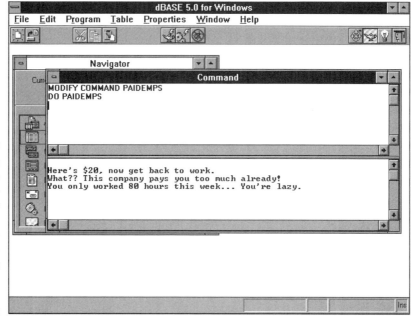

Figure 15-8:
The results
of this pro-
gram show
how each
employee
object can
have its
own PayMe
method.

MethodName is the name of the method in the super-class that you want to execute.

As shown in the following example, once the method of the super-class is executed, the method of the sub-class can take over:

```
SET TALK OFF

NormalEmployee = NEW Employee()
NormalEmployee.PayMe()

AbnormalEmployee = NEW SubEmployee()
AbnormalEmployee.PayMe()

CLASS Employee
  Procedure PayMe
     ? "Here's $20, now get back to work."
ENDCLASS

CLASS SubEmployee OF Employee
  Procedure PayMe
     SUPER::PayMe()
     ? "Thanks for the $20, I quit."
ENDCLASS
```

Figure 15-9 shows the results of this program. Notice that the PayMe method of the Employee class is executed twice. It's executed once by the NormalEmployee object, and once by the AbnormalEmployee object. Then, the AbnormalEmployee object extends the PayMe method of the Employee class by quitting. Wouldn't you?

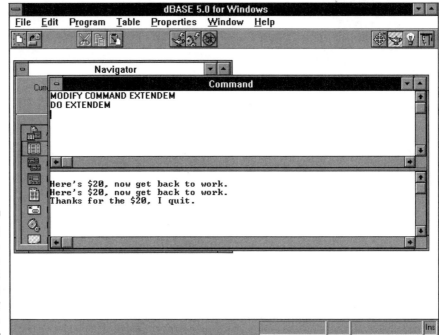

Figure 15-9:
The methods of a super-class can be extended by a sub-class.

The concepts in this chapter can help you release the true power of the dBASE for Windows programming language. You now know how the Form Designer works. As a result, you can modify the Form Designer-generated code. You can also create entirely new classes when the built-in ones aren't enough. The next chapter continues your adventure in programming with dBASE for Windows.

Chapter 16

Programming with Class

. . . .

. . . .

So far, this book has showed you the nitty-gritty basics of programming in dBASE for Windows. This chapter covers some of the finer points, including how to write procedures and functions that aren't methods and aren't tied to events. You learn about the dBASE for Windows compiler and what it can do for you. You also find out how to move information around in your program.

You Can't Get There from Here

Sometimes, you need to write procedures and functions that can be used by your program, but they don't really fit anywhere. For example, you might create a function that calculates how many shopping days are left until your birthday, only to find that this function doesn't fit in the class definitions of the objects you have designed for your application. Never fear, you can still include this function in your application.

When your application includes procedures and functions that are not included in class definitions, they are called *stand-alone procedures* and *stand-*

alone functions. Writing these procedures and functions isn't much different from creating event procedures and member functions.

You can store stand-alone procedures and functions in two places:

- ✔ The file that contains your class definitions. In this case, they must be included outside of the CLASS...ENDCLASS definitions, either before the first CLASS command or after the last ENDCLASS command.
- ✔ A separate *procedure file*, which you create specifically for storing stand-alone procedures and functions.

Whether you store your procedures and functions in the file with your class definitions or create a separate procedure file, you need to issue the SET PROCEDURE command before you try to use your stand-alone procedures and stand-alone functions.

To see how this works, let's use the Form Designer to create a form called SPUDS.WFM. This form lets couch potatoes track whether their favorite television shows are playing new episodes or reruns.

In addition to the tracking form, our application will include a stand-alone procedure that connects the T.V. remote control to the serial port on the computer, and allows the user to change the channel. As detailed in the following sections, you can either include this procedure in the file that contains the class definition for your form, or you can create a separate file for storing your stand-alone procedure.

Storing stand-alone procedures with class definitions

Let's start building the couch potato application:

1. Create a form in the Form Designer by entering the command CREATE FORM in the Command window.

2. Find the Controls window and place a Text control on your form. Click on this Text control in the Form Designer, find the Properties window, and change the Text control's Text property to "Favorite T.V. show:". Although it isn't necessary for this example, you can add some more controls to the form.

3. Save the form and close the Form Designer by pressing Ctrl-W. When prompted for a filename, enter SPUDS. The form is saved with the filename SPUDS.WFM. Now you can add your stand-alone procedure to this file.

4. To edit the code that was just created by the Form Designer, enter the following command in the Command window and press Enter:

```
MODIFY COMMAND SPUDS.WFM
```

5. The SPUDS.WFM file is opened in the Command Editor. Enter the command, SET PROCEDURE TO SPUDS.WFM just before the LOCAL command in SPUDS.WFM. Here's what the code should look like in the Command Editor (you'll actually see more code than this; we only listed the important parts):

```
** END HEADER — do not remove this line*
* Generated on 08/29/94
*
SET PROCEDURE TO SPUDS.WFM
LOCAL f
f = NEW SPUDS()
f.Open()

CLASS SPUDS OF FORM
...
```

6. Now you need to add your stand-alone procedure to SPUDS.WFM. Remember that you enter stand-alone procedures and functions outside the class definition. Enter the following procedure immediately after the ENDCLASS command:

```
PROCEDURE RemoteControl
IF Show = Favorite
    Blah Blah Blah
ENDIF
```

7. Save your program file by pressing Ctrl-W.

The following code shows the key elements of the SPUDS.WFM file, which now contains our RemoteControl procedure as well as the class definition for this form:

```
** END HEADER — do not remove this line*
* Generated on 08/29/94
*
SET PROCEDURE TO SPUDS.WFM
LOCAL f
f = NEW SPUDS()
f.Open()

CLASS SPUDS OF FORM
  this.Top =        2.00
  this.Width =     40.00
```

```
this.Text = "Spuds"
this.Height =          15.00
this.Left =            2.00

DEFINE TEXT TEXT1 OF THIS;
    PROPERTY;
    Top           0.63,;
    Width           14.75,;
    Text "Favorite T.V. show:",;
    ColorNormal "N/W",;
    Height          1.56,;
    Left           1.63,;
    Border .F.
ENDCLASS

PROCEDURE RemoteControl
IF Show = Favorite
  Blah Blah Blah
ENDIF
```

In addition to the class definition and the stand-alone procedure, this file includes the comments that are generated by the Form Designer. (Now you know when this chapter was written.) After the comments, you inserted the following command:

```
SET PROCEDURE TO SPUDS.WFM
```

This command tells dBASE for Windows where to look for stand-alone procedures and functions. In this case, they are found in the form file, SPUDS.WFM.

You also inserted the RemoteControl procedure immediately after the class definition. In the interest of full disclosure, we must admit that the statement "Blah Blah Blah" in this procedure doesn't actually connect the T.V. remote control to the serial port on the computer. As mentioned, you might add several procedures to a file.

Storing stand-alone procedures in a separate file

Instead of adding the RemoteControl procedure to SPUDS.WFM, you might decide to create a separate file for storing your stand-alone procedures and functions. To create a procedure file:

1. Enter the command, MODIFY COMMAND *MyProc* in the Command window. *MyProc* represents the name you choose for your procedure file.

This command opens the dBASE for Windows Command Editor, and you can start entering your stand-alone procedures and functions.

2. Enter as many procedures and functions as you want. Remember to include the keyword PROCEDURE or FUNCTION before each one. In addition, functions always end with the command RETURN, followed by a value.

3. Save your procedure file by pressing Ctrl-W. The procedure file is saved with the extension .PRG.

4. Enter the SET PROCEDURE command in the program that uses the stand-alone procedures or functions that are stored in your procedure file. For example, let's assume you stored the RemoteControl procedure in a procedure file named MyProc.prg. To use this stand-alone procedure in the example application, you need to add the following command to SPUDS.WFM (the .prg extension is optional):

```
SET PROCEDURE TO MyProc.prg
```

You should insert this command near the beginning of the main program file. As shown in Figure 16-1, this command allows a program file to use procedures and functions that are stored in a separate procedure file. Whether the main program is stored in a .PRG file or a .WFM file, the program file needs to know where to find your new procedures.

The Form Designer creates files with the extension .WFM. When referring to these files, you must include the .WFM extension. Program files that are not created by the Form Designer have the extension .PRG. If a program filename doesn't include a .WFM extension, the .PRG extension is assumed. ▨

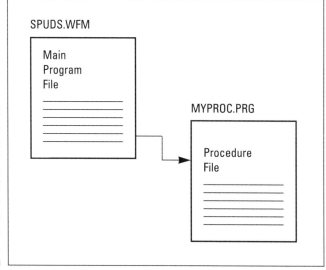

Figure 16-1:
You can create a procedure file to hold stand-alone procedures and functions.

SPUDS.WFM

Main
Program
File

MYPROC.PRG

Procedure
File

Go Out for a Pass!

The term *passing* means moving information around in your application. The information you pass around is called a *parameter*. You can pass parameters to both procedures and functions. In fact, you can have a nice game of catch with a function, because functions always return a value to the programs that call them. As a result, you can pass a parameter to a function and you can be sure it will pass back a value.

Whether you are playing football or writing dBASE for Windows programs, a good pass requires a quarterback and a receiver. The following sections describe both ends of a completed pass in dBASE for Windows.

Please pass the parameter

As shown in the following examples, there are two ways to pass parameters to a procedure:

- ✔ Do MyProc WITH Value1, Value2, Value3
- ✔ MyProc (Value1, Value2, Value3)

By including the keyword WITH in a command, you are telling dBASE for Windows that the values that follow are parameters. The keyword WITH can be followed by any number of parameters, which are separated by commas. The second example shows that you can also pass parameters to procedures by enclosing the parameters in parentheses.

The following example shows how you pass parameters to a function:

```
MyFunction(Value1, Value2, Value3)
```

Parameters can be variables, fields, objects, or values. The following example calls a function, and passes it a variable, a field, an object, and a value:

```
MyFunction(nValue1, Animal->Name, MyForm, {01/05/95})
```

Catch as catch can

The procedure or function that is receiving the parameters can do so in one of two ways:

- ✔ Using the PARAMETERS command followed by the variables that will receive the parameters. For example, the following command will receive a parameter called MyParam:

```
PARAMETERS MyParam
```

✔ Enclosing variable names in parentheses after the name of the receiving procedure or function. The parentheses should contain a variable for each passed parameter. For example, the following procedure will accept a parameter called MyParam:

```
PROCEDURE ExampleProcedure(MyParam)
```

The following example shows how parameters can be passed to a function, received, and used:

```
cMolecule = "CH₄"

IDENTIFY(cMolecule)

FUNCTION IDENTIFY(cStuff)

DO CASE
CASE cStuff = "CH₄"
  cName = "Methane"
CASE cStuff = "C₈H₁₀O₂N₄H₂O"
  cName = "Caffeine"
ENDCASE
RETURN cName
```

This example shows how an unknown gas might be passed to an IDENTIFY function, which accepts the parameter as cStuff. The IDENTIFY function then identifies the gas and returns its name.

As shown in the following example, you can also receive parameters and assign them to variables by using the PARAMETERS command. However, the PARAMETERS command is provided only for compatibility with older versions of dBASE. Although you really should use the approach that's demonstrated in the preceding example, here's how the PARAMETERS command is used (in case you're interested):

```
cMolecule = "CH₄"

IDENTIFY( cMolecule )

FUNCTION IDENTIFY
PARAMETERS cStuff
DO CASE
CASE cStuff = "CH₄"
  cName = "Methane"
CASE cStuff = "C₈H₁₀O₂N₄H₂O"
```

```
      cName = "Caffeine"
   ENDCASE
   RETURN cName
```

When you want to receive a value that is returned by a function, you set a variable equal to the result of the function. The following example shows you how to receive the value that's returned by the IDENTIFY( ) function:

```
   cTheName = IDENTIFY(cMolecule)
```

This statement creates a variable called cTheName, which receives the value that is returned by the IDENTIFY function. In this example, the IDENTIFY function is used both to accept a parameter and return a value.

If you are creating a procedure that is to return a value, you should write it as a function. Returning a value is what functions do best. We recommend using the right tool for the right job. ■

Playing Catch with the Form

The preceding section shows you how information is passed to and from procedures and functions. You can also pass information to and from a form. You use this capability when you want to set the properties of the form or one of its controls. For example, you can set the text property of a form by passing the text as a parameter in the NEW command:

```
   Myform = NEW FORM("This is a test form")
```

To return information from a form, you must use a special method to open the form. So far in this book, you have opened forms by using the Open( ) method. If you need to return a value, you open the form using the Read-Modal( ) method. The behavior of this method differs from the Open( ) method in two important ways:

✔ When a form is opened with ReadModal( ), you can't access any other forms or windows until this window is closed. You might say that the form is opened in jealous mode.

✔ ReadModal( ) can return a value. If no return value is specified, Read-Modal( ) returns the name of the last object to have focus in the form before it closed. For example, if you close the form using a button named OKButton, this name is the value that is returned by ReadModal( ).

You can use the ReadModal( ) method to open forms in which the user must make a choice, or selection. These forms are sometimes called *pop-up windows*. For example, you might have a form with a ListBox full of state names.

The user selects a name from the ListBox, the form goes away, and the selected state name is returned to the program.

When creating a form that will be opened with the ReadModal( ) method, you must set the MDI property to .F. (false). The ReadModal( ) method will not work correctly if the form's MDI property is .T. (true).

Let's create a form that returns a value:

1. Open the Form Designer to create a new form by typing CREATE FORM in the Command window.

2. You need to change the MDI property of the form. Click on the form with your right mouse button, and select Object Properties from the pop-up menu that's displayed. In the Properties window, select .F. from the drop-down ListBox to the right of the MDI property.

3. Find the Controls window and add some controls to your form.

4. The last control you add to the form should be a PushButton. Select the PushButton icon in the Controls window and click in the Form Designer to place a PushButton on the form. In the following steps, we'll make this control an OK button that the user clicks to close the form.

5. With the PushButton selected, choose the Events tab in the Properties window.

6. Click the tool icon for the OnClick event. This opens the Procedures window.

7. In the Procedures window, enter the following code:

```
Form.Close("Hi there!")
```

8. Save the form by pressing Ctrl-W. When prompted for a filename, enter MyForm.

9. To open this form with the ReadModal( ) method, you need to modify the code that the Form Designer has created. To open this file in the Command Editor, type the following command in the Command window and press Enter:

```
MODIFY COMMAND MyForm.WFM
```

10. Replace the call to the f.Open( ) method with the following code:

```
MyVariable = f.ReadModal()

? MyVariable
```

11. Save your .WFM file and exit the Command Editor by pressing Ctrl-W.

With a few exceptions, this is how you have created many other forms. The first difference is that you changed the value of the MDI property to .F. (false). This makes it possible to open the form using the ReadModal( ) method.

Aside from the text you included in the parentheses of the CLOSE( ) method, the PushButton that closes the form is a lot like any other PushButton you have created. This text is the value that will be returned when a user closes the form. If we left this out, the return value would be the PushButton's name.

To change the way the form is opened, you modified the Form Designer code by replacing the Open( ) method with the ReadModal( ) method. You also created a new variable named MyVariable, and set it equal to the value that's returned by the ReadModal( ) method. The next line you added prints the value of MyVariable in the Results window so you can see what gets returned.

When you run this form, you should see "Hi there!" printed in the Results window after you click the PushButton.

Using the Procedure Editor to Simplify Programming

In Chapter 15, you learned how to write stand-alone procedures and functions using the dBASE for Windows Command Editor. You may decide that you want to write those procedures while you are still using the Form Designer.

To write stand-alone procedures and functions in the Procedure Editor while you are using the Form Designer:

1. Open the Procedure Editor by double clicking the form with your left mouse button.

2. As shown in Figure 16-2, there is a ListBox in the upper-left corner of the Procedure Editor. Click the down-arrow icon and select (General).

3. Enter your procedures and functions in the Procedure Editor. They will be saved in the (General) section of the .WFM file, which is outside of the Form's class definition. When you're done, close and save the form using Ctrl-W, just as you always do. The .WFM file is saved, including all of the stand-alone procedures and stand-alone functions.

As shown in Figure 16-3, a .WFM file has three sections. You use the (Header) section to set environment variables such as SET TALK OFF and SET PRINTER TO LPT2. As explained in the next section, you can also define constants or include files.

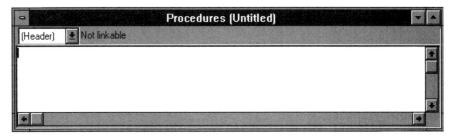

Figure 16-2: You can use the Procedure Editor to write stand-alone procedures and functions.

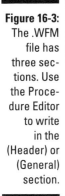

Figure 16-3: The .WFM file has three sections. Use the Procedure Editor to write in the (Header) or (General) section.

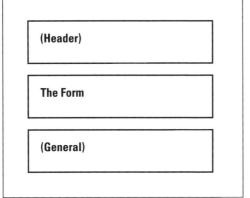

The Form section of the .WFM file is generated by the Form Designer. This section includes the class definition of the new Form, the code for creating the new Form object, and the code for opening the Form. You can use the Command Editor to modify this section. You can't edit the Form section of the .WFM file with the Procedure Editor.

The (General) section of the .WFM file is used to create stand-alone procedures and functions, or more class definitions.

Putting It All Together

dBASE for Windows uses something known as a *compiler* to read through your programs and translate them into a language the computer can understand. No matter how smart you think your computer is, it can't speak English, or even the dBASE for Windows Command Language. Your computer relies on dBASE for Windows to create programs that it can understand. This process is called *compiling*.

dBASE for Windows automatically compiles program files when you run them. Table 16-1 lists the file types that can be compiled. The first time you run a program, it takes a little longer because dBASE for Windows compiles the program. The compiler also reports errors when it finds them. Figure 16-4 shows the dialog box the compiler uses to tell you what the problem is and where to find it.

Table 16-1: Program file types that can be compiled

File Type	Compiled Version	Description
PRG	PRO	Program file created with the Command Editor
WFM	WFO	Form file created with the Form Designer
QBE	QBO	Query file created with the Query Designer
H	O	Header file created with the Command Editor
CC	CO	Custom Control file created with the Command Editor
MNU	MNO	Menu file created with the Menu Designer
FMT	FMO	dBASE IV form file
FRG	FRO	dBASE IV report file
LBG	LBO	dBASE IV label file

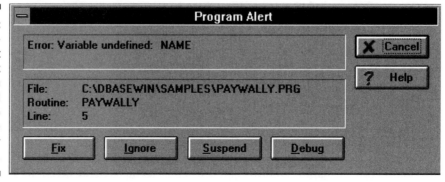

Figure 16-4: The Program Alert dialog box tells you when and where to find the bugs in your program.

I'm sorry Dave, I'm afraid you can't do that

If a program file contains an error, the compiler tells you what the error message is, and on what line you can find the problem. The compiler also gives you the option of fixing the problem. If you click the Fix button, the compiler opens the Command Editor and takes you right to the problem. After you fix the problem, dBASE for Windows tries to recompile the program. You can also try ignoring the problem. If the bug isn't too serious, sometimes you can get away with choosing Ignore.

You can also Suspend execution of the program without taking the program out of memory. You can only use the Suspend option if the error message appears while your program is running. This is also true of the Debug option. When your program fails while executing, you have the option of starting the dBASE for Windows Debugger.

Smile rhymes with compile

You'll smile, too when you learn that dBASE for Windows automatically recompiles your program every time you make a change. When you run a program, dBASE for Windows compares the date and time on the compiled version of the program file with the date and time on the uncompiled version. If the files have different date and time indicators, dBASE for Windows runs the compiler.

You can run the compiler yourself. This is useful for checking your program without running it. For example, if the program takes a long time to run, and you want to use the compiler to catch any obvious bugs, you can enter the COMPILE command in the Command window, followed by the name of your program file:

```
COMPILE SourceFile
```

As shown in Figure 16-5, the compiler displays a status window that lets you see what's happening while the compiler checks your program.

Remember, the compiler automatically recompiles whenever you make changes to any of the file types listed in Table 16-1. If your changes aren't appearing and you get the feeling that the compiler isn't recompiling your program, you should exit dBASE for Windows and restart the application. Sometimes, dBASE for Windows gets confused.

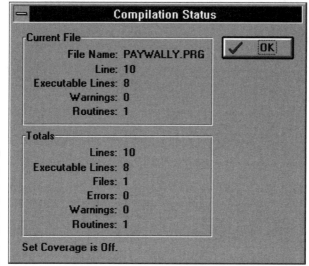

Figure 16-5:
The Compiler keeps
you up to
date on its
progress.

For More Power, Press the # Key

The really wonderful thing about dBASE for Windows is that the more you know, the easier it gets. Although the feature we discuss in this section has a big, scary name—*preprocessor directives*—it's really very simple.

A preprocessor directive is a command that tells the compiler what to do. You can use several preprocessor directives in your applications. Whenever your application is compiled, these preprocessor directives talk to the compiler and tell it important things about your program.

dBASE for Windows has several preprocessor directives, including:

- ✔ #define, which is used for controlling program compilation or defining constants.
- ✔ #ifdef, which tells the compiler to compile a section of code only if an identifier has been defined with #define.
- ✔ #ifndef, which tells the compiler to compile a section of code only if an identifier has not been defined with #define.
- ✔ #undef, which "un-defines" an identifier created with #define.
- ✔ #include, which tells the compiler to insert the contents of another file into the program.

A very defined way to do things

The #define preprocessor directive (which is pronounced pound-define) usually appears at the beginning of your program, or in the (Header) section of a .WFM file. As shown in the following example, you use this preprocessor directive to create an identifier that is usually written in uppercase letters:

```
#define MYIDENTIFIER
```

With this preprocessor directive, our program now includes an identifier that is meaningful only to the compiler. The first use of this identifier is in directing how the compiler compiles our program. This is demonstrated in the following example, which also uses another of the preprocessor directives:

```
#define DEBUG

#ifdef DEBUG
   SET TALK ON
   ? "Program started in Debug mode"
#else
   SET TALK OFF
#endif
```

In this example, we create an identifier called DEBUG. When this file is compiled, the compiler sees this identifier and remembers it. Remember, the #define command talks directly to the compiler. At this point, the compiler is translating our program into computerese.

Next, the compiler sees the preprocessor directive #ifdef. This preprocessor directive means, "if DEBUG is defined (which it is), then compile the program using the code that follows, otherwise compile the program using the code after the #else." Because the DEBUG identifier is defined in the first line of this file, the commands SET TALK ON and ? "Program started in Debug mode" will be compiled.

This is a handy way to switch between debugging a program and using it normally. You can add preprocessor directives such as these when you'd like to do something differently while you're debugging than when you're running the program normally. By simply adding or removing the line #define DEBUG in the beginning of the program, you can tell your program whether you're debugging it or running it normally. Your program will alter its behavior accordingly.

Depending on your needs, you might use the #ifndef, or if not defined, directive. You can also undefine the identifier with #undef.

You can constantly make things better

The preceding section describes how you can use #define to control compilation of your program. You can also use #define to create constants. For example, assume that the sales tax in your state is 8%. If you apply the sales tax by multiplying everything in your program by .08, you'll have to make numerous changes in your program every time the tax rate changes.

You can eliminate this maintenance headache by using #define to create a constant called SALESTAX. With #define, you can define the sales tax as a constant at the beginning of your program. The compiler replaces this value during compilation, before dBASE for Windows runs your program. If the constant needs to be changed, you make the change in one place, at the beginning of your program. Here's how it's done:

```
#define PRICE_WITH_TAX 1.08

PROCEDURE Calculate_Price
ThePrice = Inventory->Price
NewPrice = ThePrice * PRICE_WITH_TAX
```

First, you create an identifier called PRICE_WITH_TAX. Because this identifier is followed by a value, dBASE for Windows uses the identifier as a constant. The value can be any variable type. The value in our example is numeric. After creating this identifier, you can use PRICE_WITH_TAX as a constant in your program to calculate the total price with tax.

If a very long expression is used in several places in your program, you can save the expression as a constant. As demonstrated in the following example, this can reduce the possibility of making typing errors and it makes your program more readable:

```
#define CREDIT_RISK CUSTOMER->BALANCE > 10000 .AND.;
 CUSTOMER->TERMS< 30 .AND.(DATE() - CUSTOMER->LASTPAID) > 90

IF CREDIT_RISK
  ? "CREDIT DENIED"
ELSE
  ? "CREDIT APPROVED"
ENDIF

SET FILTER TO CREDIT_RISK
GO TOP
```

Using the Other Person's Controls in Your Program

You can install custom controls in dBASE for Windows. These control objects aren't usually found in the Controls window. A custom control might be a PushButton with a special graphic that prompts the user. For example, a large red hand might mean STOP!

Custom controls allow you to add controls to your forms other than the simple PushButtons, ListBoxes, and EntryFields you've worked with so far. For example, a custom control might be a large clock that allows the user to pick the current time by clicking on the clock face. Custom controls can be created using either Visual Basic or dBASE for Windows.

Installing custom controls

You can use the custom controls that come with dBASE for Windows, or you might choose to create and load your own custom controls. dBASE for Windows' custom controls are stored in files with the .CC extension. The custom controls that come with dBASE for Windows are found in a file called BUTTONS.CC. If you're interested, you can use the Command Editor to examine the contents of BUTTONS.CC.

When you install custom controls, they appear in the Custom tab of the Controls window when you are using the Form Designer.

To install custom controls:

1. Open the Form Designer by issuing the CREATE FORM command in the Command window.

2. From the dBASE for Windows menu, select File | Set Up Custom Controls. As shown in Figure 16-6, a pop-up window is displayed.

3. Select a Custom Control file using the pop-up window that's displayed. Once you've set up custom controls, you'll have access to them each time you use dBASE for Windows. You don't need to set them up again.

You can use Microsoft Visual Basic to create custom controls. Visual Basic controls, or VBX controls as they are called, have become a de facto industry standard. No Windows development environment would be complete without the ability to use VBX controls. You can install custom VBX controls by following the steps described in this section and selecting the desired VBX file.

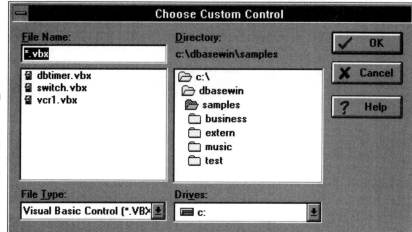

Figure 16-6:
This win-
dow allows
you to
choose a
file contain-
ing custom
controls.

Using custom controls

To use custom controls in dBASE for Windows, you must create a class definition that describes them. (Refer to Chapter 15 for more information on creating class definitions.) Definitions for custom controls are usually stored in a
file with a .CC extension, which stands for none other than Custom Controls.
Nothing bad will happen if the file that contains your custom control class
definitions doesn't have this extension. It's just another way of keeping your
program organized.

Here's an example of a class definition for a custom control:

```
CLASS OKButton (f,n) of PUSHBUTTON (f,n) CUSTOM
  this.Height  = 2
  this.Width = 10
  this.UpBitmap = "Resource #20 DBAS0009.DLL"
  this.DisabledBitmap = "Resource #21 DBAS0009.DLL"
  this.Text = "&OK"
ENDCLASS
```

This class definition is similar to the class definitions you've already seen in
this book. However, this class definition includes the keyword CUSTOM in
the first line, which tells dBASE for Windows that this is a custom control.

To define which graphics will appear on this PushButton, the class definition
specifies the Bitmap properties of this custom control . The graphics in this
control are loaded from a special library supplied with dBASE for Windows
called a dynamic linked library, or DLL. These libraries contain resources you
can link into your program.

The UpBitmap property in this class definition uses Resource number 20 of the DLL named DBAS0009.DLL. As shown in Figure 16-7, this property puts a green check mark on the PushButton (take our word for it; the check mark is green).

Figure 16-7: Give your program that special look with custom controls.

Using VBX custom controls is a little less work. You don't have to create class definitions for VBX controls because they come ready to use. You will have to refer to the documentation that comes with your VBX controls for more information on their use. You can also refer to the dBASE for Windows programming manual for an example of their use.

The techniques in this chapter can help give your program more power and pizzazz. You know how to create stand-alone procedures and functions as well as procedure files. You also know how to compile your programs and use preprocessor directives to control your compiler. By adding custom controls to your program, you can give them a professional appearance that will impress your friends and make your mother proud.

Part VI
More About Data

The 5th Wave   By Rich Tennant

" RIGHT NOW I'M KEEPING A LOW PROFILE. LAST NIGHT I
CRANKED IT ALL UP AND BLEW OUT THREE BLOCKS OF
STREETLIGHTS."

In This Part...

You already know a lot about creating data tables and using them with forms. This part of the book goes into even greater detail on processing the information that is stored in tables. You also find out how to use tables over a network.

Chapter 17

Data Processing and Other Mating Rituals

● ●

In This Chapter

▶ Getting information out of a table

▶ Putting information into a table

▶ Processing information

▶ Getting data from the user

▶ Getting data from a file

● ●

*O*ne of the most important topics in data management involves knowing what to do with data once you have it. You already know how to access your data by building a form and linking its controls to fields in your tables. However, building a form isn't always practical. This chapter shows you how to gain direct access to the data in your table. This chapter also shows what you can do with the data once it resides in variables or a table.

Putting Data in a Table

As detailed in Table 17-1, there are many ways to get data into a table.

The AUTOMEM commands listed in Table 17-1 are holdovers from the original Arago product, which was an ancestor of dBASE for Windows. The AUTOMEM commands create variables with the same names as the fields in a table. You can change the values of those variables and restore them into a table using one of the AUTOMEM commands listed in Table 17-1.

Two of the most commonly used commands listed in Table 17-1 are APPEND BLANK and REPLACE. APPEND BLANK is used to add a new record to the end

---

Table 17-1: Commands for putting data in a table

Command	Purpose
APPEND BLANK	Add a blank record
APPEND FROM	Add data that is stored in a different file or table
APPEND AUTOMEM	Add a record and fill it with data from Automem variables
IMPORT	Create a dBASE for Windows table from a Quattro Pro or Lotus 1-2-3 spreadsheet file
INSERT BLANK	Insert a blank record at the record pointer
INSERT AUTOMEM	Insert a record at the record pointer and fill it with data from Automem variables
REPLACE	Replace existing field data
REPLACE AUTOMEM	Replace existing field data with data from Automem variables
REPLACE FROM ARRAY	Replace existing field data with data from an array

---

of the current table. REPLACE allows you to place values in a table's fields without using a BROWSE window or a form and controls.

Using the APPEND BLANK command is simple. You just type the following command in the Command window or use it in a procedure, and a new record is appended to the end of the active table:

```
APPEND BLANK
```

The REPLACE command has the following syntax:

```
REPLACE FieldName WITH value
```

For example, the following command replaces the contents of a character field named CITY with the value "San Diego":

```
REPLACE CITY WITH "San Diego"
```

You can also use the -> sign to refer to a field within a particular table. The following example replaces the contents of a character field named CITY, which is located in a table called Clients, with the value "San Diego":

```
REPLACE Clients->CITY WITH "San Diego"
```

You can use the REPLACE command to replace the contents of fields in more than one record. You do this by including a scope modifier with the REPLACE command:

```
REPLACE ScopeModifier FieldName WITH value
```

Table 17-2 lists the scope modifiers you can use with the REPLACE command.

Table 17-2: Scope modifiers for the REPLACE command

Scope Modifier	Description
NEXT *x*	Replaces the contents of a field in *x* number of records, in sequence, starting with the current record
ALL	Replaces the contents of a field in all records
REST	Replaces the contents of a field in the rest of the records in the table, starting with the current record

For example, the following command replaces the contents of the CITY field, which is located in a table called Clients, with the value "San Diego" for the next 13 records:

```
REPLACE NEXT 13 Clients->CITY WITH "San Diego"
```

If you don't know which records contain the fields that you want to replace, dBASE for Windows can decide for you. Instead of a scope modifier, you can use the REPLACE command with a FOR *Condition* modifier:

```
REPLACE FOR Condition
```

For every client with a last name of "Smith", the following command replaces the contents of the CITY field in the Clients table with "San Diego":

```
REPLACE FOR Clients->LASTNAME = "Smith" Clients->CITY WITH "San Diego"
```

The chances that every client with the last name Smith will move to San Diego are probably very low, but you get the idea.

When you replace the contents of a key field in a table—that is, a field for which you have created an index—it's sometimes necessary to rebuild the affected indexes. To do this, you need to include the REINDEX keyword when using the REPLACE command:

```
REPLACE FieldName WITH value REINDEX
```

The REINDEX keyword causes dBASE for Windows to rebuild any indexes that are affected by the REPLACE command. You can use the REINDEX keyword with a scope modifier or a FOR *Condition* modifier.

You can also replace the contents of multiple fields using a single REPLACE command. You do this by listing a series of *FieldName* WITH *value* combinations, separated by commas:

```
REPLACE FieldName1 WITH value1, FieldName2 WITH value2, ...
```

The following example shows how you can replace the contents of a CITY field, a STATE field, and a COUNTRY field, all with a single command:

```
REPLACE CITY WITH "San Diego", STATE WITH "CA", COUNTRY WITH "USA"
```

Data isn't always entered directly by the user of your program. The information might be stored in another dBASE for Windows table, or in an external file. You can use the APPEND FROM command to retrieve data from other tables and files.

The table or file from which you are appending data should have the same structure as the table in which you are appending the data. dBASE for Windows performs the APPEND operation regardless of whether the structures match. If the structures don't match, information might be lost or corrupted. For example, if character values in the table or file you're appending from exceed the length of the character field in which they're being placed, the character values will be chopped off after they've filled the character field. Unless this is the result you desire, it's best to make sure that the data structures match before using the APPEND FROM command. ■

The APPEND FROM command has the following general form:

```
APPEND FROM FromWhere TYPE WhatType
```

FromWhere is the name of the table or file from which you are appending data. *WhatType* identifies the type of table or file from which you are appending data. You can append data from the following types of files:

- dBASE tables (type = DBASE)
- Paradox tables (type = PARADOX)
- System Data Format, fixed-length fields (type = SDF)
- Delimited files (type = DELIMITED)

The following example shows how you use the APPEND FROM command to put data from one table, OtherTable, into the current table, MyTable:

```
USE MyTable

APPEND FROM OtherTable TYPE DBASE
```

Notice that the table or file from which you are appending must be closed. You cannot append from an open dBASE for Windows table.

When you use the APPEND FROM command, it's a good idea to include the REINDEX keyword. This keyword tells dBASE for Windows that it should append all of the records before updating the index. Without the REINDEX keyword, dBASE for Windows tries to update the index after appending each record. If the table has multiple indexes, this process could take a long time. Here's how you use the REINDEX keyword with the APPEND FROM command:

```
APPEND FROM FromWhere TYPE WhatType REINDEX
```

Fishing for Data

There are only a few ways to get data out of a table. As shown in the following example, the most common approach involves setting the value of a variable equal to a field:

```
USE Favorite
FavrtColor = Favorite->Color
FavrtFood = Favorite->Food
```

When processing data, you don't need to store field values in variables before you start working with them. Instead, you can simply use the values stored in fields as though they are variables. The following example shows that both of these approaches produce the same result:

```
mValue = MyTable->Value  && Store the field value in a variable
NewValue = mValue * 10   && Create a new variable by multiplication

* Here is a simpler equivalent

NewValue = MyTable->Value * 10
```

The STORE AUTOMEM command automatically creates variables with the same names as the fields in the table you are using. You can refer to these variables by preceding the names with M->.

You can also get data out of a table by copying it to an array. The COPY TO ARRAY command has the following general form:

```
COPY TO ARRAY ArrayName FIELDS FieldList
```

ArrayName is the name of the array that you want to fill with data. *FieldList* is a list of the fields that you want to copy. If you don't specify FIELDS, the default is every field in the table that the array can hold.

The COPY TO ARRAY command doesn't create an array; it copies data from a table into an array. Before using the COPY TO ARRAY command, you need to create the array by entering the DECLARE command.

If you are going to copy multiple fields from multiple records, the array must be a two-dimensional array. For example, if you are copying four fields from five records, you must declare the array as follows:

```
DECLARE MyArray[4,5]
```

The following command copies data from a table into an array called MyArray:

```
COPY TO ARRAY MyArray
```

MyArray is simply filled with as many fields as possible, depending on the size of the array and the size of the table. If you want to copy just the contents of a field called MyField, use the following command:

```
COPY TO ARRAY MyArray FIELDS MyField
```

You can also add a FOR *Condition* modifier to the COPY TO ARRAY command. This modifier allows you to copy only the fields that meet your requirements. (The use of the FOR *Condition* modifier is detailed earlier in this chapter.) For each record in which the LastName field equals "Jones", the following example copies data from a table into an array called MyArray:

```
COPY TO ARRAY MyArray FOR LastName = "Jones"
```

COPY can be used to copy data to more than just arrays. Using COPY, you can create tables or files in several formats. Table 17-3 lists the file types you can create using the COPY command.

The COPY command for creating one of the file or table types listed in Table 17-3 has the following form:

```
COPY TO FileName FIELDS FieldList TYPE FileType
```

Table 17-3: The COPY command can copy data to these file types

File Type	Description
SDF	System Data Format, with fixed-length fields. Field lengths in the SDF file will match the field lengths in the table.
DBMEM03	dBASE III Plus format files with .DBF and .DBT extensions
PARADOX	Borland Paradox table
Delimited	File containing fields separated by delimiters. Comma delimited is the default, but you can specify your own delimiter.
dBASE	dBASE Version 5.0 file format. If no type is specified, this is the default file format.

FileName is the name of the file or table you'd like to create using the copied data. Note that COPY can only create new files. If you need to copy data into an existing table, use the APPEND FROM command.

FieldList is a list of the fields you want to copy to the new file or table. Again, if FIELDS are not specified, the default is the entire table.

FileType is one of the file types listed in Table 17-3.

For example, the following command copies an entire table to a new table named NewTable:

```
COPY TO NewTable TYPE dBASE
```

Like the REPLACE command described earlier in this chapter, the COPY command also accepts a scope modifier. For example, the following command copies the next 13 records from a table to a new Paradox table called ParaTab:

```
COPY TO ParaTab NEXT 13 TYPE PARADOX
```

You can also use a FOR *Condition* modifier with the COPY command. For more on the FOR *Condition* modifier, see the discussion of the REPLACE command earlier in this chapter.

Working with Data

Once you get some data, you will want to do something with it. Data processing usually involves one or several of the following actions:

- ✔ Reading data from one or more fields in a table
- ✔ Writing data to one or more records in a table
- ✔ Receiving data that a user has entered
- ✔ Receiving data from a file
- ✔ Working with the data

The following example reads data from a field, processes it, and then stores the processed value into another field:

```
USE Amount                && Use the table

DO WHILE .NOT. EOF()              && Skip through the entire table
  IF Amount->Total > 0   && If the total is greater than zero
     nTot = Amount->Total      && Store the total in a variable
     NewTot = nTot * 10 && Create a new variable by multiplication
     REPLACE Amount->GrandTotal with NewTot    && Store the result
  ENDIF
  SKIP                    && Skip to the next record
ENDDO

Use in Amount             && Close the table
```

This is a very simple example of data processing. However, you can make this example even simpler. The following example uses the REPLACE command more effectively:

```
USE Amount

* Notice that you can continue commands on the next line by breaking
* the line with a semicolon.

REPLACE Amount->GrandTotal WITH Amount->Total * 10 ;
FOR Amount->Total > 0

USE in Amount
```

TIP

After you write a program, it's always a good idea to read through your program and look for ways to make it more concise. As you become more proficient using dBASE for Windows, you'll be able to use the language more efficiently and write more streamlined programs. ▪

AUTOMEM is a dBASE for Windows feature that can help you write more efficient code. AUTOMEM lets you create a complete working copy of a particular record, and automatically copies the field values into memory variables with the same names as the fields. This capability is a tremendous time-saver if your table contains lots of fields.

By using AUTOMEM, you can work with the variables it creates instead of the information in the table. For the following reasons, working with variable data is preferable to working with the field data:

✔ The data in the table remains safe while the user modifies the data in the variables. If the user's work is aborted, the table remains unchanged.

✔ In a network environment, records don't need to be locked for as long a period of time.

The following example shows how you can use the AUTOMEM commands:

```
Use MyTable
STORE AUTOMEM              && Make working copies of the field data

* Use variables with the same names as the fields except they are
* preceded by M->.

M->Total = M->Value1 + (M->Value2 / 3)

REPLACE AUTOMEM   && Store the data back in the same record
USE in MyTable           && Close the table
```

Without AUTOMEM, you would need to write a separate line of code to store the data from each field in a variable. After working with the data, your program would have to include separate lines of code to store the variable data back in each field of the table. In other words, AUTOMEM helps you protect your data tables and it saves you from writing many lines of code.

Working with strings

A character variable is often referred to as a *string*, or a *string of characters*. For a change of pace, we use the term string here in place of character variable. Besides, it's easier to write string than it is to write character variable.

Some of the more common things you can do with strings are:

- ✔ Change the string to upper- or lowercase letters.
- ✔ Check the length of a string.
- ✔ Chop a big string into several little strings.
- ✔ Find little strings embedded in big strings.
- ✔ Trim off the blank spaces at the beginning or the end of a string.

Changing strings to upper- or lowercase letters is useful when you need to search for something the user has entered in a table. If the user enters the information in lowercase letters and the data is stored in uppercase, you would have to search in the table for an uppercase version in order to find a match. You can overcome this problem by using either the UPPER( ) function or the LOWER( ) function.

The following example shows how you can use the UPPER( ) function. In this example, the user has entered character data in entryfield1 on a form. The program in this example is supposed to find the same value in a table. For some reason, the programmer who created this data entry form didn't use the Picture or Function properties of the EntryField to format the data. As a result, the program must use the UPPER( ) function to convert both the value entered by the user and the value in the table to uppercase letters:

```
USE MyTable

cCharData = form.entryfield1.value  && Store value into a variable
LOCATE FOR UPPER(MyTable->Field1) = UPPER(cCharData)
* The field and the variable are both converted to uppercase
```

Being able to check the length of a string can be very useful. In the following example, a user has typed information in an EntryField. This value is going to be displayed in a Text control. To make sure the Text control is long enough, this example uses the LEN() function to check the length of the string, multiplies the result by 1.5 (just to be safe), and then sets the Width property of the Text control:

```
DisplayValue = form.entryfield1.value
Length = LEN(DisplayValue)
form.text1.Width = Length * 1.5
form.text1.Text = DisplayValue
```

Three different functions let you chop big strings into little strings:

📌 ✔ SUBSTR( ) extracts a string from anywhere in a string.

📌 ✔ LEFT( ) chops off a string from the left side of a string.

📌 ✔ RIGHT( ) snips off a string from the right side of the string.

The following example uses the LEFT( ) and SUBSTR( ) functions to cut a proper name into first and last names. To find the space between the first and last names, this example also uses the AT( ) function, which finds little strings in bigger strings:

```
FullName = "Willie Walker"

TheSpace = AT(" ",FullName)
FirstName = LEFT(FullName,TheSpace - 1)
LastName = SUBSTR(FullName,TheSpace + 1)
```

The first command sets FullName equal to "Willie Walker". Next, TheSpace is set equal to the location of the first space within FullName. Then, FirstName is set equal to every letter on the left side of FullName up to the first space. Finally, LastName is set equal to every letter in FullName after the space. When these commands are executed, FirstName will contain "Willie" and LastName will contain "Walker". Oh, in case you were wondering, TheSpace will contain the number 7.

The TRIM( ) function gives your string an aircut by lopping off the useless air or spaces at the end of a string. Adding first and last name fields to form a proper name can be a pain if the first name ends up half a page away from the last name. You can solve this problem by using the TRIM( ) function to trim off the trailing spaces of the first name field:

```
USE MyTable

FirstName = MyTable->First
LastName = MyTable->Last

FullName = TRIM(FirstName) + " " + LastName
```

Working with numbers

As most accountants will tell you, you can do many things with numbers. dBASE for Windows has functions for trigonometry, calculating payments, conversions, square roots, pi, logarithms, modulus, and rounding. There's a function for almost any numeric need you could have. These functions are listed in detail in the dBASE for Windows Language Reference.

One of the most common numeric functions is the VAL() function, which converts character data into numeric data. If an EntryField isn't DataLinked to a field in a table, anything the user enters in the EntryField is considered character data. As shown in the following example, you must convert this character data to numeric data before you can use it in any math operations:

```
NewValue  = form.entryfield1.value
NumValue = VAL(NewValue)

* NumValue is now Numeric type data
```

To tell an EntryField that isn't DataLinked which type of data it should accept, set the EntryField's Value property equal to a value. For example, if you want an EntryField that accepts only numeric data, you can enter the following example before the EntryField is used in your procedure:

```
form.EntryField.Value = 0
```

If you are creating games of chance or decision support tools, you might need to use the RANDOM() function. As shown in the following example, this function returns a random decimal number between 0 and 1:

```
* Personnel Equal Opportunity Numerics System

RandValue = RANDOM(-4)   && -4 is a randomizing seed value
Do Case
CASE RandValue < .1 .and. RandValue > 0
  Decision = "Hire applicant"
CASE RandValue < .2 .and. RandValue > .1
  Decision = "Call applicant for second interview"
CASE RandValue < .3 .and. RandValue > .2
  Decision = "Cancel interview for no reason"
CASE RandValue < .4 .and. RandValue > .3
  Decision = "Send rejection letter"
CASE RandValue < .5 .and. RandValue > .4
  Decision = "Offer a ridiculously low salary"
CASE RandValue < .6 .and. RandValue > .5
  Decision = "Make them the CEO"
CASE RandValue < .7 .and. RandValue > .6
  Decision = "Yawn. Let the resume fall into the waste can."
OTHERWISE
  Decision = "We have other qualified applicants to interview"
ENDCASE
```

The RANDOM( ) function accepts one parameter, which is called a *seed value*. In the preceding example, the seed value is -4. The RANDOM( ) function isn't truly random. How is that possible? Well, computers can't just "think of a number" like you can; they have to use calculations to come up with a number. Even the RANDOM( ) function uses calculations to return a number between 0 and 1. As outlined in Table 17-4, the seed value affects how RANDOM( ) picks a number.

Table 17-4: How the seed value affects the RANDOM() function

Seed Value	Result
Positive value, such as 2 or 300	Returns a single value based on the seed value. RANDOM() always returns the same number when given the same positive seed value. For example, RANDOM() will always return 0.0111758696 when given a seed value of 2.
Zero or no seed value	Uses the last number that RANDOM() returned as the seed value.
Negative value, such as –4	Returns a value based on the number of seconds in the computer's internal clock. This is as random as RANDOM() can get.

As mentioned, there are many functions for working with numbers. If we tried to cover them all, we would run out of space, and you would run out of patience. By the way, the interview system listed in this section is probably illegal in most states.

Working with dates

No, we aren't talking about dating your coworker. In earlier versions of dBASE, the most important date function turned character information into date information. You can still find this function in dBASE for Windows. If you're curious, look for the CTOD( ) function in the on-line help.

Instead of using the now-obsolete CTOD( ) function, you can transform character information into a date by enclosing it with braces. Oh no, a date with braces!

```
* Add braces to turn character information into an important date.
* My parents turned this into an important date.
{06/19/54}
```

To get the current date from your computer, you can use the DATE( ) function. However, if your computer has the wrong date, this function will return the wrong date. You can use the SET DATE TO command to reset the system date on your computer.

Most of the other date functions are used for formatting date information. The DAY( ) function returns the day in the specified date as a number. For example, DAY({06/19/54}) returns 19 as a number.

One of our favorite date functions is the CDOW( ) function, which stands for Character Day Of the Week. CDOW( ) evaluates a date value and returns the day of the week on which the date falls.

CDOW( ) returns the day of the week as a character value. If you want the number for the day of the week (1-7), use the DOW( ) function. You can amaze your friends with the following example, which tells you on which day of the week you were born:

```
? CDOW({Birthday})
```

Birthday represents your birth date. For example, the following command prints the day of the week for January 1, 2000 in the Results window:

```
? CDOW({01/01/2000})
```

January 1, 2000 happens to be a Saturday. Wow, just think of the parties people will have on New Year's Eve, 1999! It's even a Friday!

The big switcheroo

You already know how to change character data to a numeric value. As listed in Table 17-5, this is only one of several changes you can make.

Table 17-5: Functions for converting data types

Function	Description
ASC()	Returns the ASCII value of a character
CHR()	Returns the character that corresponds to an ASCII value
CTOD()	Changes a character value to a date
DTOC()	Changes a date to a character value
DTOS()	Converts a date value to character data in YYYYMMDD format
FLOAT()	Changes a numeric value to a float value
HTOI()	Converts hexadecimal data to an integer value
ITOH()	Converts an integer value to hexadecimal
STR()	Changes a numeric value to a string value
TYPE()	Identifies the data type
VAL()	Converts character data to numeric data

Accepting User Data Entry

Most applications allow the user to enter data. As a result, data processing usually includes procedures for checking the validity of the data entered by the user.

There are two main schools of thought on when you should validate the data that is entered by a user:

- When the user first enters data
- When leaving the Form

The preferred method is to validate data when the user first enters it. You can do this by writing an event procedure for the Valid event in a control. Your Valid event procedure checks the data the user has entered and returns .T. if the data is acceptable, or .F. if it's not. The following steps describe the approach you'd take to write a Valid event procedure for a control:

1. Create your Form and its controls using the Form Designer.

2. While in the Form Designer, click the control for which you'd like to add a Valid event procedure.

3. Find the Properties window and click the Events tab.

4. Click the Valid event and then click the tool icon that's displayed.

5. Write your procedure in the Procedures window. Remember to use the RETURN command to return .T. if the data is acceptable or .F. if the data is incorrect.

6. Click the Properties tab in the Properties window and find the ValidRequired property.

7. Change the ValidRequired property to .T. This causes the control to pay attention to your new Valid event procedure.

8. If you'd like, you can edit the ValidErrorMsg property to change the error message that is displayed if the Valid event procedure returns .F.

Time is an important consideration when you are writing data-entry validation rules. If the validation takes too long, users might think the program isn't working and start throwing their lunches at the screen, or at you. If you want to keep users happy, make your validations concise and quick. For example, ListBox or ComboBox controls are useful because the control displays a list of the valid options the user can choose.

Although validating data when the user first enters it is the preferred method, there are cases in which you'll want to wait until leaving the Form before validating the data. One reason you might want to do this is that users won't mind as much if they have to wait a while once they've finished entering data. On the other hand, making them wait each time they enter something will drive them nuts. One way to validate data when leaving the Form is to create a procedure in the Form's OnClose event that checks the contents of each control.

Don't make your validations too restrictive. A data entry screen that doesn't allow some flexibility is a nightmare for users. Remember, this is not a perfect world. In most cases, users won't have all the information requested on the data entry form. In such cases, users will need to save their work and return later to complete the Form. If your application forces users to choose between entering everything or nothing at all, it will cause them to go prematurely gray and require you to wear a bullet-proof vest. ■

You can also speed data entry and keep the user on the right track by using the Picture and Function properties of the EntryField control. Formatting the data as it is entered simplifies data entry and helps eliminate data entry errors.

Data validation and formatting is an art. Too much or too little can make for an inefficient application and unhappy users. With just enough formatting and validation, you might be a hero to the users. On the other hand, they might despise you because of your dBASE for Windows prowess. Sometimes, you just can't win.

Processing data is the most important part of using dBASE for Windows. This chapter covers getting at the data, working with it, checking it before you put it in the table, and updating the table. You will be working with data most of the time. As you have seen, many different functions can help you work with the data. For a complete list of the functions by category, refer to the dBASE for Windows Language Reference.

If you are a loyal dBASE user from way back, or you have used other data management programs or spreadsheets, you will find that dBASE for Windows has opened many doors. You are no longer limited to working with data from tables and flat files. You can share data with many other types of programs. You get to explore some of these possibilities in the following sections of this book. For example:

- ✔ Working with images, sounds, and other binary data
- ✔ Linking and embedding documents from other applications using Object Linking and Embedding (OLE)
- ✔ Sharing data with other applications using Dynamic Data Exchange (DDE)

These are some of the things you can look forward to learning.

Chapter 18

Committing Your Data and Other Crazy Things

In This Chapter

▶ Keeping your tables clean and free from debris

▶ Reducing data entry errors

▶ Applying good housekeeping in your applications

*W*hen you write real applications that are to be used by real people, you can be sure that those real people are going to make real mistakes. When users make mistakes, they're usually the first to know about it. Users don't like to make mistakes, so they generally do one of two things:

> ✔ Figure out how to stop and remove the mistakes as quickly as possible, so nobody sees them.
>
> ✔ Make sure there's someone else to blame.

You can't do much to help users who would rather blame someone instead of correcting mistakes. However, you can help users avoid making mistakes. If they manage to make a mistake anyway, you can also make it easy for them to correct the mistake.

Saving and Undoing Changes to Your Tables

One of the easiest ways to prevent mistakes is to carefully control which changes are saved in your tables (and which ones aren't). To do this, you can group a set of changes to form a *transaction*. Then, if there's a mistake somewhere in a transaction, you can simply undo the whole mess.

Transactions work best when the changes are somehow related. For example, in an order processing system that allows the user to enter new orders, each order could be a transaction. If an order contains a mistake, you can remove the entire order from your tables all at once.

To use transactions in dBASE for Windows, you simply mark the beginning of a transaction. You end a transaction by either saving the changes in the transaction or removing them. That's all there is to it!

Beginning and ending transactions

When you're in the checkout line at the supermarket, you use a rubber divider to separate your groceries from those of the person in front of you. When your groceries reach the front of the line, the clerk sees the rubber divider and knows to begin a new transaction. You end a transaction at the supermarket by paying the nice cashier. Sometimes you end a transaction by turning red and running from the store because you forgot to bring your wallet. In this case, your groceries are placed back on the shelf, and the cashier cancels the transaction on the cash register.

Beginning and ending transactions in dBASE for Windows is similar to your shopping experience. Instead of a rubber divider, you use the following function to mark the beginning of a transaction:

```
BEGINTRANS()
```

Once you start a transaction with the BEGINTRANS() function, any modifications to tables will be part of the new transaction. It's a good idea to use the BEGINTRANS() function before you make critical changes to your tables. This way, if you accidentally change 10,000 records in 12 tables, you can easily undo the mistake.

The following example creates a new transaction and makes three changes to a table:

```
USE Inventory
BEGINTRANS()
APPEND BLANK
Inventory->Item = "Pet Rock"
Inventory->Color = "Dirt Gray"
```

As in your shopping experience, a transaction must be completed before the next one can begin. Before your transaction can begin, the person ahead of you in the checkout line must either pay the nice clerk or run out of the store in a panic.

There are two ways to end a transaction in dBASE for Windows. You can either accept the changes that were made during a transaction, or you can cancel them. When you accept the changes in a transaction, it's called *committing*. Canceling the changes is called *rolling back*.

To commit or to roll back, that is the question

Two functions allow you to end transactions. One function ends the transaction by committing changes; the other function ends the transaction by rolling back changes:

- ✔ COMMIT( )
- ✔ ROLLBACK( )

There's not a lot to say about these two functions. You either use the COMMIT( ) function to finalize changes in a transaction, or you use the ROLLBACK( ) function to cancel the changes. It doesn't get much easier than this.

In dBASE for Windows, all sales are final. When you commit your transaction, dBASE for Windows enters the changes in your tables. You can't wiggle out of the transaction at this point. Similarly, once you've rolled back a transaction, your changes are gone. If you change your mind and decide that you want to make the changes, you'll have to re-enter them in a new transaction.

If a system error occurs or you try to exit the program before a transaction has properly ended, dBASE for Windows displays the window shown in Figure 18-1. This window notifies you that a transaction is still in process, and allows you to either commit or roll back the changes in the transaction.

Figure 18-1: The Transaction Pending window lets you commit or roll back changes in the current transaction.

If you receive this message when you try to exit dBASE for Windows, you can click the Cancel button to remain in dBASE for Windows. However, if you receive this message because a system error has occurred, you won't be able to cancel. If a system error occurs, you should either commit or roll back the current transaction.

Commands to avoid when using transactions

While a transaction is open, you can't use any command or function that would do something drastic, such as close all of the open tables, clear the contents of memory, or hijack an airplane and take hostages. You can't use the following commands and functions while a transaction is open:

- ✔ BEGINTRANS( )
- ✔ CLEAR ALL
- ✔ CLOSE ALL
- ✔ CONVERT
- ✔ CREATE FROM
- ✔ DELETE TAG
- ✔ INDEX
- ✔ MODIFY STRUCTURE
- ✔ PACK
- ✔ USE (if the command would close an open table)
- ✔ ZAP

If you try to use one of these commands, dBASE for Windows displays the Alert window shown in Figure 18-2.

You won't do any damage by trying to use one of these commands. After the Alert is displayed, the command is simply aborted without affecting anything. If dBASE for Windows displays this Alert window when you enter a command, you should end the current transaction using COMMIT( ) or ROLLBACK( ) before you use the command again.

Figure 18-2: This Alert window is displayed if you enter a command that can't be used in a transaction.

Using Transactions with Your Forms

You can create a more stable application with fewer bugs by adding transactions to your forms. Transactions are a useful, but not essential, part of a dBASE for Windows program. If you want to apply transactions in your data entry forms, here's how you do it:

1. Create your forms as you usually do.

2. Enter the following lines in the OnOpen event procedure of each form, replacing *Table* with the names of each of the tables you need to access in the form:

```
BEGINTRANS()
SELECT Table
SELECT Table
...
```

3. In the OnClick event procedure of your OK PushButton (or, if the form doesn't have an OK PushButton, in the procedure that is executed when the user is done entering data), enter the following function to end the transaction:

```
COMMIT()
```

4. In the OnClick event procedure of your CANCEL PushButton (or the procedure that is executed when the user cancels, or closes the form), enter the following function to end the transaction:

```
ROLLBACK()
```

With these additions to your application, any changes to tables using the form are saved only if the user accepts the changes. If the user cancels the changes that are entered on the form, all of the changes are discarded. A new transaction begins automatically each time the user opens one of the forms in your application.

To demonstrate how you use transactions with forms in an application, the following section shows you how to add transactions to the sample program you developed in Chapter 10.

Transactions in Action

Before we get started, let's take another look at the forms you created for the sample application in Chapter 10. Figure 18-3 shows the employee data entry form, and Figure 18-4 shows the employee time report data entry form.

Figure 18-3:
The
employee
data entry
form from
the sample
application.

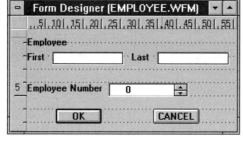

Figure 18-4:
The
employee
time report
data entry
form from
the sample
application.

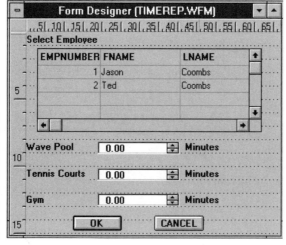

To open the Form Designer and start modifying the employee data entry form, enter the following command in the Command window:

```
MODIFY FORM Employee
```

The forms in this application should start a new transaction by using the BEGINTRANS( ) function. The application should start a new transaction each time a user opens either of your forms. In other words, you need to add the BEGINTRANS( ) function to the OnOpen event procedures of both forms.

Find the Properties window and click the Events tab. Open the Procedures window by clicking the OnOpen event and then clicking the tool icon. The Procedures window already contains the following code:

```
select employee
append blank
```

As mentioned, you need to change this event procedure so that it begins a new transaction before changes are made to the EMPLOYEE table. As shown in Figure 18-5, your new event procedure should contain the following code:

```
begintrans()
select employee
append blank
```

The BEGINTRANS( ) function starts a new transaction. Next, the command SELECT EMPLOYEE selects the EMPLOYEE table. Finally, the APPEND BLANK command creates a new record in the EMPLOYEE table.

Remember to save the employee data entry form by pressing Ctrl-W.

Figure 18-5:
A new transaction is started by the employee data entry form's new OnOpen event procedure.

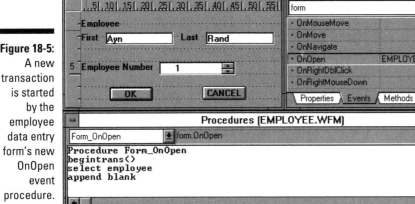

You need to make similar changes to the employee time report data entry form. To open the Form Designer and start modifying this form, enter the following command in the Command window:

```
MODIFY FORM TIMEREP
```

You need to edit this form's OnOpen event procedure. Find the Properties window and click the Events tab. Open the Procedures window by clicking the OnOpen event and then clicking the tool icon. The Procedures window already contains the following code:

```
select timerep
append blank
```

You need to change this event procedure so that it starts a new transaction before any changes are made to the EMPLOYEE table or the TIMEREP table. As shown in Figure 18-6, the new event procedure for the employee time report data entry form should contain the following code:

```
begintrans()
select timerep
append blank
```

The BEGINTRANS( ) function starts a new transaction. Next, the TIMEREP table is selected. Finally, a new record is created in the TIMEREP table with the APPEND BLANK command.

Figure 18-6: With this new OnOpen event procedure, the application starts a new transaction when a user opens the time report form.

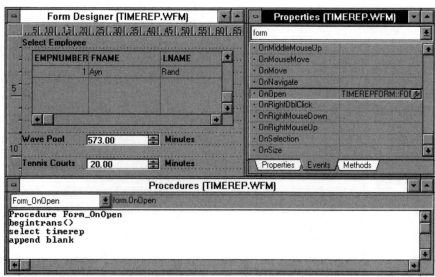

All you need to do now is end the transaction somewhere. You do this by adding either COMMIT( ) or ROLLBACK( ) to the OnClick event procedures for the two PushButtons on each form. You're already working on the employee time report data entry form, so let's start with the PushButtons on that form:

1. In the Form Designer, click the form's OK PushButton.

2. Find the Properties window, click the Events tab, and then click the OnClick event.

3. Click the tool icon to open the Procedures window, and change the event procedure to:

```
replace timerep->empnumber with employee->empnumber
COMMIT()
form.close()
```

4. Back in the Form Designer, click the CANCEL PushButton, find the Properties window, and click the OnClick event.

5. Click the tool icon to access the Procedures window, and change the event procedure to:

```
ROLLBACK()
form.close()
```

6. Save the employee time report data entry form by pressing Ctrl-W. Because this command closes the Form Designer, you need to enter the following command to open the Form Designer and start modifying the employee data entry form:

```
MODIFY FORM EMPLOYEE
```

7. In the Form Designer, click the form's OK PushButton. Find the Properties window, and click the Events tab. Click the OnClick event, and then click its tool icon, which opens the Procedures window.

8. Change the OK PushButton's OnClick event procedure to:

```
COMMIT()
form.close()
```

9. In the Form Designer, click the CANCEL PushButton. In the Properties window, click the OnClick event, and then click the tool icon. In the Procedures window, change the CANCEL PushButton's OnClick event procedure to the following:

```
ROLLBACK()
form.close()
```

10. Save the form and exit the Form Designer by pressing Ctrl-W.

When a user runs this application, a new transaction will automatically begin when the user opens one of the forms, and a transaction automatically ends when the user closes either form.

Transactions are a handy tool that can help you develop quality applications. When transactions are used appropriately, they prevent errors and useless data from accumulating in your tables.

Chapter 19

Getting Along on the Computer Party Line

*N*etworks have been installed in most large businesses, many smaller businesses, some homes, and our boat. Networks tie computers together, allowing them to share such resources as:

- ✔ Printers
- ✔ Hard drives
- ✔ Modems

A computer that provides resources to other computers is called a *server*. Other computers connected to the server are known as *network nodes*. When you use dBASE for Windows on a network, several challenges emerge. For one thing, you most likely share tables and other dBASE for Windows files with other people on the network. As you've probably discovered in life, sharing isn't always easy. When dBASE for Windows is used on a network, sharing becomes essential.

Sharing with Friends

If your computer is a node on a network, you probably use a printer that is attached to a server. If so, you probably have to go down the hall to pick up your printouts. Some computers are connected to a network solely for sending and receiving e-mail. In this case, your computer is a *mail client*.

In addition to using the printer that's attached to a server and getting your e-mail, a network node can also use hard disks that are being shared by a server. This capability makes it appear as though your computer has several disk drives. If your computer has drive letter designations from E: through Z:, you are probably using these shared hard disks, which are known as *network drives* or *virtual drives*. The files that you store on these drives do not reside in your computer. They live on another computer somewhere else.

"Somewhere, out there..."

Network drives are simply disk drives in the computer that is acting as a server. Your network administrator has configured the network software so that users on the network can share all or part of each of these disk drives.

Network software has its own built-in security system. The network administrator can set access rights on the disk drives or directories that are shared on the network. If your computer has access rights, it can "use" a disk drive or directory that is shared on the network. When your computer uses a network drive, a new drive letter is assigned to distinguish the network drive from other drives. In other words, your Q: drive might actually be the root directory on a server somewhere in the network.

Disk drives and directories aren't the only things that can be shared by a server over a network. As we mentioned earlier in the chapter, printers are the most common resource shared over networks. Some networks are installed simply to cut down the number of printers a company must buy. Figure 19-1 shows the layout of a typical network that uses a *network hub*. A network hub is a device that allows the computers in the network to communicate with each other.

For more information on setting up network printers, refer to the Windows manual or contact your network administrator.

This is an EXCLUSIVE place

A network is sometimes known as a *shared environment*, or cyberspace. In a shared environment, you need to know how to assert yourself. With dBASE for Windows applications, it's particularly important to control who uses your information and when they can use it.

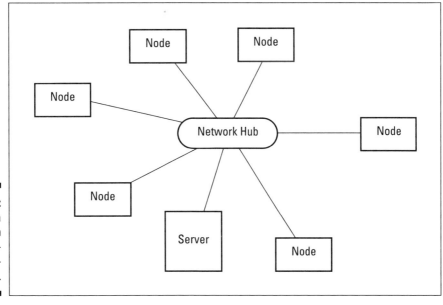

Figure 19-1:
The star is a
common
type of net-
work con-
figuration.

To protect the information in your tables, you can tell dBASE for Windows that you want exclusive use of your tables. When you have exclusive use of your tables, the other computers on the network can't access the information in those tables.

To open a table exclusively, you can include the EXCLUSIVE keyword when you enter the USE command:

```
USE MyTable EXCLUSIVE
```

Or, you can enter the command SET EXCLUSIVE ON. Any tables that are opened after you issue this command are opened exclusively.

The following dBASE for Windows commands work only when a table is opened exclusively:

- ✔ CONVERT
- ✔ COPY INDEXES
- ✔ DELETE TAG
- ✔ INDEX ON...TAG
- ✔ INSERT
- ✔ MODIFY STRUCTURE

- ✔ PACK
- ✔ REINDEX
- ✔ RESET
- ✔ ZAP

For example, if you want to re-index your tables, you must open them with the EXCLUSIVE keyword before issuing the REINDEX command. If your tables are already in use, they must be closed and then reopened exclusively.

IDAPI, you DAPI, and we DAPI, too

When you installed dBASE for Windows, you were asked where you wanted to install IDAPI. You probably didn't even know you wanted to install IDAPI.

IDAPI might surpass WYSIWYG and become a new high in the world of acronyms. IDAPI stands for different things, depending on whether you're reading the IDAPI help file or the dBASE for Windows help file. According to the IDAPI help file, the acronym stands for Independent Database Application Programming Interface.

This is the database engine that accesses and delivers information. In other words, IDAPI is the part of dBASE for Windows that allows you to access tables. Like most things in computers, especially when acronyms are involved, you may need to configure IDAPI to fit your particular needs.

Configuring IDAPI makes it possible to:

- ✔ Include OLE fields in your dBASE for Windows tables
- ✔ Fix data access problems if they arise
- ✔ Use SQL database servers on the network
- ✔ Use Paradox tables in dBASE for Windows when your computer is on a network
- ✔ Occupy yourself when you're bored and need to look busy

Before you can configure IDAPI, you must exit dBASE for Windows. After exiting dBASE for Windows, here's how you configure IDAPI:

1. In Windows, double click the IDAPI Configuration Utility icon, which is found in the dBASE for Windows program group. The icon is shown in Figure 19-2.

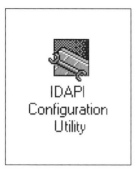

2. As shown in Figure 19-3, the IDAPI Configuration Utility window is displayed. The tabs at the bottom of this window let you select several categories of parameters. To see a different group of parameters, click the
appropriate tab. The Drivers tab should be selected. In the ListBox of
Driver Names, select dBASE. dBASE and Paradox are the only drivers
installed when you first install dBASE for Windows. Other drivers can be
installed later.

3. Most of the parameters are set to default values. To use OLE fields in
your tables, make sure that the LEVEL parameter is 5, not 4.

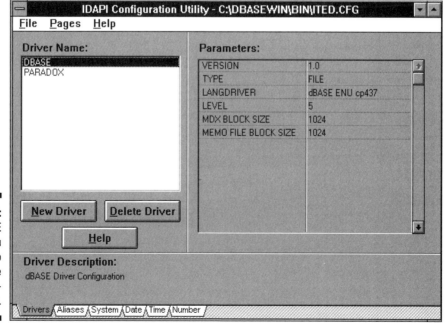

4. To use Paradox tables on a network, select the Paradox driver and set the NETDIR parameter. The NETDIR parameter should point to the directory that contains the Paradox network control files PDOXWIN.USR and PDOXUSRS.NET. dBASE for Windows needs these files to access Paradox tables on a network.

5. Select the System tab at the bottom of the IDAPI Configuration window. A new page of parameters is displayed. To share tables among several programs on your computer, set the LOCALSHARE parameter to True.

Until you become a mega-power user, this is just about all you will need to do with the IDAPI configuration. Even after you become a dBASE for Windows programming guru, you won't change much from the default settings.

Goldilocks, Do You?

You might be wondering what happens when two people on different computers try to change the same information at the same time. We hope this question hasn't kept you awake at night. This problem is known as a network *deadlock*. Although deadlocks were common in the early days of networks, they don't happen as much anymore. Programs that operate over networks have become more sophisticated. Now, whoever saves their information last wins.

This might be fair, but it can cause great consternation to the person who saved their information first. For this reason, there is something known as a *network lock*. A network lock keeps other people from making changes to data in a table until you release the lock. There are two levels of network lock:

✔ File lock, which locks an entire table

✔ Record lock, which locks one or more records

When certain commands are issued, dBASE for Windows automatically tries to lock a file or record. Depending on the command or how many records the command will affect, dBASE for Windows might try to lock the entire table or a single record. The following commands cause dBASE for Windows to attempt an automatic lock:

✔ APPEND

✔ APPEND FROM

✔ AVERAGE

✔ BLANK

✔ BROWSE

- ✔ CALCULATE
- ✔ CHANGE
- ✔ COPY
- ✔ COPY STRUCTURE
- ✔ COUNT
- ✔ DELETE
- ✔ EDIT
- ✔ INDEX
- ✔ JOIN
- ✔ LABEL FORM
- ✔ RECALL
- ✔ REPLACE
- ✔ REPORT FORM
- ✔ SORT
- ✔ SUM
- ✔ TOTAL
- ✔ UPDATE

In a shared environment, it's important to remember that dBASE for Windows attempts record locking. If you issue one of these commands and dBASE for Windows can't lock the file or record because it is locked by someone else, you will see a message telling you that the file or record is currently being used by someone else.

To disable the automatic locking feature before issuing one of these commands in a program, you can issue the SET LOCK OFF command.

If you turn off the automatic locking feature in dBASE for Windows while using information shared over a network, you must issue record and file locks in your program, as described later in this chapter. Otherwise, your data could become corrupt. Isn't corrupt a funny word? It sounds like your data will start taking bribes and robbing houses. It might be better to say, "Otherwise, your data might be wrong!" ■

I'm busy, come back later

When a table is locked with a file lock, other users on the network can't access that table. If they try, they receive a nasty message telling them that someone else is already using the table.

For several dBASE for Windows commands, the table you're working with must be locked because the command operates on the entire table. For example, the REINDEX command rebuilds the table's indexes. If changes are made to the table while an index is being created, the index will become confused. To avoid this, the table file must be locked before the index can be created. When you issue the REINDEX command, dBASE for Windows automatically tries to lock the file.

You can manually lock a table's file by using the FLOCK() function. This function returns true if it successfully locks the file, and false if it isn't able to lock the file. To use the FLOCK() function:

1. First, make sure the table that you want to lock is in use. USE the table or SELECT it to make it the active table.

2. Use the FLOCK() function to lock the entire table:

   ```
   FLOCK()
   ```

As shown in the following example, if you don't want to SELECT the table before you lock it, you can pass the number of the table's work area as a parameter to the FLOCK() function:

```
FLOCK(1)
```

Or, you can pass the table's alias to FLOCK(), enclosed in quotation marks:

```
FLOCK("MyTable")
```

Once you've locked a table's file, remember that nobody else can access it until you're done. If you only need to change a few records in a table, it's better to lock only the records you need instead of the entire table. The following section shows you how to do this.

Locking records

If your computer is on a network, it's a good idea to lock records while you are editing them. By doing so, you prevent other users from changing the information while you are editing it.

The following scenario shows the problems that arise when you don't lock records:

> A salesperson is taking an order for one widget. At the same time, another salesperson is trying to make a major killing by selling seven widgets. According to the inventory forms displayed on both salespersons' computers, seven widgets are in stock.
>
> The first salesperson enters the order for one widget, and the inventory system adjusts the on-hand total accordingly.
>
> The second salesperson closes the deal for seven widgets and proudly presses the Enter key. This salesperson's hair stands on end when the inventory system displays a message saying the transaction has been rejected because there aren't enough widgets in stock to fill the order. The salesperson calls the customer to explain that only six widgets are available, and the customer cancels the entire order in disgust.

This problem would have been avoided if the inventory application locked the record when it was accessed by the first salesperson. If the inventory record was locked, the second salesperson couldn't access the record until the first salesperson finished entering the order for one widget.

You can lock one or more records by using the RLOCK() function in your program. When you are using the dBASE for Windows user interface, you can also lock records by moving the record pointer to the record you want to lock and pressing Ctrl-L.

If you lock a record in which the information you are viewing has been changed by another user, dBASE for Windows displays a message informing you that the "Record has been changed by another." If this message is displayed, you must click OK before continuing. When you click OK, dBASE for Windows refreshes the information displayed on your screen to reflect the changes.

If you are using either the EDIT command or the BROWSE command, dBASE for Windows automatically locks the records you are editing.

When you lock records in a table that is related to another table with the SET RELATION command, dBASE for Windows automatically locks the records in the related table that correspond to the key field. ■

Unlocking your data so others can play, too

As mentioned, dBASE for Windows automatically tries to lock a file or record when you issue certain commands. After executing any of those commands, dBASE for Windows automatically unlocks the records or files. However, if you use the FLOCK() or RLOCK() functions to create a lock, the lock sticks around until you tell it to unlock.

You can unlock records and tables by issuing the UNLOCK command in your program or in the Command window. The following command unlocks every lock created with FLOCK() or RLOCK():

```
UNLOCK ALL
```

You can also unlock any locks created using FLOCK() or RLOCK() within a single table. If you use the UNLOCK command by itself, every lock in the current table is removed. To unlock every lock in another table, issue the following command:

```
UNLOCK IN "TableAlias"
```

TableAlias is the alias of the table in which every lock should be removed. The alias should be enclosed in quotes.

Sharing tables locally

In some cases, you might need to share dBASE for Windows tables with more than one program at a time on your computer. To share tables in this way, you need to use the locking techniques described in this chapter, even if you aren't on a network. In addition to using the correct locking techniques, the following actions are required if you need to use the same table in more than one program on your computer at the same time:

- ✔ The SHARE.EXE command must be issued at the DOS prompt or in your AUTOEXEC.BAT file. See your system administrator if you need help editing your AUTOEXEC.BAT file.
- ✔ As described earlier in this chapter, IDAPI must be configured so that LOCALSHARE is true.

While dBASE for Windows is running, you might switch to the Windows Program Manager and double click the dBASE for Windows icon. If you do this, you will have two *instances* of dBASE for Windows running on your computer at the same time. This is an example of a situation in which SHARE.EXE and

LOCALSHARE must be set up correctly in order to use the same table from both instances of dBASE for Windows.

Convert your tables

If you write programs that are going to be used primarily over a network, you should consider using the CONVERT command. To store information about locking and update status, this command adds a _dbaselock field to your existing tables.

As shown in the following example, you can control how much information is stored in the new _dbaselock field by specifying its width when you issue the CONVERT command:

```
CONVERT TO 30
```

This command creates a _dbaselock field with a width of 30 characters. This field should be wide enough to hold the following information, which is automatically stored by dBASE for Windows:

- ✔ The date and time of the last record lock.
- ✔ The status of changes since the record information was last displayed.
- ✔ The network ID of the person who last locked or changed the record.

 To track and display the user ID of the person who updates or locks a record, you must create a _dbaselock field that's at least eight characters wide. The correct field width depends on the length of user IDs on your network. Setting the width of this field to 25 to 30 characters is usually sufficient. ■

The _dbaselock field is also useful for keeping track of who changes your information. It isn't as secure as creating a log file of changes, but it does let you know who last changed the record.

You can use the following dBASE for Windows functions to read the information stored in the _dbaselock field:

- ✔ LKSYS( ), which returns the date and time of the last record lock, and the user ID of the person who locked the record.
- ✔ CHANGE( ), which returns true if the record has been changed since you last displayed it.

The REFRESH command updates your display when changes have occurred. If you issue the SET REFRESH command, dBASE for Windows automatically refreshes the data that appears in your display. As shown in the following example, the SET REFRESH command is followed by the number of seconds in the interval between display refreshes:

```
SET REFRESH TO 60
```

This command refreshes your display every 60 seconds. The maximum is 3,600 seconds, or one hour.

The amount of time users spend on networks grows daily. Connectivity is the buzzword of the 1990s. How often have you heard the term *information super-highway?* Whether you're in the fast lane of the information superhighway or on a small network in your home or office, this chapter can help you manage your information. dBASE for Windows manages much of the network locking you will need. It also gives you the opportunity to write applications that can manage shared information in a very sophisticated manner.

Part VII
Talking to Other Applications

The 5th Wave   **By Rich Tennant**

5th Wave PowerTip: To increase application speed, punch the Command Key over and over and over as rapidly as possible. The computer will sense your impatience and move your data along more quickly than if you just sat and waited. Hint: This also works on elevator buttons and crosswalk signals.

In This Part...

dBASE for Windows has the tools necessary for establishing connections with other software packages. You can share information with word processors, spreadsheets, graphics programs, and many other types of Windows programs. As described in the following chapters, you don't have to limit your dBASE for Windows applications to simple database processing tasks. With the tools described in this part of the book, your dBASE for Windows programs can include the processing power of many other applications.

Chapter 20

Object Linking and Embedding: The Windows Application Superhighway

● ●

In This Chapter

▶ Learning the superhighway lingo

▶ Placing documents from other Windows applications in a table

▶ Using other applications from within dBASE for Windows

● ●

*O*bject linking and embedding (OLE) is a Windows tool that allows different programs to work together. With OLE, you can store a document from one Windows application inside a document from another application.

For example, you might create a dBASE for Windows table in which a field contains an entire document such as a spreadsheet that you have created with another application. By linking documents in this way, you can extend the power of your dBASE for Windows applications to include the capabilities of your favorite word processing, spreadsheet, and graphics programs.

After 19 chapters about tables, records, fields, and forms, you might find it a bit strange that we are suddenly talking about documents. When you are using OLE, the term *document* doesn't necessarily mean a file you create with your word processing program. To Windows, dBASE for Windows tables are documents too.

Following a brief vocabulary lesson, this chapter shows you how to use OLE in your dBASE for Windows applications.

Link, Embed, and Be Merry

The process of linking and embedding in dBASE for Windows can best be explained by breaking down the words *object*, *linking*, and *embedding*. Each file that is created by an OLE server application is an object. As detailed in Table 20-1, the term *OLE server* simply refers to the Windows application that creates this document, or object. Objects might be image files from Windows Paint, text files from a word processor that supports OLE, spreadsheet files, or any other type of document from an OLE server application. Of course, dBASE for Windows tables are documents, too.

You can link this file, or object, to a file from a completely different application. The application that creates the file to which you are linking the OLE object, or document, is an OLE client application.

OLE servers create documents that can be stored in other files that are created by OLE client applications. Some applications have the ability to act as both an OLE server and client. dBASE for Windows is an OLE client application. "It is far better to receive than to give." (anonymous realist) ▪

If you are feeling artistic, you might create some artwork in the Windows Paint program. You can link your masterpiece to an OLE field in a dBASE for Windows table. Instead of the entire graphics file, the OLE field contains only

Table 20-1: OLE terminology

Term	Description
Document	A file created by a Windows applicatio;. Windows documents include dBASE for Windows tables, spreadsheets, word processing files, image files, and sound files.
Object	A document
OLE Server	An application that creates documents that can be embedded or linked into another application's documents
Client	An application, such as dBASE for Windows, that stores OLE documents within its own files or documents
Linking	Storing a link to the document in the client file, rather than the entire document
Embedding	Storing the entire document in the client file
Package	A wrapper around the OLE object that makes it possible to access the server application that created the document

a link to that image. If you edit the Paint file, your changes are reflected when you display the image in your dBASE for Windows application.

Remember, you aren't storing the image, only a link to it. If you move the image, the link will be corrupted. In other words, it's important to store your OLE files where they can stay for a while.

Embedding an object is another story. If you embed your Windows Paint file, the entire bitmapped picture is stored in the OLE field of your table. Embedding takes considerably more room in your table, but you don't have to worry about someone inadvertently moving your file, changing it, erasing it, or otherwise messing with it.

Linking a document to your table

To link an OLE document into a table, the first thing you need is an OLE field. You can refer to Chapter 3 for detailed information on the mechanics of table creation. When you create or modify your table, one or more fields should be OLE-type fields.

In the event of an IDAPI error when you try to save your table structure, you must exit dBASE for Windows and change the IDAPI configuration. In the IDAPI Configuration Utility, select dBASE from the list of driver names. Next to the driver names is a list of parameters. The LEVEL parameter sets compatibility to either dBASE version 4 or version 5. Make sure LEVEL is set to 5. If it is set to 4, you can't add an OLE field. Save this setting and restart dBASE for Windows. Try creating or modifying your table again. ■

Now that your table has an OLE field, dBASE for Windows is ready to receive. The OLE game has three players:

✔ A dBASE for Windows table with an OLE field (the client)

✔ A document from an OLE server application

✔ The Windows clipboard (the go-between)

Your OLE field is going to contain a link to a document from an OLE server application. As an example, create a picture in Windows Paint. With the picture on the screen, use the cut tool and select Edit | Copy from the Paint menu. Most Windows applications have this menu choice. The Edit | Copy menu choice sends a copy of the selected graphics or text to the Windows clipboard, which acts as a storage place, or go-between.

The last step in the process is to create the link between the object and the dBASE for Windows table:

1. Bring up dBASE for Windows. If it is running in the background, you can press Alt-Tab until dBASE for Windows is on top. If it isn't already running, start dBASE for Windows in the usual manner.

2. Use the table that contains the OLE field. Add a record if necessary.

3. Browse the table and double click the OLE field to bring up the OLE Viewer.

4. Select Edit | Paste Link from the dBASE for Windows menu.

This menu choice establishes the link to the OLE object. Because the clipboard isn't erased until you copy another object or exit Windows, you can continue pasting this OLE object into as many records as you want.

Embedding a document in your table

Embedding OLE documents into dBASE for Windows tables is almost identical to linking them. Embedding has the advantage of greater portability. Sharing tables is much easier because you don't need to worry about the location of the files. You know they are in your table, safe and sound. The disadvantage of embedding is the increased disk space needed for storing the file or document in your table. However, this is usually a very small disadvantage.

To embed a document, follow all of the steps for embedding, until you are ready to paste the document into the OLE Viewer. Rather than choosing Edit | Paste Link, you should choose Edit | Paste.

Be careful when choosing either Paste or Paste Link from the Edit menu. It's easy to accidentally choose the wrong option. As a result, you may believe a file is embedded when it is only linked. It can be a little tricky figuring out which option you chose. One way to determine whether a file is linked or embedded is to move the file or temporarily change its name. If you can still access the file after moving it or renaming it, your document is embedded. ▪

If all this switching to and from other applications has you feeling like a whirling dervish, there is a way to start an OLE server application from within dBASE for Windows:

1. Browse a table that contains an OLE field.

2. Double click the OLE field to bring up the OLE Viewer.

3. Select Edit | Insert Object. The window shown in Figure 20-1 is displayed.

4. Choose the application you want as a server for your OLE object from the window shown in Figure 20-1.

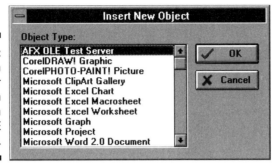

Figure 20-1:
Choose an
OLE server
application
to create a
new OLE
object.

The application you choose as the server for the OLE object starts, and it appears on your screen. If you create a document in the server application and then return to dBASE for Windows, the document will be embedded in the OLE field of your table.

When you install Windows-based programs on your PC, a little-known program called Regedit is automatically updated. Regedit keeps track of your Windows programs, their paths, and their capabilities. When you choose to insert an OLE object and dBASE for Windows displays the list of possible server applications, this list comes from Regedit. If an application that you know to be an OLE server doesn't seem to work as one, you probably need to check Regedit. Similarly, if the application doesn't appear on the list of possible OLE servers in dBASE for Windows, it might not be properly registered with Regedit. Your Windows manual has more information on manually updating your Regedit list. ▪

Watch, it comes when I call it

There are two ways to access an OLE object after you have linked it to your table or embedded it in your table:

✔ Open a Browse window and double click the OLE field

✔ Open a Browse window, select the field, and press F9

Either approach opens the OLE Viewer and displays the linked or embedded object. For example, if you created the OLE document in the Windows Paint application, bringing the document up in the OLE Viewer displays the Paint image.

This is only half the fun. Behind the scenes, dBASE for Windows begins a session with the OLE server application. If your trigger finger isn't in spasms from all the double clicking, double click the document that appears in the

OLE Viewer window. What do you think happens? The OLE server application starts so you can modify your OLE document. You don't have to choose the application from a list, dBASE for Windows already knows which application created the embedded or linked object.

It's All in There

So far, this chapter has showed you how to use OLE objects through the dBASE for Windows user interface. Because this is a book on programming, you probably want to know how you can include this feature in you applications.

 Chapter 14 introduced you to class definitions, which are recipes for building objects. You can use the dBASE for Windows help system to display a list of all the pre-defined classes. To display this list, select Search from the Help menu and type the word CLASS. Notice that there is an OLE class. You can also find information about the OLE class definition in the dBASE for Windows Language Reference. ■

When designing a form, you can select an OLE object from the Controls Palette and place it somewhere on your form. You need to make sure that the OLE control has enough room for your OLE object. If your object doesn't fit, dBASE for Windows automatically displays vertical and horizontal scroll bars.

Once the OLE object is on your form, use the Properties window to change its properties. The very first property you need to change is the DataLink property. To be useful, the OLE object must be DataLinked to an OLE field. After specifying the DataLink, you will notice that the following properties are automatically filled in and can't be modified:

- LinkFileName
- OleType
- ServerName

These properties identify the document and its OLE server. These properties are updated automatically. For example, if a graphic image is stored in record 1 of your table, and a word processing document is stored in record 2, these properties change as the current record changes. Figure 20-2 shows a form with an OLE document created in Windows Paint.

You can modify several other properties to customize your OLE object. For the most part, these properties determine the size, border, and placement of the OLE object on the form.

You can control the server application with the DoVerb( ) member function. The DoVerb( ) function starts an action in an OLE server application. The verb you send to your object is a number that the application understands. All OLE objects understand at least one verb, while others understand quite a few more. Generally, the one command that is common to most applications is the number zero (0), the edit command. However, this may vary between applications.

To find out which verbs are accepted by your OLE server application:

1. Open the OLE Viewer with a document from your OLE server application.

2. Select Edit from the dBASE for Windows menu.

3. Click the last item in the Edit menu. This is the OLE object. If the OLE server application accepts more than one verb, the verbs are listed in a sub-menu. Otherwise, the OLE server application only accepts the one default verb, edit.

The DoVerb( ) function accepts two parameters. The first parameter is the verb number; the second is a character string you would like to appear as the title in the OLE window. That's assuming that your OLE object has a window. Some OLE objects are not visual, and therefore do not appear on the screen.

You can give users of your applications more control over the behavior of OLE objects by adding the DoVerb( ) function to the OnClick events of Push-Buttons on your form.

Application development is changing to create an environment in which applications can work together. Microsoft created Object Linking and Embedding to meet this need. OLE currently allows many Windows applications to share information, start applications from within other applications, and create a truly integrated information system within Windows.

It is also possible to share information with other applications without storing their documents. This capability is known as dynamic data exchange (DDE), and it is covered in the next chapter. OLE and DDE are powerful tools for expanding the capabilities of your programs. Use both or choose the class type that provides the greatest flexibility for your application.

Chapter 21

Exchanging Data with Other Windows Applications

· ·

In This Chapter

▶ Finding out if an application supports dynamic data exchange

▶ Using information from another Windows program in your dBASE for Windows application

▶ Using dBASE for Windows information in another Windows application

· ·

*T*he preceding chapter introduced OLE, a Windows tool that allows different programs to work together. Dynamic data exchange (DDE) provides another way to share information between Windows applications. DDE allows Windows applications to make specific information requests of other Windows applications. For example, dBASE for Windows could ask a spreadsheet application to open a budget spreadsheet and return the amount that's budgeted for surfboard wax. dBASE for Windows could then use the value returned by the spreadsheet application to make decisions, perform calculations, or even store the value in a table. Without DDE, this type of data exchange isn't possible.

This chapter shows you how to use DDE to request data from other Windows applications. You also find out how other Windows applications can request data from dBASE for Windows. First, you need to know how DDE works and how you start a DDE conversation, called a *DDE link*, between two Windows applications.

How DDE Works

There are two sides to a DDE link: the server side and the client side. The server side receives and acts upon instructions and data-exchange requests.

The client side sends the instructions and data-exchange requests. For example, dBASE for Windows might act as the client side of a DDE link, sending the instruction "open the file called BUDGET" to a spreadsheet application that is acting as the server side of the DDE link. Once the spreadsheet application follows this instruction, dBASE for Windows can ask the spreadsheet application for information from the BUDGET file using a data-exchange request.

To get things started, the client application sends a request asking a DDE server application to create a DDE link. If the client asks nicely and the server feels the client is worthy, a DDE session is established. Once the connection is made, the client can start sending DDE messages to the server.

First Things First

To start a DDE link between two applications, the following criteria must be met:

- ✔ Both applications must have DDE capabilities.
- ✔ Both applications must be registered in Regedit.
- ✔ One application must be able to operate as a DDE server and the other must be able to function as a DDE client. One server can't talk to another server. A server can only talk to a client, and vice versa. Some programs are both servers and clients.

To find out if the application with which you want to exchange data has DDE capability, you should consult the user manual of that product. Check the index of the manual for any signs of DDE capabilities.

You can also find out if an application is DDE-aware by using the Regedit application. If the software with which you are trying to establish a DDE link was properly installed, it is registered with Regedit, the Windows registration utility.

To start Regedit:

1. Switch to the Windows Program Manager.

2. Select File | Run... from the Windows menu.

3. In the Run window, click the Browse button, and then find and select REGEDIT.EXE in the Browse window that's displayed.

4. Click the OK button in the Browse window, then click OK in the Run window. As shown in Figure 21-1, Regedit displays a list of the registered file types.

Figure 21-1:
You can use
Regedit to
find out if
your appli-
cation is
registered
as DDE-
enabled.

Scroll through this list until you find the file type for the application that you want to use as part of your DDE link. Double click this file type with your left mouse button. For example, we selected WordPerfect Document (6.0) in Figure 21-1.

Figure 21-2 shows the dialog box that Regedit displayed when we selected WordPerfect Document (6.0) from the list of registered file types. As you can see, a CheckBox indicates that WordPerfect 6.0 uses DDE. The lower part of the dialog box contains DDE information.

Once you're sure that both applications use DDE, they're both registered in Regedit, and one of them can be a DDE server, you're ready to start a DDE connection.

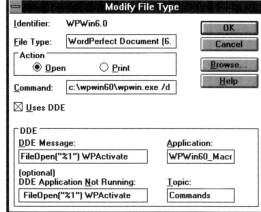

Figure 21-2:
Regedit
shows you
if an appli-
cation uses
DDE.

The client is always right

dBASE for Windows can be both a DDE client and a DDE server. Two special classes make it easy for you to start using DDE.

To use dBASE for Windows as a DDE client, you create a DDELINK object from the DDELINK class.

You create an object from a class definition. When you create a DDELINK object, it will have all of the attributes and capabilities designed into the DDELINK class definition. ■

To create a DDELINK object, type the following line in the Command window and press Enter:

```
MyDDELINK = NEW DDELINK()
```

As described in the following section, you can now use the INITIATE() method of the DDELINK object to begin the DDE link to the other application.

Start your engines

The INITIATE() method of the DDELink object takes two parameters:

- ✔ *Server.* This is the name of the executable file for the server application.
- ✔ *Topic.* This is the name of the data file that you want to open in the server application.

The following example shows how you use the INITIATE() method of the DDELINK object to start the DDE link to the other application:

```
Result = MyDDELINK.INITIATE("WPWIN", "MYFILE")
```

This example runs the INITIATE() method of the DDELINK object. A link is requested with the server application, WordPerfect for Windows 6.0. If Word-Perfect isn't already running in Windows, this method attempts to start it. The second parameter of the INITIATE() method tells WordPerfect that dBASE for Windows would like it to open MYFILE. This file must already exist.

The INITIATE() method returns .F. (false) if the connection isn't established, and .T. (true) if the DDE connection starts successfully. Result will contain either .T. or .F. to let you know whether a DDE connection exists.

Make it so

To send a command or instruction to another application, you use the EXE-CUTE() method of the DDELink object. For a list of the commands or instruc-tions that the other application understands, you should refer to that application's manual or on-line help.

The following example uses the EXECUTE() method with WordPerfect 6.0 to insert a hard return into MYFILE:

```
MyDDELINK.EXECUTE("HardReturn()")
```

The following example adds text to the WordPerfect document through your DDELINK:

```
MyDDELINK.EXECUTE('Type ({"HELLO WORDPERFECT!"})')
```

This example uses the WordPerfect Type macro to insert text. There are many things you can do with a DDELINK. In theory, you're only limited by the DDE capabilities of the programs in a DDELINK!

dBASE for Windows has a sample application called NameInfo.WFM, which provides a complete example of using the EXECUTE() method in an applica-tion. This example creates a link with WordPerfect using the WordPerfect macro language. For a detailed description of the WordPerfect macro lan-guage, see MACROS in the WordPerfect on-line help or the WordPerfect manuals. ▪

Table 21-1 lists the other methods available with the DDELink object and describes their use.

Table 21-1: DDELink methods

Method	Description
Advise()	Creates a DDE hot link, which means the DDE server notifies dBASE for Windows when changes occur in the server's document
Peek()	Retrieves a data item from the DDE server
Poke()	Inserts data into a server document
Terminate()	Ends a DDE session
Unadvise()	Stops notifying the client application of changes in the server's document

Hanging up

When you're done with a DDELINK session, you end the connection by typing the following line in the Command window and pressing Enter:

```
MyDDELINK.Terminate()
```

This ends the DDE connection established by the MyDDELINK object. In our example, WordPerfect will still be running in Windows, but the DDE connection between dBASE for Windows and WordPerfect is terminated.

May I Be of Service?

dBASE for Windows can also act as a DDE server application. As a server application, dBASE for Windows performs the following tasks:

✔ Receiving commands and instructions from client applications

✔ Allowing client applications to access dBASE for Windows tables

✔ Performing any special tasks you program into it as a DDE server

A special DDE class allows dBASE for Windows to be a DDE server. The class is called DDETOPIC, and an object from this class must exist in order for dBASE for Windows to act as a DDE server.

To create an object from the DDETOPIC class, enter the following line in the Command window and press Enter:

```
MyDDEServer = NEW DDETOPIC("MyDDETopic")
```

Because a DDETOPIC object must exist in order for dBASE for Windows to be a DDE server, any client application that needs to start dBASE for Windows must execute a special program that you write to create a new DDETOPIC object. dBASE for Windows refers to this special program as an initiation-handler routine. The following section describes how to create such a routine.

Starting a dBASE for Windows DDE server from a client application

Before dBASE for Windows can be a DDE server, you must write an initiation-handler routine that creates a new DDETOPIC object and gives your object the ability to respond to DDE requests. To create an initiation-handler routine:

1. Start dBASE for Windows (if you haven't already).

2. Type the following command in the Command window and press Enter:

```
MODIFY COMMAND INIT.PRG
```

3. dBASE for Windows displays the Program Editor. Type the following program:

```
SET PROCEDURE TO INIT.PRG ADDITIVE

PUBLIC DDEServerObject

_app.DDEServiceName = "DBASEDDE"
_app.OnInitiate = INITFUNC

FUNCTION INITFUNC(Topic)
   DDEServerObject = NEW MyDDEClass(Topic)
   ? "DDE server ready for topic: ", DDEServerObject.Topic
RETURN .T.

CLASS MyDDEClass(Topic) of DDETOPIC(Topic)
   FUNCTION OnExecute(CommandToExecute)
      IF CommandToExecute = "HELLO"
         ? "HELLO WORLD"
      ELSE
         ? "UNKNOWN COMMAND"
      ENDIF
   RETURN .T.
ENDCLASS
```

4. Press Ctrl-W to save your new initiation-handler routine.

When a DDE client application needs to use dBASE for Windows as a DDE server, it must first start dBASE for Windows and include the filename of your initiation-handler routine as a parameter. Applications differ when it comes to executing external commands. When you find out how to execute an external command in your client application, you need to execute the following command:

```
DBASEWIN YourInitiationHandlerFilename
```

YourInitiationHandlerFilename is the filename of your initiation-handler routine. For example, the one you just created is INIT.PRG. Before we describe the contents of this file, let's see it in action. In the following section, you get to experiment with using DDE in dBASE for Windows.

Experimenting with DDE the easy way

By far the easiest way to see DDE work is to use dBASE for Windows as both a DDE client and DDE server application. That's right, dBASE for Windows can talk to itself using DDE. Here's how you do this:

1. Create a "scratch" table with which we can experiment by typing the following command in the Command window:

   ```
   CREATE DDETEST
   ```

2. The Table Designer is displayed. Enter TEST as the name of field 1, and press Ctrl-W to save the DDETEST table.

3. Close the DDETEST table by entering the following command in the Command window:

   ```
   USE
   ```

4. You need to create a DDELINK object, which allows dBASE for Windows to act as a DDE client. To create a DDELINK object, enter the following command in the Command window:

   ```
   MyDDELink = NEW DDELINK()
   ```

5. The RUN() function allows you to execute an external Windows command from within dBASE for Windows. To run a new instance of dBASE for Windows that will act as the DDE server, enter the following command in the Command window:

   ```
   RUN(.T.,"DBASEWIN INIT.PRG")
   ```

6. Your screen resembles the example in Figure 21-3. This is your new instance of dBASE for Windows. The INIT.PRG initiation-handler program was executed, so this instance is ready to be a DDE server application.

7. Press Alt-Tab to go back to the original instance of dBASE for Windows. Your screen should look like Figure 21-4.

8. To establish a DDE link with the dBASE for Windows DDE server, enter the following command in the Command window:

   ```
   MyDDELink.Initiate("DBASEDDE","DDETEST.DBF")
   ```

9. Your mouse cursor changes to an hourglass while dBASE for Windows establishes a DDE link. When your mouse cursor returns to a pointer, click in the Command window. To send a HELLO Execute request to the DDE server, type the following command in the Command window:

   ```
   MyDDELink.Execute("HELLO")
   ```

10. Press Alt-Tab twice to see the results of your HELLO Execute request.

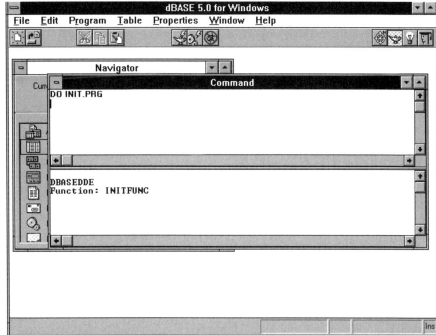

Figure 21-3:
When the INIT.PRG program is executed, dBASE for Windows becomes a DDE server.

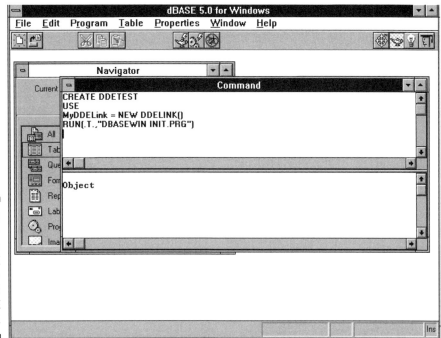

Figure 21-4:
Your original instance of dBASE for Windows will be the DDE client.

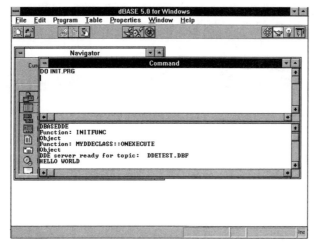

Figure 21-5:
The HELLO
Execute
request was
received by
the dBASE
for Win-
dows DDE
server.

As shown in Figure 21-5, HELLO WORLD is printed in the Results window in response to the HELLO Execute request. This simple example shows how you can use dBASE for Windows as both a DDE server and a DDE client application.

Understanding the initiation-handler

The initiation-handler is the key to turning dBASE for Windows into a useful DDE server. The DDETOPIC object you create in the initiation-handler determines the capabilities that dBASE for Windows has when functioning as a DDE server. If you want dBASE for Windows to perform really useful tasks, such as searching for information in a table and returning that information to the client program, you need to write your own initiation-handler that uses tables and responds to several DDE messages. To do this, you need to understand how an initiation-handler works and how the DDETOPIC class is used.

Let's take another look at the simple initiation-handler you created earlier in this chapter:

```
SET PROCEDURE TO INIT.PRG ADDITIVE

PUBLIC DDEServerObject

_app.DDEServiceName = "DBASEDDE"
_app.OnInitiate = INITFUNC

FUNCTION INITFUNC(Topic)
  DDEServerObject = NEW MyDDEClass(Topic)
  ? "DDE server ready for topic: ", DDEServerObject.Topic
```

```
RETURN .T.

CLASS MyDDEClass(Topic) of DDETOPIC(Topic)
  FUNCTION OnExecute(CommandToExecute)
    IF CommandToExecute = "HELLO"

      ? "HELLO WORLD"
    ELSE
      ? "UNKNOWN COMMAND"
    ENDIF
  RETURN .T.
ENDCLASS
```

First, the command SET PROCEDURE TO INIT>PRG ADDITIVE tells dBASE for Windows to search INIT.PRG (in addition to any other files it currently searches) for class and function definitions. This is an extremely important command in an initiation handler. Without this command, dBASE for Windows cn't find the function called INITFUNCT, and your initiation handler won't work.

Then, a public variable called DDEServerObject is created. This is the variable used to store the MyDDEClass object reference when the object is created in the INITFUNC function. This variable must be public so that it will exist in dBASE for Windows after the initiation handler has finished handling. For dBASE for Windows to act as a DDE server, a DDETOPIC object or an object inherited from DDETOPIC must exist in dBASE for Windows. If the DDEServerObject variable isn't public, it disappears after the initiation handler has finished running.

Next, the routine sets the DDE Service Name using _app.DDEServiceName. This allows the client application to refer to the dBASE for Windows DDE server by name.

The _app.OnInitiate variable is set to the INITFUNC function so that initiation occurs automatically. This step is required in any initiation-handler routine.

The INITFUNC function simply creates a new object from the class we've defined, using the DDETOPIC class as a starting point. Once this is done, dBASE for Windows becomes a DDE server. Sometimes it's handy to print a message in the Results window when a DDE link is established, so the INITFUNC function does this as well.

Finally (this is the really important part), we use inheritance to define a new class from the DDETOPIC class. This makes it possible to create event procedures and methods to do anything we'd like in response to DDE messages.

A DDE client can send the following DDE messages:

✔ Advise ("Tell me when something changes")

✔ Execute ("Do this ...")

✔ Peek ("Show me ...")

✔ Poke ("Take that! And that!")

✔ Unadvise ("Stop telling me when things change")

When the DDETOPIC object, or an object created from a class that was inherited from DDETOPIC, receives one of these DDE messages, a corresponding event is triggered within the object. These events are:

✔ OnAdvise (for the Advise message)

✔ OnExecute (for the Execute message)

✔ OnPeek (for the Peek message)

✔ OnPoke (for the Poke message)

✔ OnUnadvise (for the Unadvise message)

In our sample initiation-handler, the class MyDDEClass is given the ability to respond to an Execute message. If the message contains the word "HELLO", a greeting is printed in the Results window; otherwise, an error message is printed. If you want your dBASE for Windows DDE server to respond to other DDE messages, you need to add functions to your class definition. Be sure to give each function the same name as one of the DDETOPIC's events, so that the function is executed each time the event occurs.

Using dBASE for Windows as a DDE client application can greatly increase the power and scope of your dBASE for Windows applications. If it makes more sense to use a word processing program for some part of your application than it does to use dBASE for Windows, DDE lets you do it. Programming with DDE takes some getting used to, and like OLE, it's a different way to think about application development. However, the advantages are well worth the mental shift.

dBASE for Windows is an extremely capable, highly flexible DDE server application. You can do just about anything you need to using dBASE for Windows as a DDE server. The key to an incredible DDE server in dBASE for Windows is a powerful initiation-handler routine. With some practice and a look at the initiation-handler routines written by other programmers, you'll be an expert initiation-handler programmer in no time.

Part VIII
The Part of Tens

"IT'S A MEMO FROM SOFTWARE DOCUMENTATION. IT'S EITHER AN EXPLANATION OF HOW THE NEW SATELLITE COMMUNICATIONS NETWORK FUNCTIONS, OR DIRECTIONS FOR REPLACING BATTERIES IN THE SMOKE DETECTORS."

In This Part...

dBASE for Windows is the culmination of many years of evolving database technology. If you have been following along with these developments, you need to upgrade from the previous version of dBASE. The first chapter in the Part of Tens helps you through the process of upgrading from dBASE III Plus and dBASE IV. You learn how to convert any existing program files to dBASE for Windows, and whether you can run them as they are.

dBASE for Windows is a powerful and useful tool. The last chapter in this book provides insight into some of the most useful functions in the dBASE for Windows language.

Chapter 22

Ten Things You Should Know about Upgrading from dBASE III Plus or dBASE IV

• •

In This Chapter

▶ How to upgrade and run your existing dBASE programs

▶ dBASE for Windows tools that can help you upgrade

▶ What's new in dBASE for Windows

• •

*U*pgrading from dBASE III Plus or dBASE IV can be very easy. In fact, many of your existing programs won't need any modifications at all before you can use them in dBASE for Windows! If you need help converting dBASE III Plus or dBASE IV programs to dBASE for Windows, this chapter shows you the way.

Upgrading Is Worth the Effort

You've probably already given some thought to the advantages offered by dBASE for Windows. If you're still wrestling with the decision to upgrade (or you need some help convincing your boss), here are some of the best reasons for making the move to dBASE for Windows:

- ✔ You can write sophisticated dBASE programs that have all the features and capabilities of Windows applications.

- ✔ With the dBASE for Windows development tools, you can quickly and easily build powerful dBASE for Windows applications.

- ✔ Your dBASE for Windows tables can store binary information, such as images and sounds.

- ✔ dBASE for Windows has a powerful report writer that makes it easy for you to create attractive, informative reports.

- ✔ You can use OLE and DDE to incorporate the capabilities of other Windows programs into your dBASE for Windows applications.

- ✔ Your dBASE for Windows programs can use Paradox tables as well as access SQL-based client-server databases.

Your Existing Programs Will Probably Work in dBASE for Windows

For the most part, dBASE for Windows is backward-compatible with earlier versions of dBASE. The people who developed dBASE for Windows put a great deal of effort into making sure that it would run a wide variety of existing programs.

Before you do anything else, try running your program in dBASE for Windows. It will probably work just fine! Because some dBASE commands behave differently than in previous versions, you might notice some slight changes in your application. If the changes are acceptable, you have the option of continuing to use your dBASE III Plus or dBASE IV program without changing a thing.

The DO command lets you run a program in dBASE for Windows. For example, you would run a program file called MYPROG.PRG by entering the following command:

```
DO MYPROG
```

When you run a dBASE III Plus or dBASE IV program in dBASE for Windows, you might be surprised by what happens. Instead of using the entire screen like it used to, your program now runs in a window. Actually, it runs in a portion of a window, which is connected to the Command window. This area is called the Results window, or the Results pane of the Command window. Figure 22-1 shows a simple dBASE III Plus program running in dBASE for Windows.

If your dBASE III Plus or dBASE IV programs work in dBASE for Windows, you're all set. If they don't, or you would rather convert them to dBASE for Windows programs, the following sections can help you.

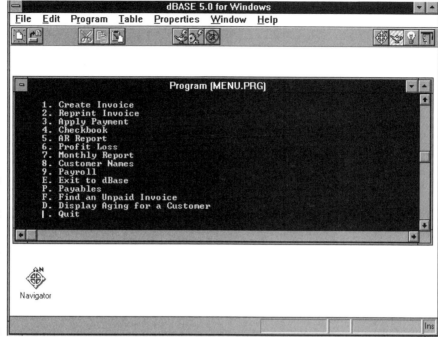

dBASE 5.0 for Windows

File   Edit   Program   Table   Properties   Window   Help

Program [MENU.PRG]

```
1. Create Invoice
2. Reprint Invoice
3. Apply Payment
4. Checkbook
5. AR Report
6. Profit Loss
7. Monthly Report
8. Customer Names
9. Payroll
E. Exit to dBase
P. Payables
F. Find an Unpaid Invoice
D. Display Aging for a Customer
|. Quit
```

Navigator

Ins

Figure 22-1:
Most
dBASE III
Plus and
dBASE IV
programs
will run in
dBASE for
Windows.

If Your Program Doesn't Work, You Can Probably Fix It

Don't despair if dBASE for Windows has problems with your dBASE III Plus or dBASE IV program. In such cases, you'll probably see an error message similar to the one shown in Figure 22-2. If dBASE for Windows displays this type of error message, click the Fix button to open the offending program file in the Command Editor. You'll be plopped down in the program on the line that caused the error.

Most conversion problems are easy to fix if you apply some patience and some elbow grease.

Figure 22-2: An error message like this one informs you that there's a problem with your program.

Some dBASE Language Elements Are No Longer Supported

If your program uses language elements that aren't supported in dBASE for Windows, nothing will happen. dBASE for Windows simply ignores commands and functions that it doesn't support. For a complete list of unsupported language elements, see Appendix A in the dBASE for Windows Language Reference.

If you are confronted with language elements that are no longer supported, be patient. dBASE for Windows probably offers a new, more efficient way to accomplish your task.

Tools Help You Convert dBASE III Plus and dBASE IV Programs

dBASE for Windows provides a conversion tool called the Component Builder. The Component Builder allows you to convert several types of files into dBASE for Windows user interface objects. The Component Builder lets you make the following conversions:

- ✔ .FMT files to Forms (.WFM files)
- ✔ .FRM files to Reports (.RPT files)
- ✔ .LBL files to Crystal Labels (.RPL files)

✔ .PRG files containing proper .FMT file syntax to Forms (.WFM files)

✔ .PRG files containing dBASE IV menu definitions to Menus (.MNU files)

There are two ways to start the Component Builder:

✔ Double-click the dBASE for Windows Component Builder icon that was created when you installed dBASE for Windows, or

✔ Change to the UTILITY directory from your dBASE for Windows directory and issue the following command:

```
DO CB.PRO
```

For more on using the dBASE for Windows Component Builder, run the Component Builder and refer to the on-line help.

The 5th Wave   By Rich Tennant

System Integration at Disney World

"LOOK, I HAVE NO PROBLEM RUNNING MICKEY-MICROS AND PLUTO-PCs THROUGH A TINKERBELL BUS, BUT WE'RE NEVER GOING TO HAVE A HUEY-DEWEY-LOUIE-LAN ON A MINNIE-MINI WITHOUT SERIOUSLY UPGRADING ALL OF OUR GOOFY SOFTWARE."

The dBASE Language Includes Numerous Enhancements

The dBASE language has been enhanced in the following ways:

- ✔ The language now supports object-oriented development.
- ✔ You can write Windows applications in the dBASE language.
- ✔ There are 14 powerful functions for handling arrays.
- ✔ The dBASE for Windows language includes bit-handling functions.
- ✔ Improvements have been made to 98 commands and functions.
- ✔ The language is unlimited because you can call functions from dynamically linked libraries.
- ✔ As detailed in Table 22-1, several dBASE specifications have been improved.

Table 22-1: Improvements in dBASE specifications

Specification	dBASE IV	dBASE for Windows
Maximum record size	4,000 bytes	32,767 bytes
Maximum number of fields	255	1,024
Maximum MDX block size	16,384 bytes	32,256 bytes
Float accuracy	15.9 places	19 places
Command line length	1,024 bytes	4,096 bytes
Maximum lines in editor	32,000 lines	unlimited
Maximum printer drivers	4	unlimited
Maximum number of work areas	40	255
Array dimensions	2	255
Elements per dimension	65,525	unlimited

You Can't Compile dBASE for Windows Programs into Executables

At least, not yet.

The current version of dBASE for Windows doesn't allow you to create Windows executables from your dBASE for Windows programs. A guy named Bruce is feverishly working on this capability, and it should be available soon.

You'll Be Writing dBASE for Windows Programs Almost Immediately

Building programs is simple using the dBASE for Windows development tools. With dBASE for Windows, the complexity of Windows programming is reduced to a couple commands and a few clicks of the mouse. Armed with a few simple concepts, anyone can start applying these development tools to creating complete dBASE for Windows applications.

You Don't Need to Know Object Orientation to Write Programs

dBASE for Windows is an object-based development tool. In other words, dBASE for Windows uses object orientation. However, you don't have to understand all the subtle intricacies of object orientation to be able to write powerful applications. The tools in dBASE for Windows do most of the work for you.

Chapter 15 explained how objects are created, and why you might want to create them. By developing an understanding of how the dBASE for Windows design tools create applications, you will eventually be able to modify the code that is created by those design tools. In this way, you can gain experience with object-oriented programming.

You Can Access Your Client-Server Database Engine

dBASE for Windows uses several programs behind the scenes to create an interface to client-server database engines. BDE (the Borland Database Engine), IDAPI (the interface definition language), and SQL Link translate dBASE for Windows commands into structured query language (SQL) syntax. The results of the queries are returned in the familiar dBASE format.

With the SQLEXEC( ) function, you can also use the dBASE for Windows language to send SQL commands to a client-server database.

Chapter 23

Ten of the Most Useful Functions in dBASE for Windows

- -

In This Chapter

▶ Figuring out how many parameters have been passed

▶ Looking up values in a table

▶ Hiding the dBASE for Windows MenuBar and SpeedBar

▶ Running a Windows application from within a dBASE for Windows program

- -

*d*BASE for Windows offers dozens of functions that can help you create powerful information-management applications. This chapter describes ten dBASE for Windows functions that we wouldn't want to do without.

Don't Count Your Parameters Before They're Hatched

Because it's possible to pass more or fewer parameters than are specified in a PARAMETERS statement, it's often important to know how many parameters were passed to a procedure or a user-defined function. For example, the same procedure might be called from many parts of your program. Each part of the program may have different requirements of your procedure. The procedure can react to new requirements based on the number of parameters that are passed to it. You can use the PCOUNT( ) function to tell your procedure how many parameters were actually passed.

As shown in the following example, you can have your procedure or function do different things based on the number of parameters that are passed to it:

1. Enter the following command in the Command window:

```
MODIFY COMMAND MYTEST
```

2. Enter the following procedure in the editor that's displayed:

```
PROCEDURE MYPROC
PARAMETERS cParam1, cParam2
nParams = PCOUNT()
DO CASE
CASE nParams = 0
   MSGBOX("You must pass at least one parameter.","ERROR",1)
CASE nParams = 1
   MSGBOX(cParam1 + " was sent.","Howdy",0)
CASE nParams = 2
   MSGBOX(cParam1 + " and " + cParam2 + " were sent.","Hello",0)
CASE nParams = 3
   MSGBOX("You sent one too many parameters.","Hey!",1)
OTHERWISE
   MSGBOX("WOW!, What's wrong with you?","Go Home",1)
ENDCASE
```

3. Save your procedure and exit the editor by pressing Ctrl-W.

4. Enter the following command in the Command window:

```
SET PROCEDURE TO MYTEST
```

5. Test your program by running it and passing it one parameter. A message box should be displayed when you enter the following command in the Command window:

```
DO MYPROC WITH "Hey diddle"
```

6. Now try sending two parameters:

```
DO MYPROC WITH "Hey diddle", "a dah dah dah"
```

7. Keep adding parameters and separating them with commas.

As this simple example shows, it's often useful to count the number of parameters that are passed to a procedure or function. You can take different actions in your program, or let the user know that not enough, or too many parameters were sent.

How Many Strings Could a Substr ( ) Chop If a Substr ( ) Could Chop Strings?

SUBSTR( ) is the most useful function for manipulating strings. You can use the substring function to extract or examine parts of a string. For example, let's assume that your company uses the following part number for a widget:

```
123DWV5CA
```

This number might actually mean something to someone in your company. (If it does, that person is paid far too little.) Let's say the first three numbers identify the color of the product. The next three letters identify the product as a digital weather vane. The 5 identifies the features, such as serial link availability, and the CA means that this product is manufactured in California. Where else?

The SUBSTR( ) function makes it pretty easy for dBASE for Windows to figure out all of this. The SUBSTR( ) function accepts three parameters:

```
SUBSTR(String, Start, Length)
```

The *String* parameter is the entire character string. The *Start* parameter is a number that tells dBASE for Windows where to start chopping the string. The *Length* parameter is a number signifying how many characters to chop out of the string. The *Length* parameter is optional. If it is left out, the SUBSTR( ) function begins chopping at the *Start* parameter and includes the rest of the string.

The following example shows how you could create variables that contain all the information you would need from the part number, 123DWV5CA:

```
cPartNum = "123DWV5CA"
cColor = SUBSTR(cPartNum,1,3)
cProductCode = SUBSTR(cPartNum,4,3)
cFeatureCode = SUBSTR(cPartNum,7,1)
cMfgLocation = SUBSTR(cPartNum,8,2)
```

The first line of this program stores the part number in the variable cPartNum. Whenever this variable is used, it is the same as saying "123DWV5CA".

The next three lines store the results of the SUBSTR( ) functions. The color starts at position 1, and it is 3 characters long. The product code starts at position 4, and it is 3 characters long. The feature code is taken from position

7, and it is 1 character. Finally, the manufacturing code begins at position 8, and it is 2 characters long. The result looks like this:

```
cColor = "123"
cProductCode = "DWV"
cFeatureCode = "5"
cMfgLocation = "CA"
```

This is also a great function for finding and separating first and last names from a single field.

In dBASE for Windows, Nothing Is Ever Half EMPTY( )

The EMPTY( ) function lets you know at a glance whether a variable, field, or expression equals zero or is blank. In many cases, you need to know whether a user has entered data in a field. In other words, you need to determine whether the value of a variable is more than 0 or blank. The EMPTY( ) function returns .T. if whatever it's checking is empty, or .F. if something is there.

Of course, you don't have to use the EMPTY( ) function to find out if the values of variables, fields, and expressions are equal to 0 or have no value. This is just a simpler, more straightforward way to do it.

When you see the EMPTY( ) function being used, there is no question about what's going on in that statement. To see the impact of this function, let's look at two examples. The first example doesn't use the EMPTY( ) function:

```
IF cFirstName > ""
   . . .
```

This is a perfectly valid expression for an IF statement. However, it doesn't scream, HEY IF THE FIRST NAME IS EMPTY..., like the following IF statement:

```
IF EMPTY(cFirstName)
   . . .
```

As you learn the dBASE for Windows language, your programs will become less cryptic and easier to read and debug. Look for functions such as EMPTY( ) that can shorten your programs or make them clearer. We like the next function for exactly the same reason.

Lost and FOUND ( )

There's no reason to be lost in your program code any longer. By using functions such as FOUND( ), you can keep the purpose of your code clear and concise.

The following dBASE for Windows commands and functions search your table looking for a match:

- CONTINUE
- FIND
- LOCATE
- LOOKUP()
- SEEK
- SEEK()

The FOUND( ) function returns .T. when these functions find what they are looking for.

The FOUND( ) function accepts one parameter, the work area number or alias of the table in which the search is performed. Searches aren't always performed in the current work area. This is especially true if tables are related. If a search is performed in a parent table, all of the child tables are also searched.

This is demonstrated in the following example, which involves two related tables. The following program searches the parent table and then looks for a match in the child table:

```
USE Child in 2
SELECT Child
SET ORDER TO ChildKey
SELECT 1
USE Parent
SET RELATION TO ChildKey INTO Child

MySearchVar = "kid123"
LOCATE FOR Child->ChildKey = MySearchVar
IF FOUND(Child)
   ...
```

The first five lines of the program open the tables and the index. Then, the program sets the relationship between the Parent and Child tables. A variable called MySearchVar is created by storing a value in it. Then, using the slow, but faithful LOCATE command, the program looks for a value in the Child table while the Parent table is the currently selected work area. If a match is found in the Child table, the FOUND( ) function returns .T. (true).

As shown in the preceding example, you might be more interested in finding a match in a child table than in the parent. If the record pointer in the parent table is moved by any means other than one of the commands and functions that are listed in this section, FOUND( ) won't tell you if there is a match in a child table.

In addition, you need to remember that the FOUND( ) function returns .T. only for an exact match. If the SET NEAR environment variable is set to ON, dBASE for Windows will settle for the nearest match if an exact one is not found. If this happens, FOUND( ) returns .F.

No More Fumbling in the Dark for Your Key

The KEYMATCH( ) function is used mainly to let you know if you are going to enter a duplicate while adding new records to your table. For example, let's assume that you are working with a table in which a filter has been set. You want to add a new record, but you can't add duplicates. What do you do?

You could remove the filter and search for the value you want to enter. If it isn't already in the table, you can enter it, and then reset the filter. What a hassle! Fortunately, the KEYMATCH( ) function offers an alternative to this approach.

The KEYMATCH( ) function looks in the index, not in the table. Indexes are not affected by commands such as SET FILTER, SET DELETED, and SET KEY.

The KEYMATCH( ) function has the following syntax:

```
KEYMATCH(Expression, .MDX filename, TAG number, Alias)
```

The KEYMATCH( ) function can accept the following parameters:

✔ *Expression* is the value you are looking for. This is the only required parameter.

✔ *.MDX filename* is the name of the index file.

> ✔ *TAG number* is the numeric position of the tag in the index file. If necessary, you can find this position by using the TAGNO( ) function with the name of the tag.

> ✔ *Alias* is the alias name of the table.

The following example shows how you can use the KEYMATCH( ) function:

```
USE MyTable
SET ORDER to Name
SET FILTER TO MyTable->Name = "Smith"

cName = "Jones"
IF .NOT. KEYMATCH(cName, TAGNO(Name))
  APPEND BLANK
  REPLACE NAME WITH cName
  ...
```

The example program begins by opening a table called MyTable, which is indexed on a field called Name. The program makes the index active and then sets a filter so that the only visible records are those in which the name is Smith.

We want to add a record in which the name is Jones, and we can't have any duplicate records. The KEYMATCH( ) function searches the Name tag for this value. The logical .NOT. operator is used to reverse the return value of the KEYMATCH( ) function. The APPEND BLANK and REPLACE commands are issued only if KEYMATCH( ) returns .F., which means that a match is not found. This function can make life a lot easier. You won't need it all the time, but when you do, you'll be glad it's there.

Big Program to Write? Don't Get Shook Up, Use LOOKUP( )

LOOKUP( ) is a handy little function for finding a specific value in your table. The beauty of LOOKUP( ) is that it does its job in one step, whereas other search methods require two steps.

You tell LOOKUP( ) three things:

1. The name of the field that contains the value you want LOOKUP( ) to return.

2. The value you want to match.

3. The name of the field in which you want LOOKUP() to find a matching value.

When LOOKUP() finds a match, it returns the contents of the field you specified. Cool, huh?

For example, let's say you found a phone number scribbled on a piece of paper and you want to know who it belongs to. The following program uses the LOOKUP() function to check your handy dBASE for Windows table of names and phone numbers:

```
USE Blakbook
SET ORDER TO Phone
cPhoneNum = "5552222"
?LOOKUP(Name, cPhoneNum, Phone)
```

In the first two lines, the program opens a table of names and phone numbers, and makes the phone tag the master index. A variable is created to store the phone number (this is optional), and the program performs the lookup. The program searches the Blakbook table, looking for a record in which the Phone field matches the value of the variable cPhoneNum. When it finds a record in which Phone matches cPhoneNum, the LOOKUP() function returns the contents of the Name field from that record.

LOOKUP() doesn't require an index. However, if you have an index on the field you are trying to match, make it active and LOOKUP() will use it. Otherwise, LOOKUP() does a sequential search just like the LOCATE command. One significant difference is that the LOOKUP() function will not move the record pointer. It stays where you last left it.

LOOKUP() won't exactly cut the size of your code in half, but every little bit helps. More concise code means fewer bugs, less writing, more readable code, faster programs, fabulous riches, and vacations in the Mediterranean. All the other search commands and functions move the record pointer until they find a match. Some of them even tell you if they find a match. However, these other search methods always require a second step to get the information you were after in the first place. Not with LOOKUP().

Let's Play Hide and SEEK ( )

We use the SEEK() function instead of the SEEK command for a couple of reasons:

✔ SEEK() returns .T. or .F., depending on whether a match is found. As a result, you don't have to use the FOUND() function after every SEEK.

✔ You can search in other work areas without selecting the work area first.

Once again, less code = happier programmer!

The SEEK() function has the following syntax:

```
SEEK(Expression, Alias)
```

The SEEK() function accepts the following parameters:

✔ *Expression* can be any value or expression you want to find. The field containing the value must be indexed, and the index tag must be the Master index when the SEEK() is performed.

✔ *Alias* is an optional alias name. If you specify an alias, dBASE for Windows searches that table for the match. Without this optional parameter, dBASE for Windows assumes that you want to search the current work area.

The following example uses SEEK():

```
USE MyGarden
SET ORDER TO Shrubs
cShrub = "Rhododendron"
IF SEEK(cShrub)
   . . .
```

In this example, the table named MyGarden has an indexed field called Shrubs. The program opens the table, makes the index active as the Master index, creates a variable, and sets it equal to Rhododendron. Then, the program performs a SEEK() for this value. SEEK() returns .T. if this lovely pink flowering shrub is found in the table. You'll be happier if you use this function instead of the SEEK command.

Playing to Win the SHELL() Game

Similar to the game in which you try to guess which shell is hiding the pea, the SHELL() function hides the dBASE for Windows interactive environment, which includes the MenuBar, SpeedBar, Command window, and Navigator. Yes, SHELL() will also "unhide" the interactive environment.

At present, you can't compile stand-alone programs with dBASE for Windows. As a result, you have to run your programs in the interactive environment.

However, this doesn't mean you have to look at it. For example, you might write an application in which you don't want the user to see or have access to the MenuBar, SpeedBar, Command window, and Navigator. In such cases, you can use the SHELL( ) function to hide all of these elements of the dBASE for Windows interactive environment.

You use the SHELL(.F.) function to hide the dBASE for Windows interactive environment. To bring back the interactive environment, you pass .T. as a parameter:

```
SHELL(.T.)
```

If your form has the MDI property set to .T., you won't get the full effect of the SHELL( ) function. In other words, dBASE for Windows won't disappear. The form's menu appears in place of the dBASE for Windows MenuBar. For the full effect, you should set the MDI property to .F.

It's a good idea to include the SHELL(.T.) function in an error-handling routine. In the event of an error, this function brings back dBASE for Windows. ■

RUN( ) Forrest! RUN( )!

When faced with the task of running a Windows application from within a dBASE for Windows program, you don't have to run. The RUN() function lets you run Windows programs, as well as DOS commands and applications, from within dBASE for Windows.

In previous versions of dBASE, you could only run DOS commands and applications. You still can. However, based on the first parameter you pass to the RUN() function, you can also run a Windows application.

The RUN( ) function has the following syntax:

```
RUN(lProgramType, DosCommand)
```

The RUN( ) function accepts the following parameters:

- ✔ *lProgramType* tells RUN( ) whether this is a Windows program. If this parameter is .T., RUN( ) thinks it is a Windows program. A value of .F. or no value means it is a DOS command or function.
- ✔ *DosCommand* is the command that starts either the Windows or DOS program.

RUN() returns a 0 if the command is successfully executed. Any other value equates to a Windows error message. The following example uses RUN() to execute the DOS command that changes the DOS directory to the root directory:

```
RUN(.F., "CD \")
```

The next example runs a Windows program and checks the return value to determine whether RUN() was successful:

```
IF RUN(.T.,"C:\SPLOTCH\SPLOTCH.EXE") < 5
  MSGBOX("Error running file.","Error",1)
  ...
```

If the return value is a number other than 0, a message box will display an error message.

Somewhere over the Rainbow

GETCOLOR() is a fun function. You can use it in the Command window to return the huge numbers that are associated with custom colors, or you can include it in your application to let users set their own colors. GETCOLOR() displays the CHOOSE COLOR dialog box, which is shown in Figure 23-1.

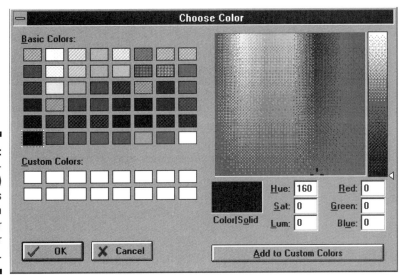

Figure 23-1:
The GET-
COLOR()
function lets
you open
this color
chooser
dialog box.

You can use the GETCOLOR( ) function in the Command window by entering the following command:

```
? GETCOLOR()
```

To use it in an application, you should create a variable from the result of the GETCOLOR( ) function:

```
NewColorString = GETCOLOR()
```

You can also pass a title for the GETCOLOR dialog box that's displayed:

```
NewColorString = GETCOLOR("Color Customizer")
```

The DEFINE COLOR command lets you use the results returned by the GET-COLOR() function in your program. Refer to the dBASE for Windows on-line help for more information on this command.

Index